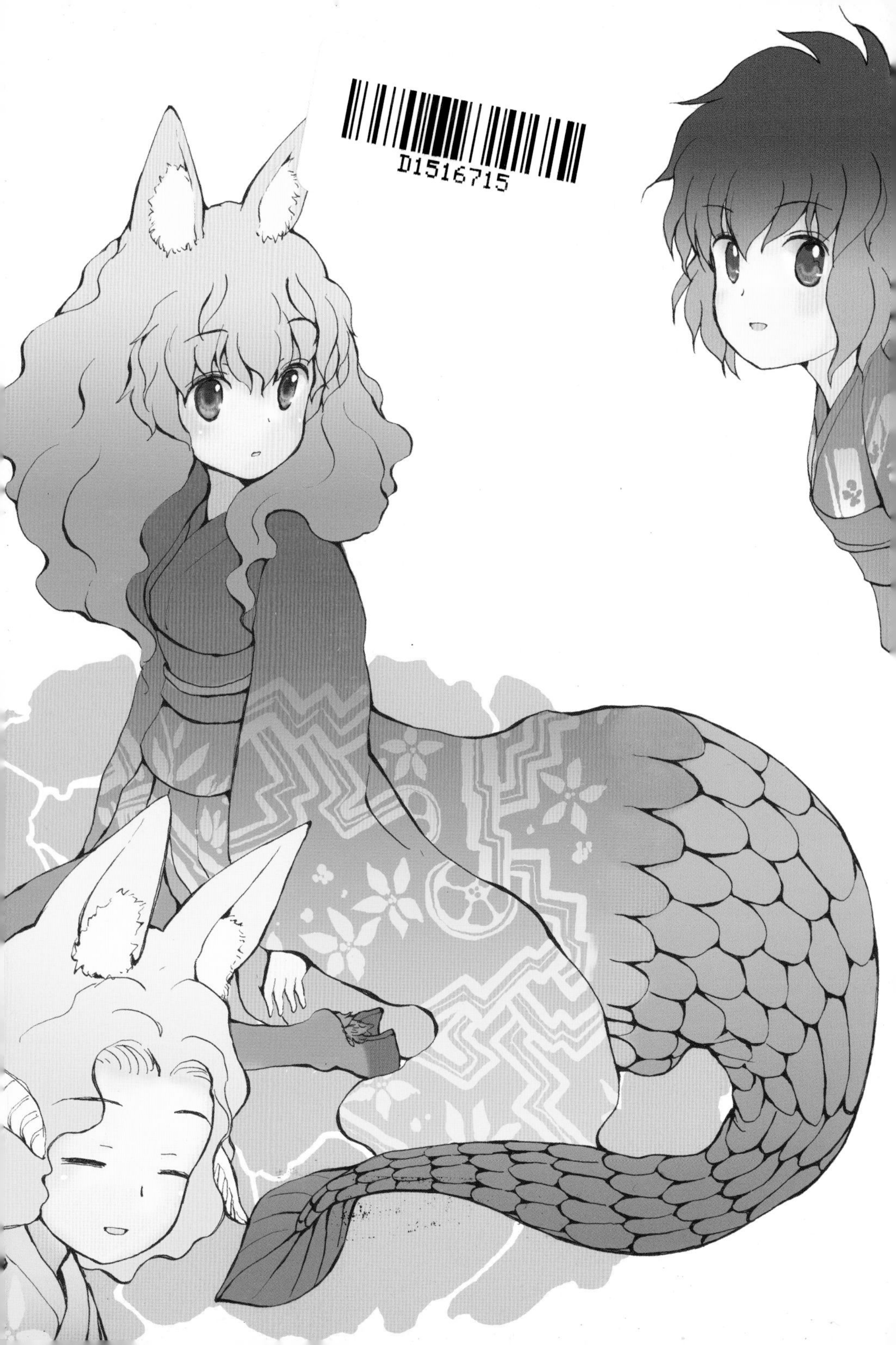

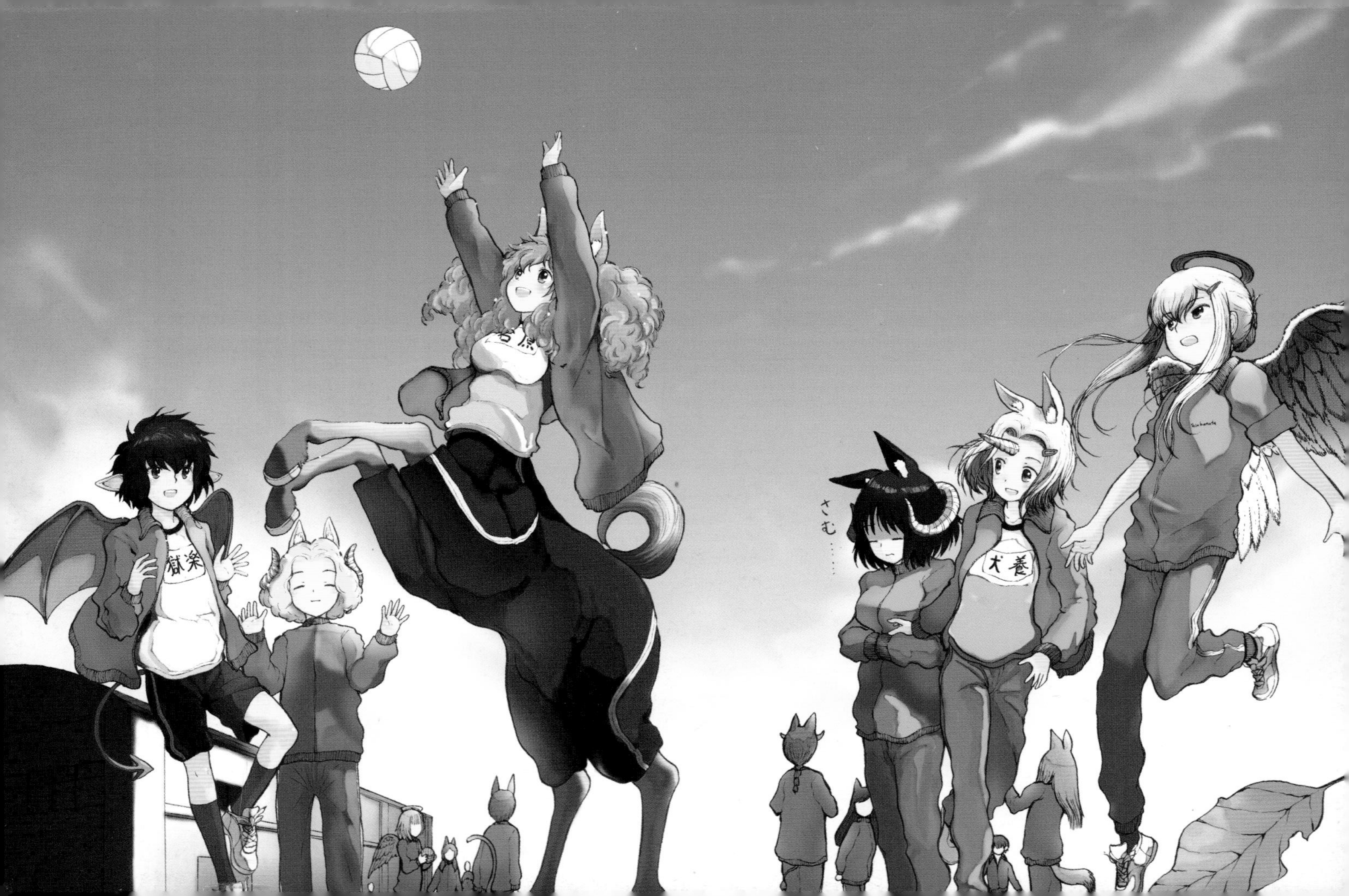
さむ……
犬養
獄楽

A Centaur's Life

Vol. 2

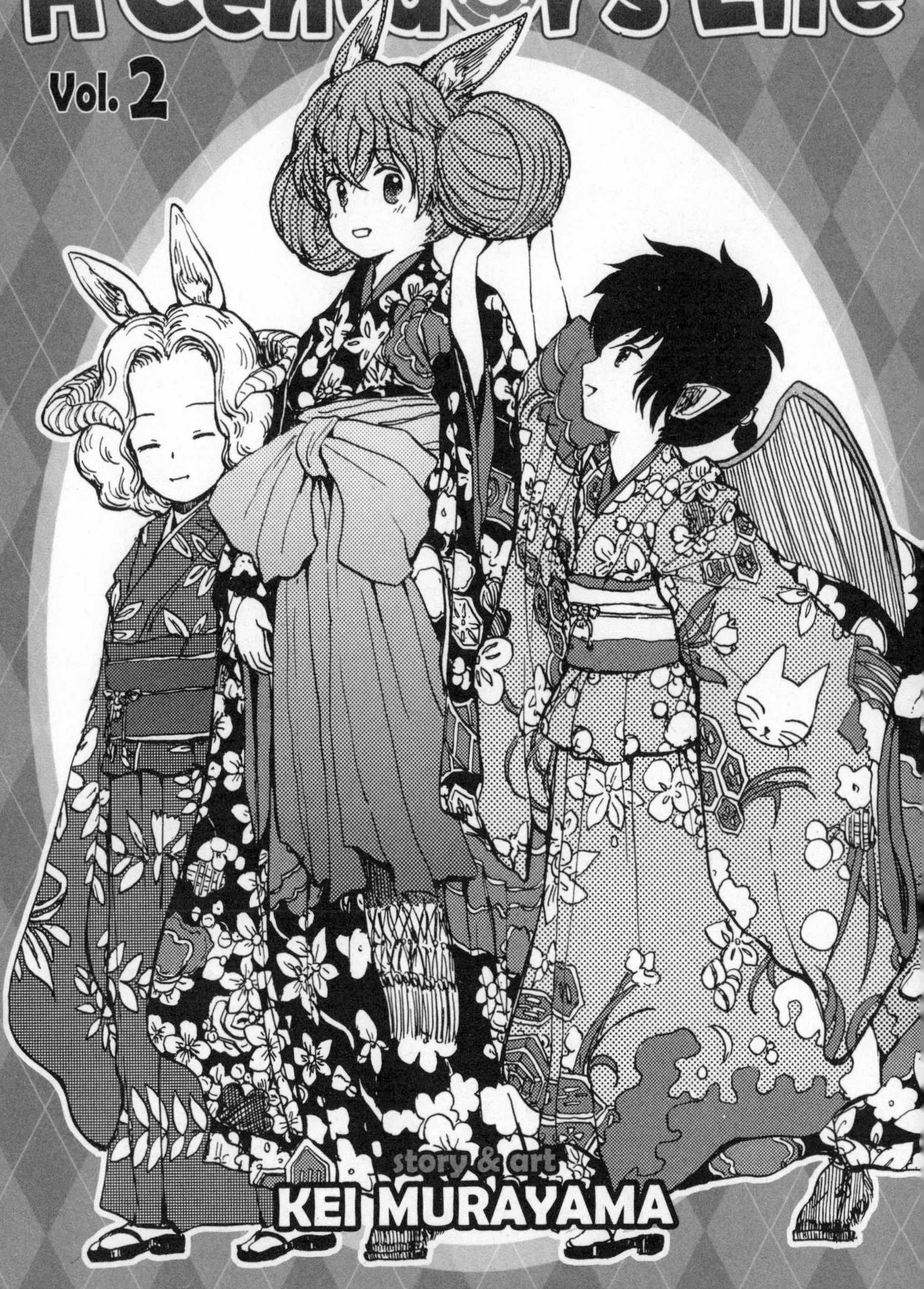

story & art

KEI MURAYAMA

SEVEN SEAS ENTERTAINMENT PRESENTS

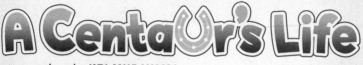

A Centaur's Life

story and art by **KEI MURAYAMA**

VOLUME 2

TRANSLATION
Angela Liu

ADAPTATION
Holly Kolodziejczak

LETTERING AND LAYOUT
Jennifer Skarupa

LOGO DESIGN
Courtney Williams

COVER DESIGN
Nicky Lim

PROOFREADER
Patrick King

MANAGING EDITOR
Adam Arnold

PUBLISHER
Jason DeAngelis

CENTAUR NO NAYAMI VOLUME 2

Originally published in Japan in 2012 by TOKUMA SHOTEN PUBLISHING CO., LTD., Tokyo. English translation rights arranged with TOKUMA SHOTEN PUBLISHING CO., LTD., Tokyo, through TOHAN CORPORATION, Tokyo.

ISBN: 978-1-626920-00-2

Printed in Canada

First Printing: February 2014

10 9 8 7 6 5 4 3 2 1

READING DIRECTIONS

This book reads from ***right to left***, Japanese style. If this is your first time reading manga, you start reading from the top right panel on each page and take it from there. If you get lost, just follow the numbered diagram here. It may seem backwards at first, but you□ll get the hang of it! Have fun!!

1
2
3
4
5
6
7
8
9

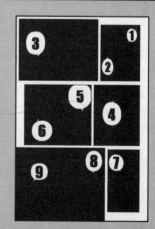

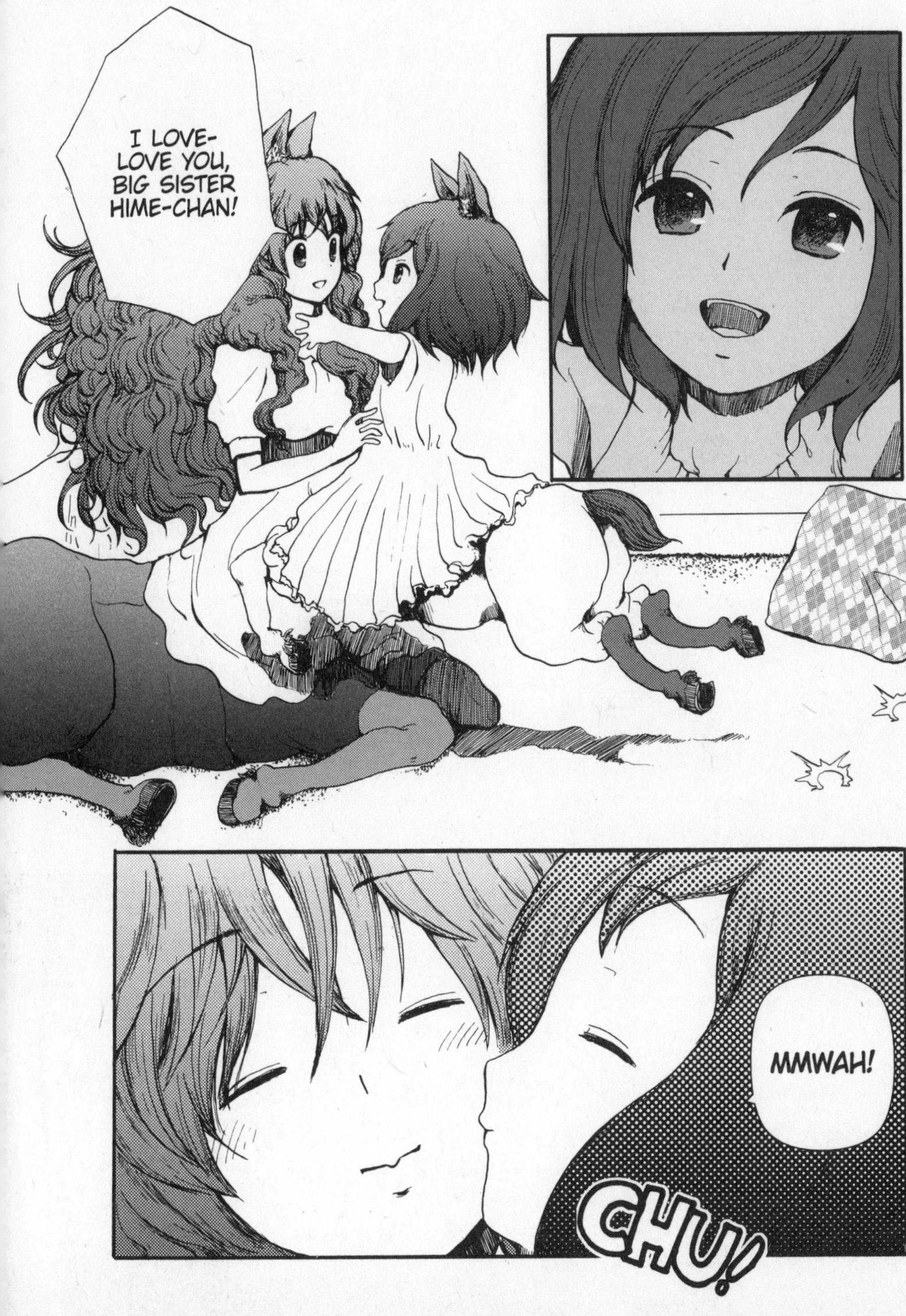
I LOVE-LOVE YOU, BIG SISTER HIME-CHAN!
MMWAH!
CHU!

CHAPTER 5

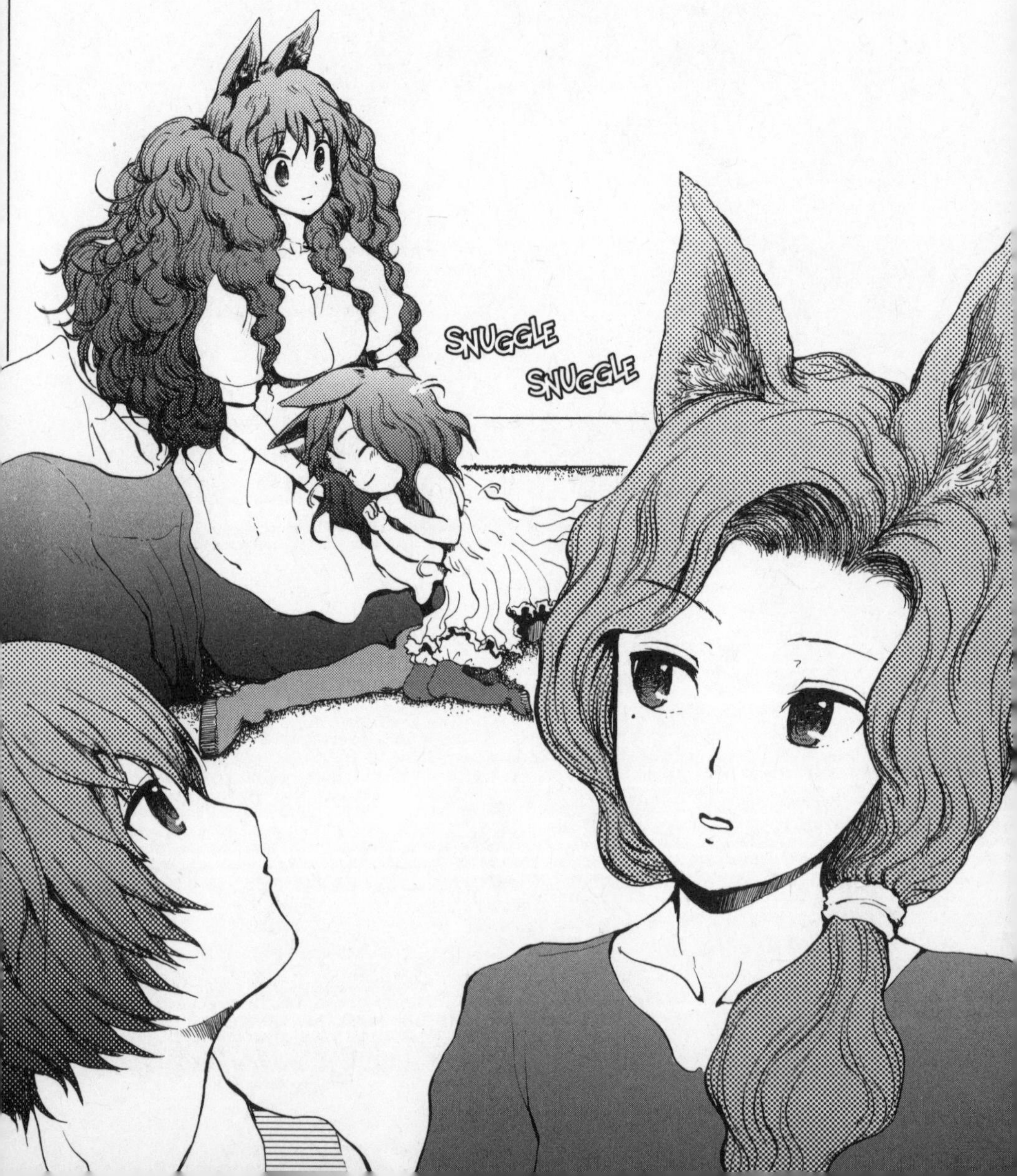
SNUGGLE
SNUGGLE

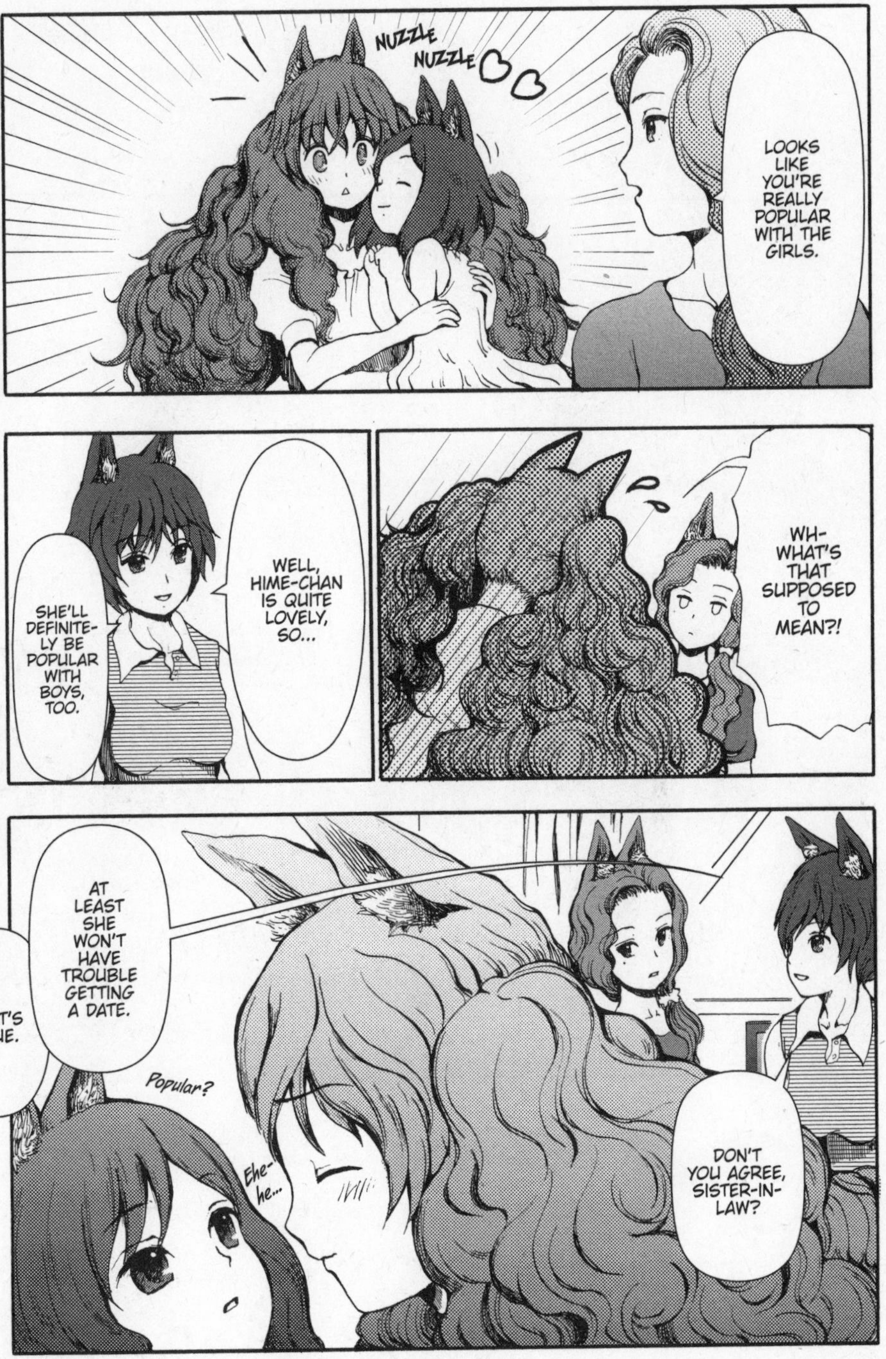
NUZZLE NUZZLE
LOOKS LIKE YOU'RE REALLY POPULAR WITH THE GIRLS.
WH- WHAT'S THAT SUPPOSED TO MEAN?!
WELL, HIME-CHAN IS QUITE LOVELY, SO...
SHE'LL DEFINITELY BE POPULAR WITH BOYS, TOO.
AT LEAST SHE WON'T HAVE TROUBLE GETTING A DATE.
DON'T YOU AGREE, SISTER-IN-LAW?
THAT'S TRUE.
Popular?
Ehe-he...

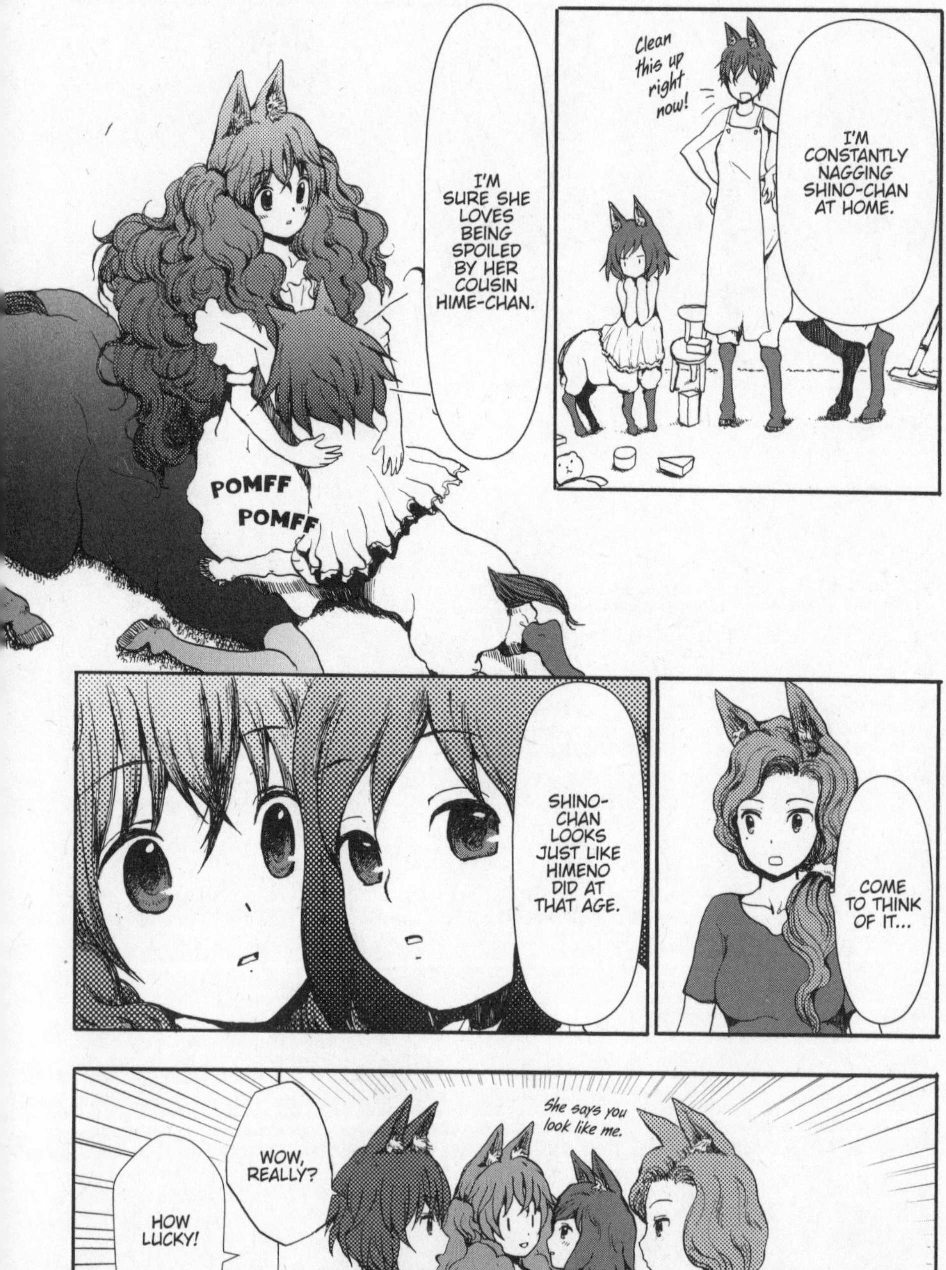
I'M CONSTANTLY NAGGING SHINO-CHAN AT HOME.
Clean this up right now!
I'M SURE SHE LOVES BEING SPOILED BY HER COUSIN HIME-CHAN.
POMFF
POMFF
COME TO THINK OF IT...
SHINO-CHAN LOOKS JUST LIKE HIMENO DID AT THAT AGE.
She says you look like me.
WOW, REALLY?
HOW LUCKY!

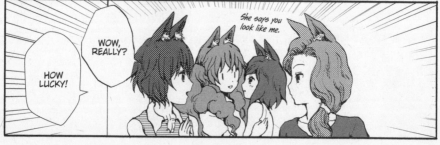

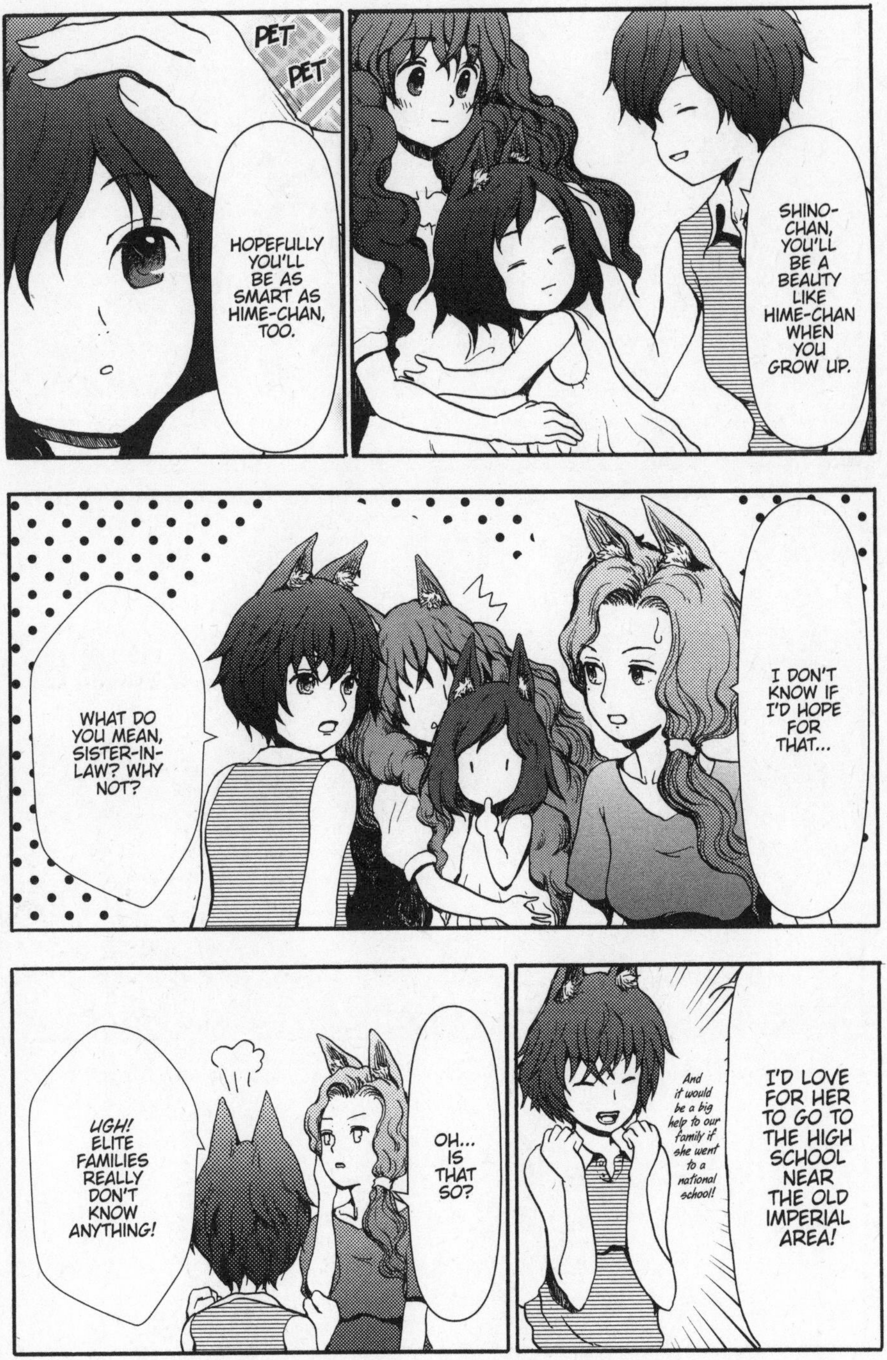
SHINO-CHAN, YOU'LL BE A BEAUTY LIKE HIME-CHAN WHEN YOU GROW UP.
PET
PET
HOPEFULLY YOU'LL BE AS SMART AS HIME-CHAN, TOO.
I DON'T KNOW IF I'D HOPE FOR THAT...
WHAT DO YOU MEAN, SISTER-IN-LAW? WHY NOT?
I'D LOVE FOR HER TO GO TO THE HIGH SCHOOL NEAR THE OLD IMPERIAL AREA!
And it would be a big help to our family if she went to a national school!
OH... IS THAT SO?
UGH! ELITE FAMILIES REALLY DON'T KNOW ANYTHING!

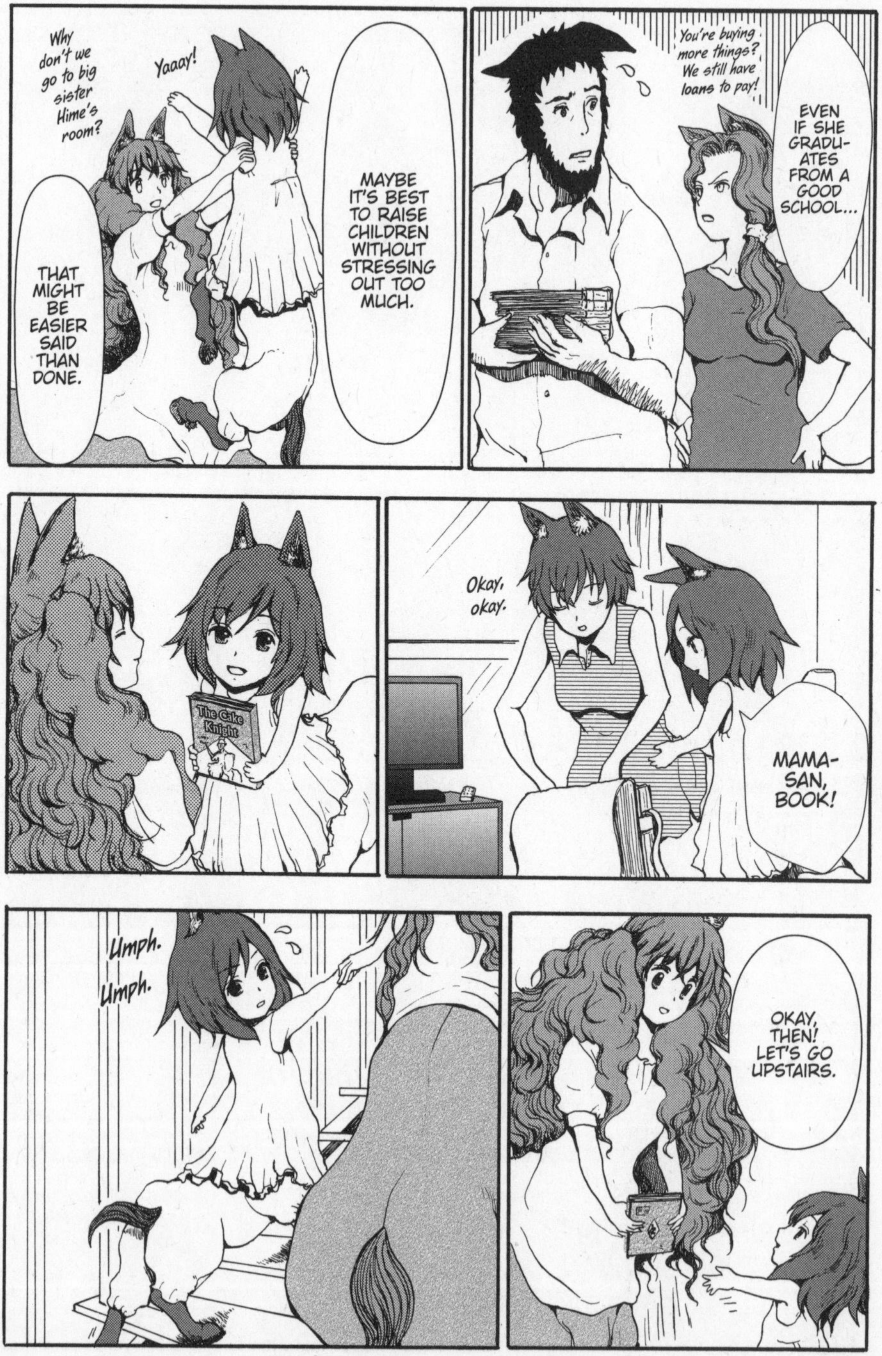
EVEN IF SHE GRADUATES FROM A GOOD SCHOOL...
You're buying more things? We still have loans to pay!
MAYBE IT'S BEST TO RAISE CHILDREN WITHOUT STRESSING OUT TOO MUCH.
Why don't we go to big sister Hime's room?
Yaaay!
THAT MIGHT BE EASIER SAID THAN DONE.
MAMA-SAN, BOOK!
Okay, okay.
The Cake Knight
OKAY, THEN! LET'S GO UPSTAIRS.
Umph.
Umph.

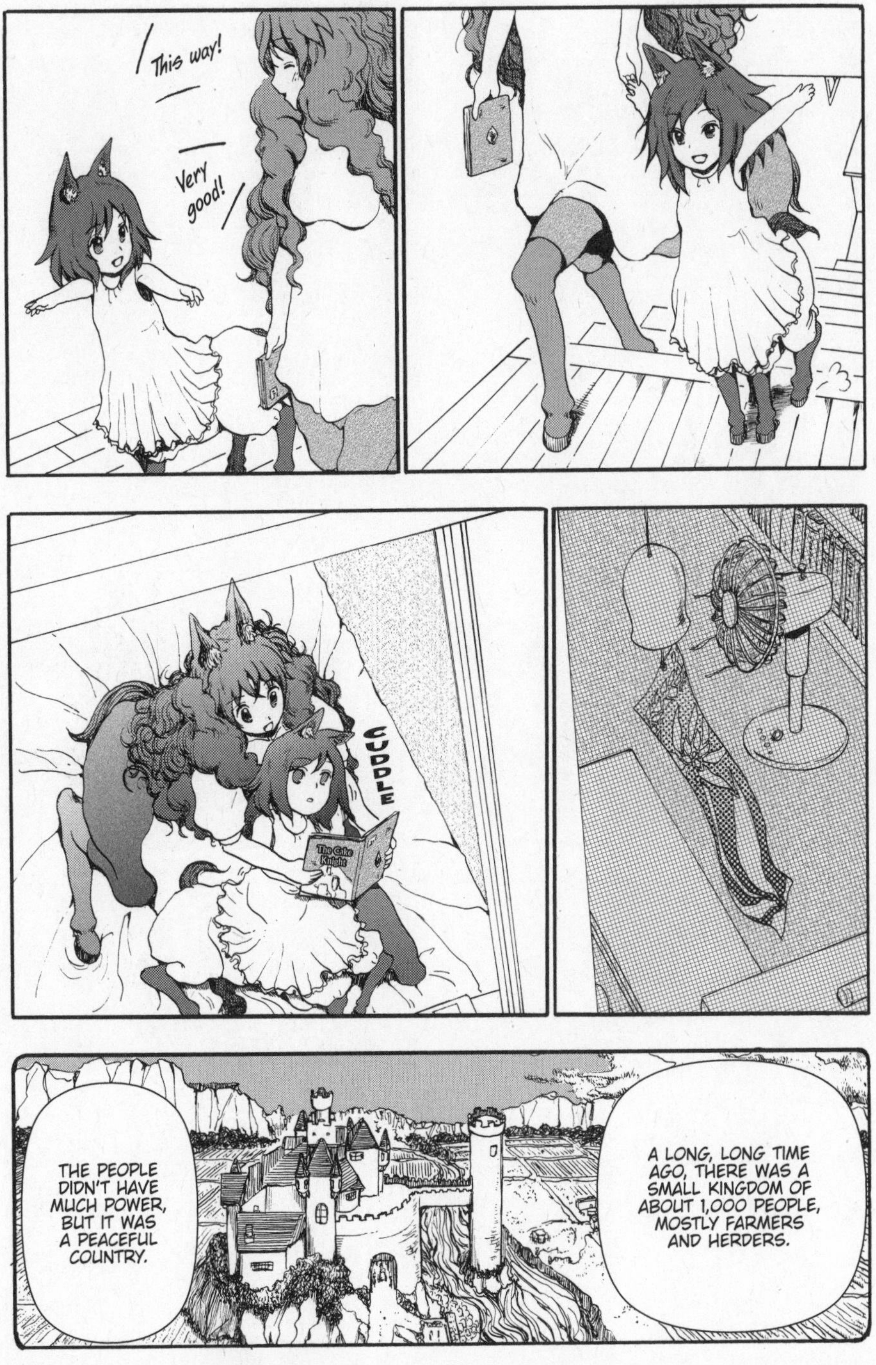
This way!
Very good!
CUDDLE
The Cake Knight
A LONG, LONG TIME AGO, THERE WAS A SMALL KINGDOM OF ABOUT 1,000 PEOPLE, MOSTLY FARMERS AND HERDERS.
THE PEOPLE DIDN'T HAVE MUCH POWER, BUT IT WAS A PEACEFUL COUNTRY.

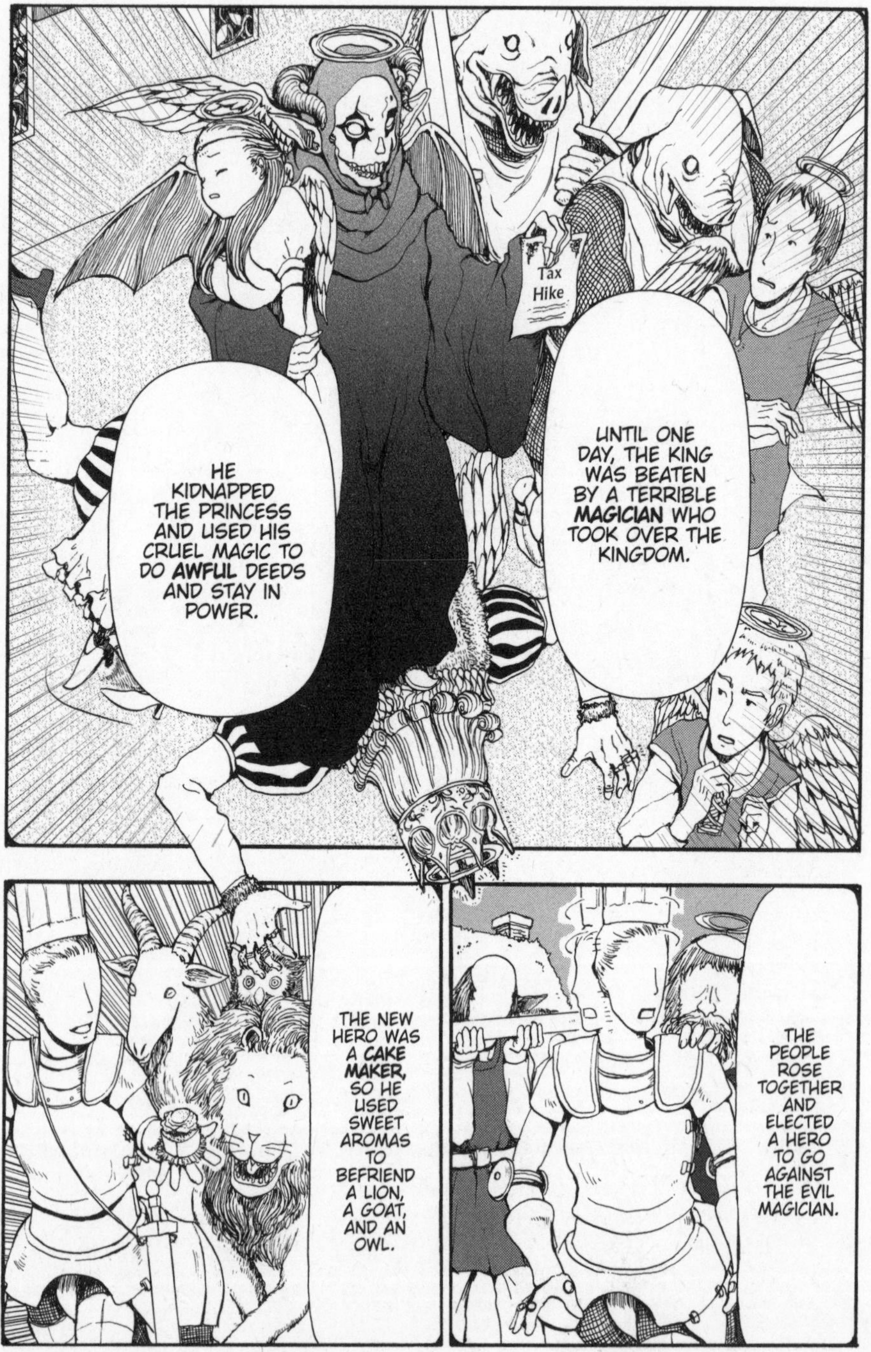
Tax Hike
UNTIL ONE DAY, THE KING WAS BEATEN BY A TERRIBLE **MAGICIAN** WHO TOOK OVER THE KINGDOM.
HE KIDNAPPED THE PRINCESS AND USED HIS CRUEL MAGIC TO DO **AWFUL** DEEDS AND STAY IN POWER.
THE PEOPLE ROSE TOGETHER AND ELECTED A HERO TO GO AGAINST THE EVIL MAGICIAN.
THE NEW HERO WAS A **CAKE MAKER,** SO HE USED SWEET AROMAS TO BEFRIEND A LION, A GOAT, AND AN OWL.

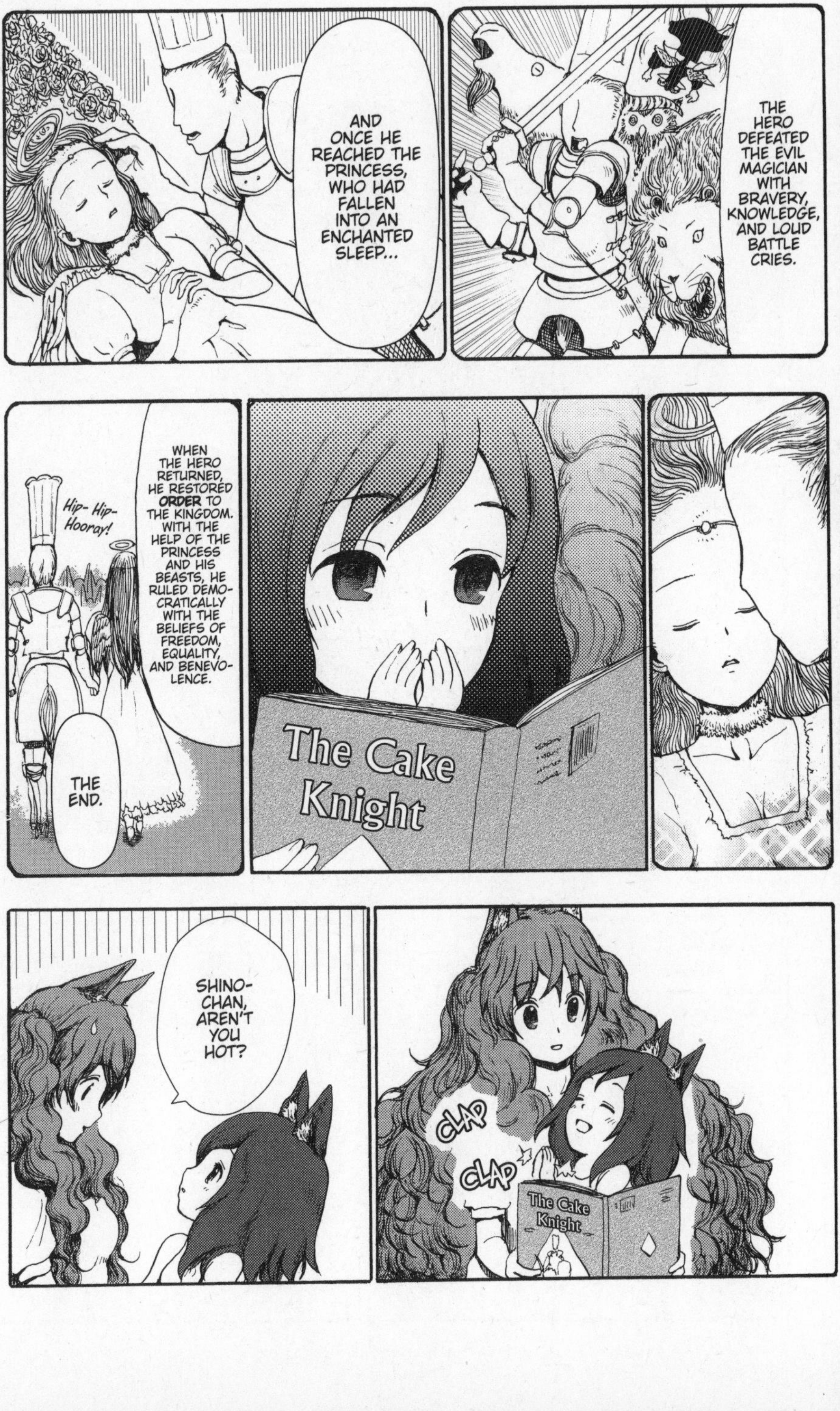
THE HERO DEFEATED THE EVIL MAGICIAN WITH BRAVERY, KNOWLEDGE, AND LOUD BATTLE CRIES.
AND ONCE HE REACHED THE PRINCESS, WHO HAD FALLEN INTO AN ENCHANTED SLEEP...
The Cake Knight
WHEN THE HERO RETURNED, HE RESTORED **ORDER** TO THE KINGDOM. WITH THE HELP OF THE PRINCESS AND HIS BEASTS, HE RULED DEMOCRATICALLY WITH THE BELIEFS OF FREEDOM, EQUALITY, AND BENEVOLENCE.
Hip-Hip-Hooray!
THE END.
CLAP
CLAP
The Cake Knight
SHINO-CHAN, AREN'T YOU HOT?

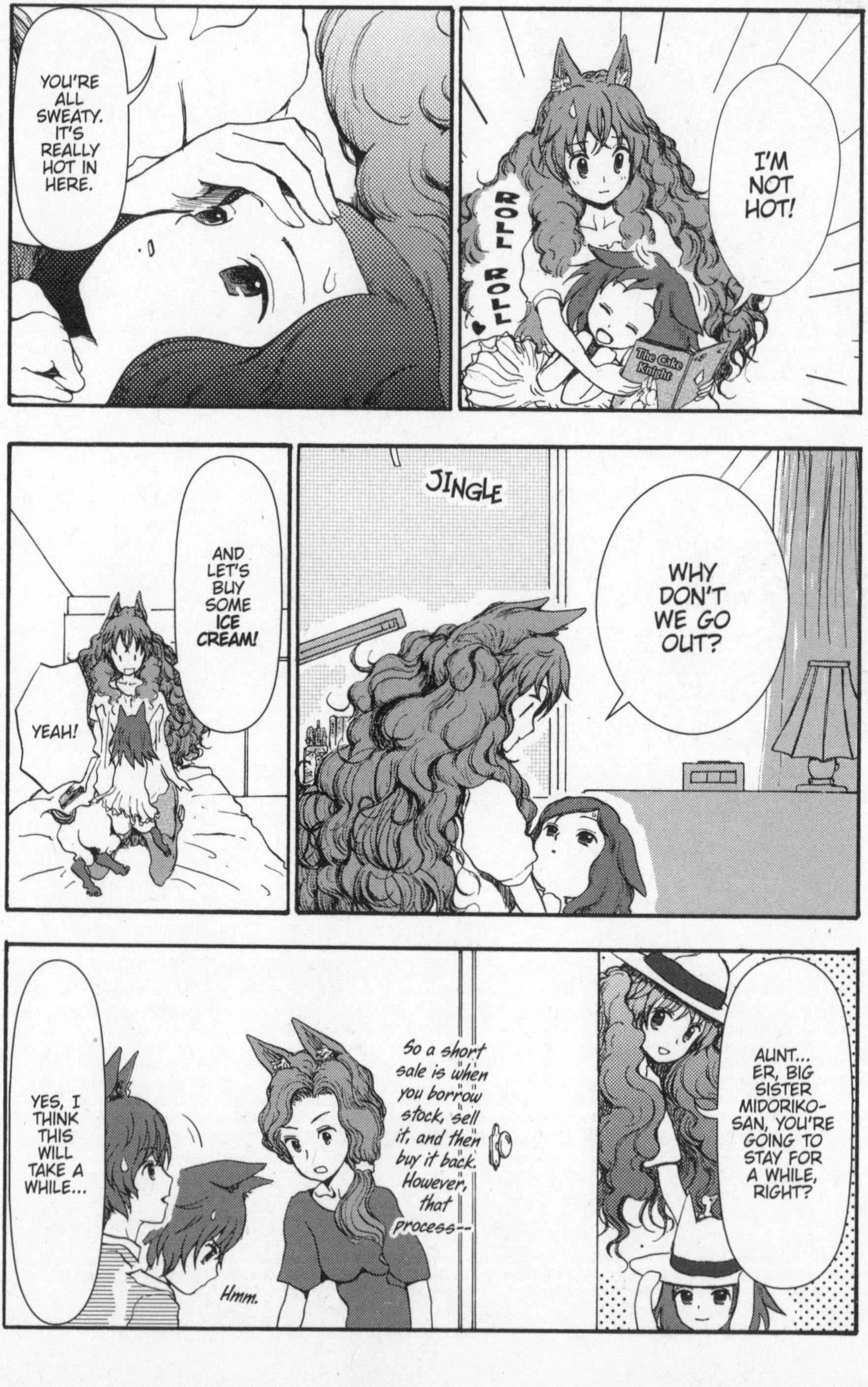
I'M NOT HOT!
ROLL ROLL
The Cake Knight
YOU'RE ALL SWEATY. IT'S REALLY HOT IN HERE.
JINGLE
WHY DON'T WE GO OUT?
AND LET'S BUY SOME ICE CREAM!
YEAH!
AUNT... ER, BIG SISTER MIDORIKO-SAN, YOU'RE GOING TO STAY FOR A WHILE, RIGHT?
So a short sale is when you borrow stock, sell it, and then buy it back. However, that process--
Hmm.
YES, I THINK THIS WILL TAKE A WHILE...

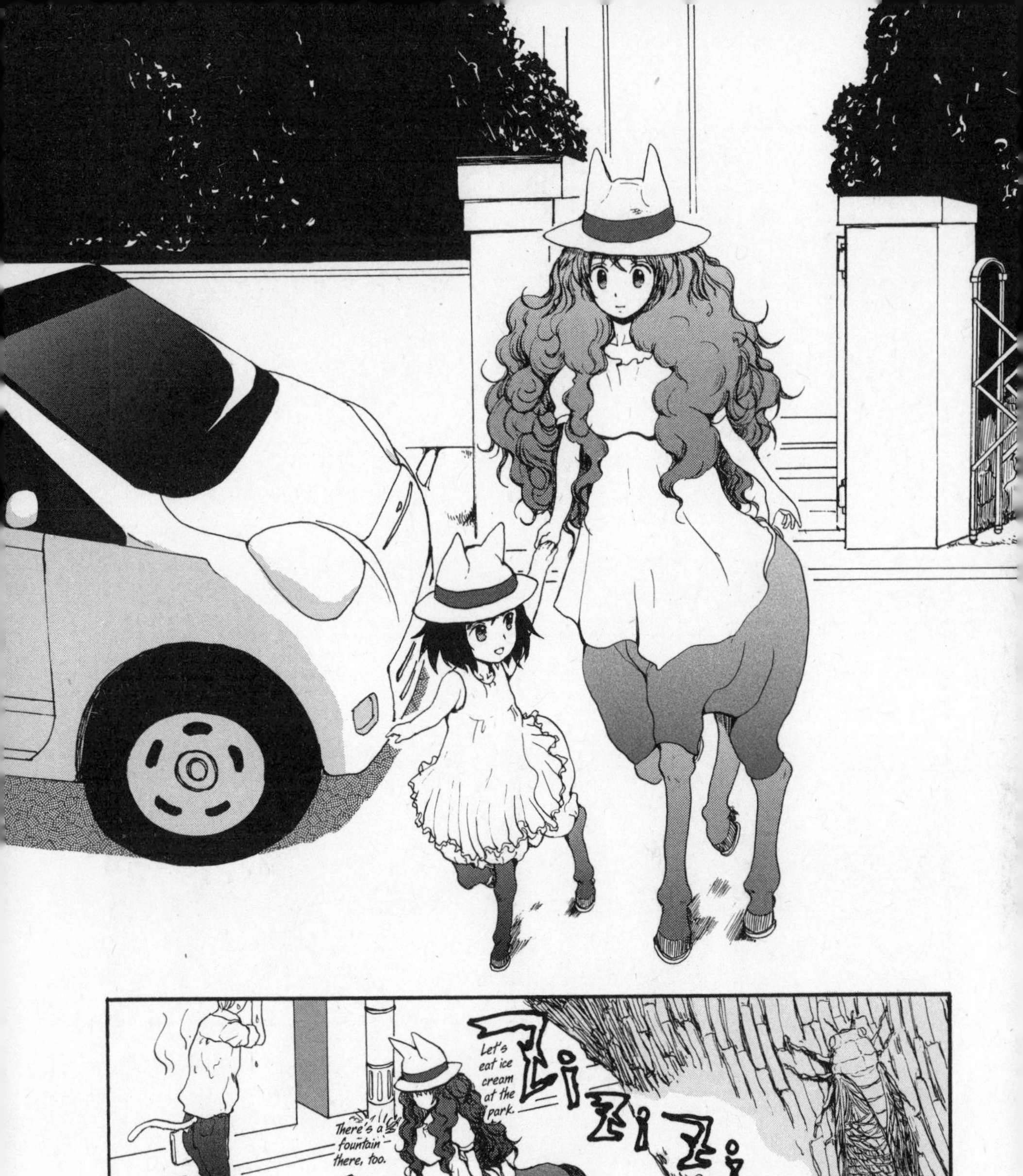

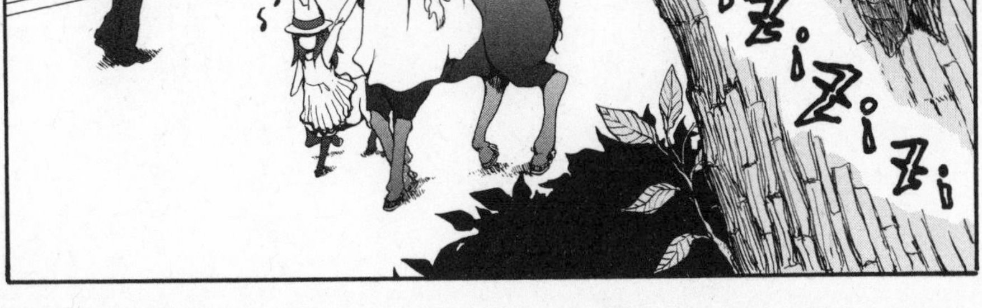
Let's eat ice cream at the park.
There's a fountain there, too.
Zi Zi Zi Zi Zi Zi

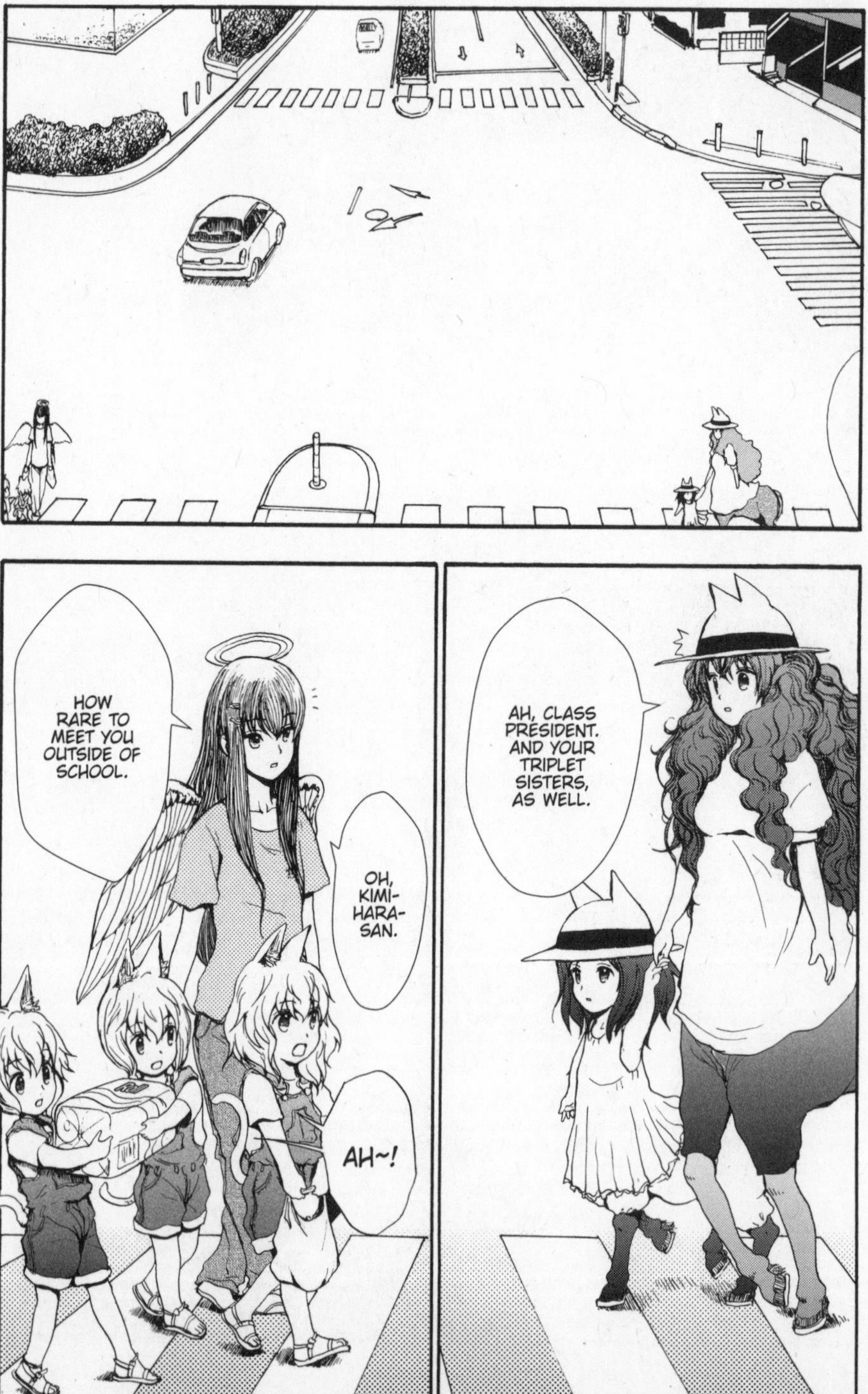
AH, CLASS PRESIDENT. AND YOUR TRIPLET SISTERS, AS WELL.
HOW RARE TO MEET YOU OUTSIDE OF SCHOOL.
OH, KIMIHARA-SAN.
AH~!

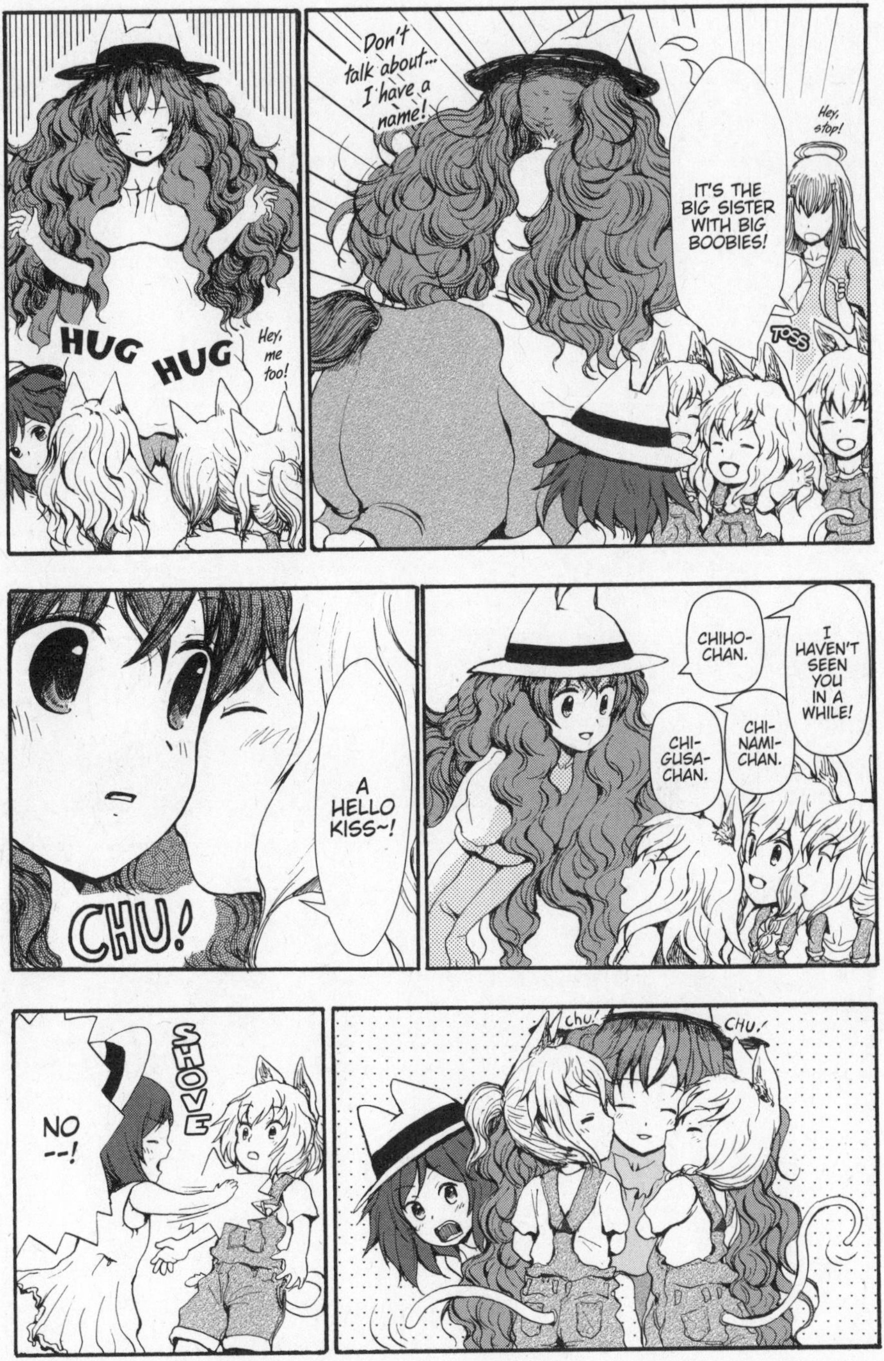

IT'S THE BIG SISTER WITH BIG BOOBIES!
Hey, stop!
TOSS
Don't talk about... I have a name!
Hey, me too!
HUG HUG
I HAVEN'T SEEN YOU IN A WHILE!
CHIHO-CHAN.
CHI-NAMI-CHAN.
CHI-GUSA-CHAN.
A HELLO KISS~!
CHU!
CHU!
chu!
SHOVE
NO--!

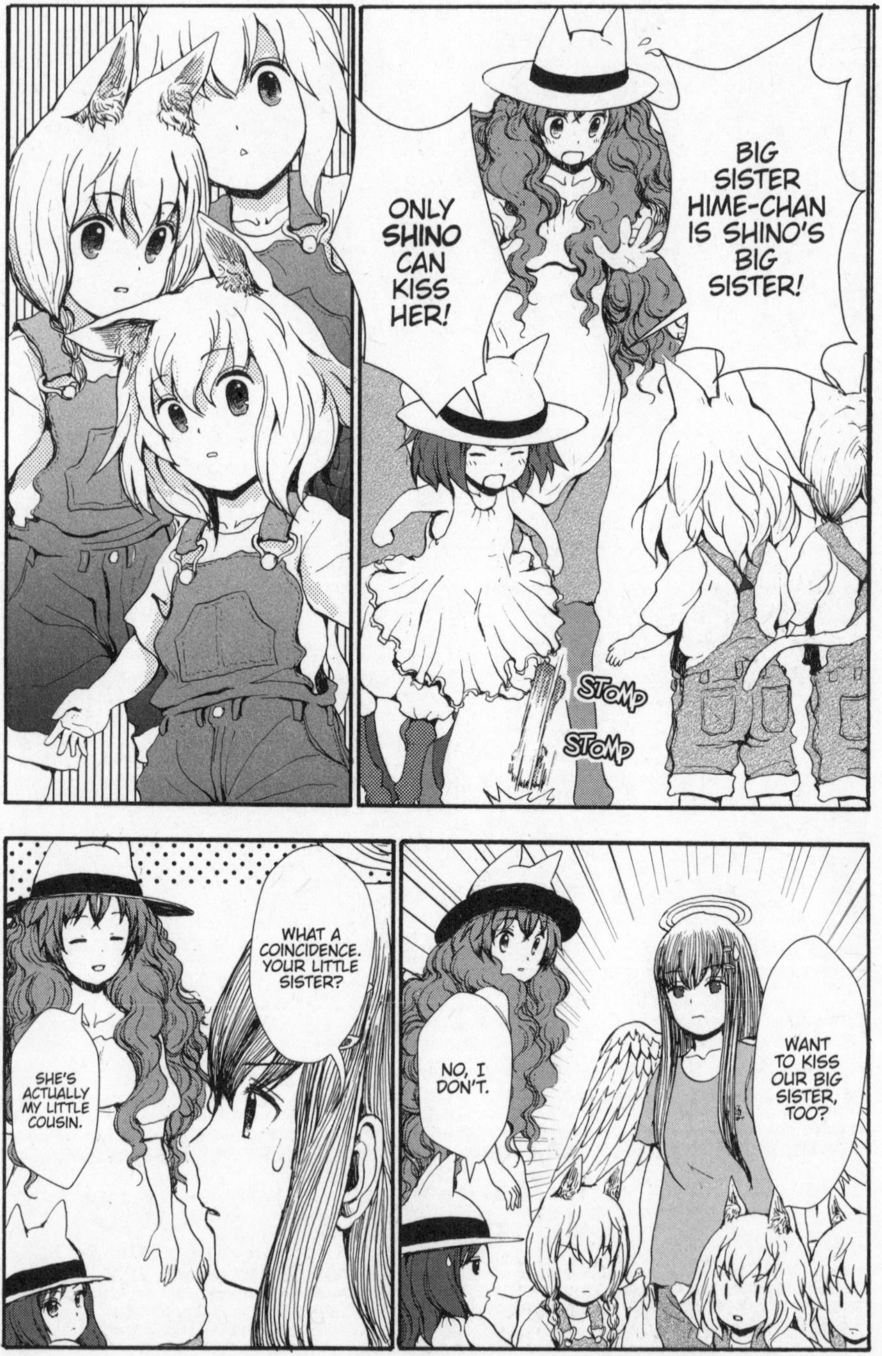
BIG SISTER HIME-CHAN IS SHINO'S BIG SISTER!
ONLY SHINO CAN KISS HER!
STOMP
STOMP
WANT TO KISS OUR BIG SISTER, TOO?
NO, I DON'T.
WHAT A COINCIDENCE. YOUR LITTLE SISTER?
SHE'S ACTUALLY MY LITTLE COUSIN.

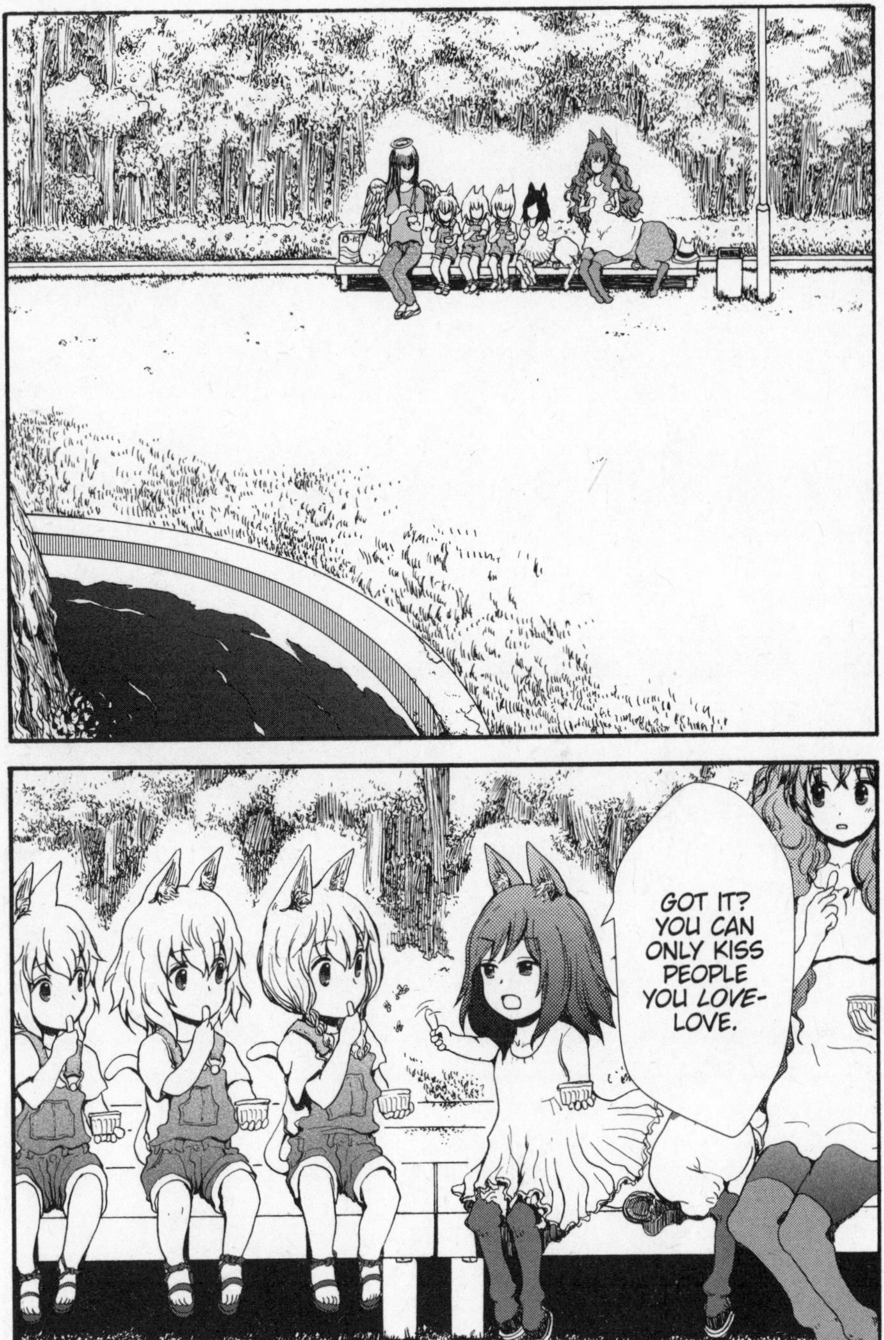
GOT IT? YOU CAN ONLY KISS PEOPLE YOU LOVE-LOVE.

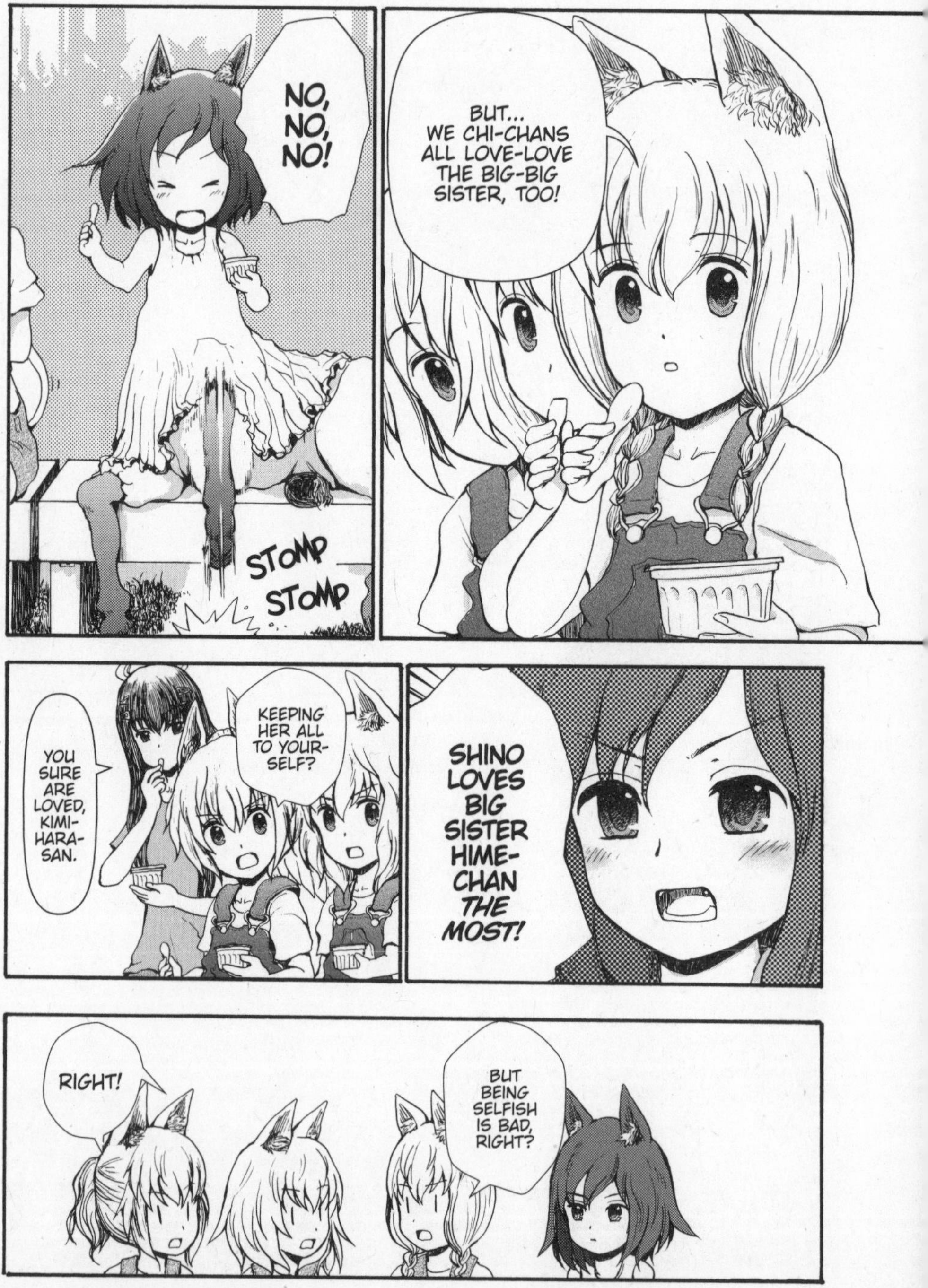
BUT... WE CHI-CHANS ALL LOVE-LOVE THE BIG-BIG SISTER, TOO!
NO, NO, NO!
STOMP STOMP
SHINO LOVES BIG SISTER HIME-CHAN *THE MOST!*
KEEPING HER ALL TO YOURSELF?
YOU SURE ARE LOVED, KIMIHARA-SAN.
BUT BEING SELFISH IS BAD, RIGHT?
RIGHT!

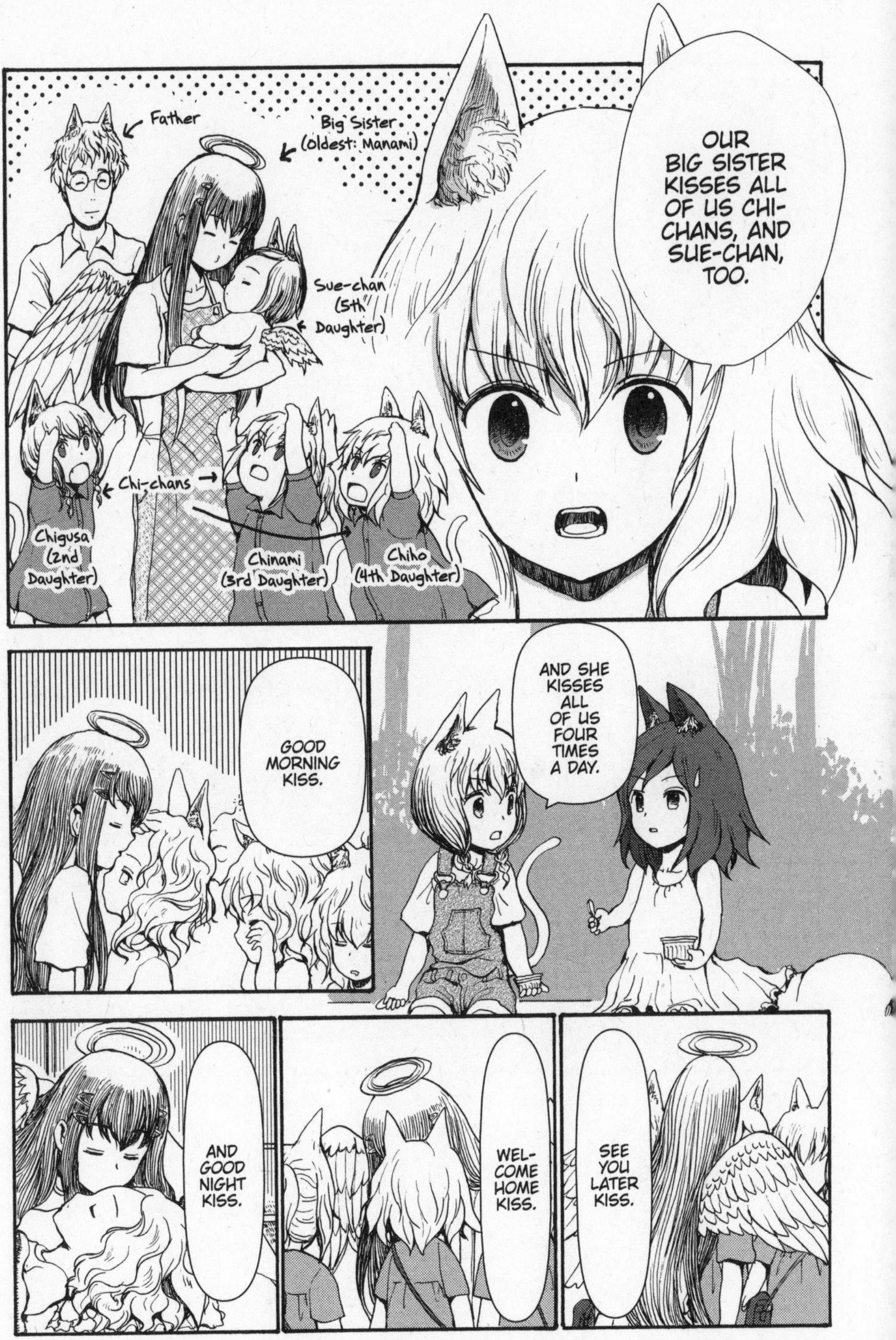
OUR BIG SISTER KISSES ALL OF US CHI-CHANS, AND SUE-CHAN, TOO.
Father
Big Sister (oldest: Manami)
Sue-chan (5th Daughter)
Chi-chans
Chigusa (2nd Daughter)
Chinami (3rd Daughter)
Chiho (4th Daughter)
AND SHE KISSES ALL OF US FOUR TIMES A DAY.
GOOD MORNING KISS.
SEE YOU LATER KISS.
WEL-COME HOME KISS.
AND GOOD NIGHT KISS.

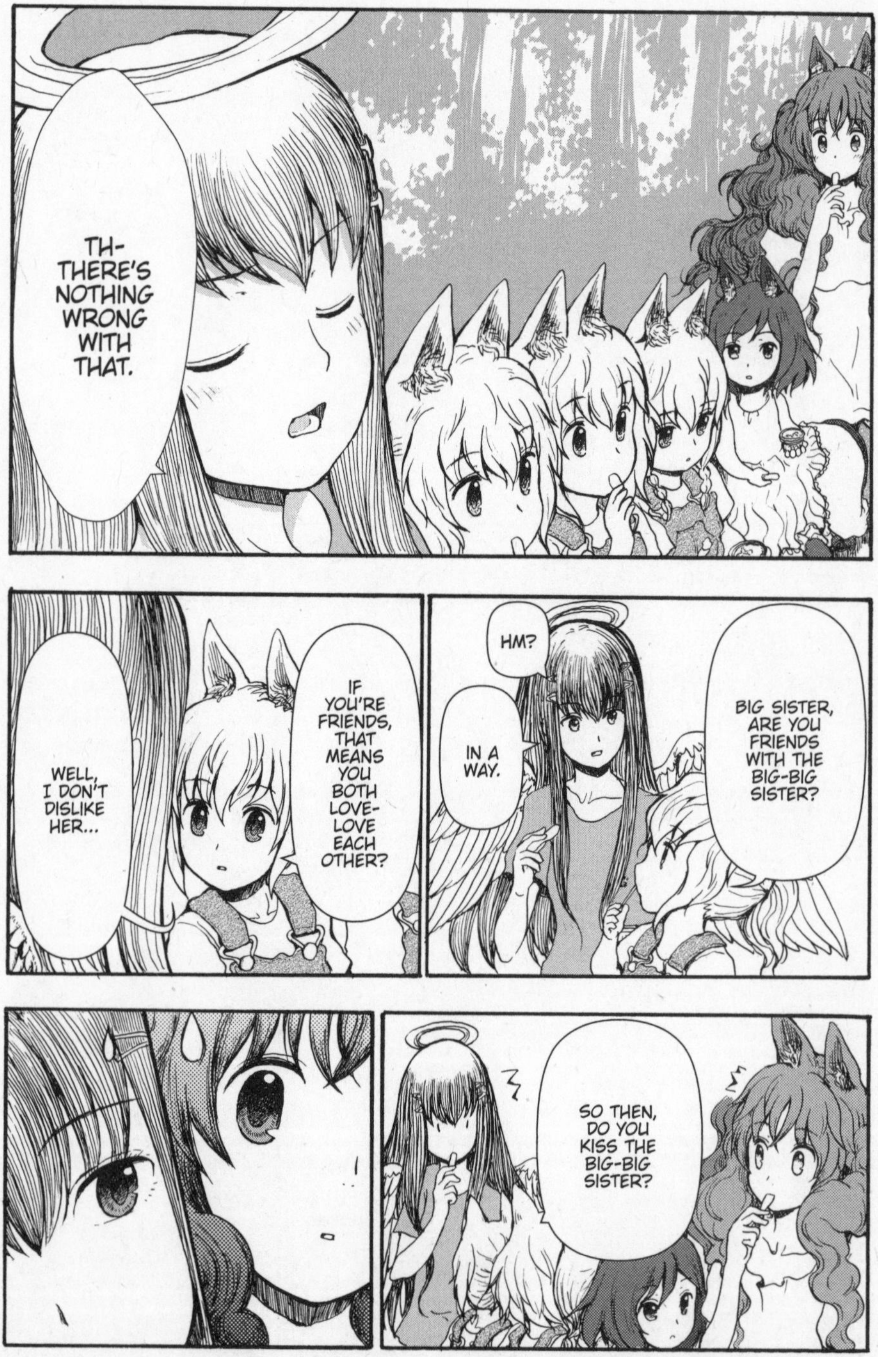
TH- THERE'S NOTHING WRONG WITH THAT.
BIG SISTER, ARE YOU FRIENDS WITH THE BIG-BIG SISTER?
HM?
IN A WAY.
IF YOU'RE FRIENDS, THAT MEANS YOU BOTH LOVE-LOVE EACH OTHER?
WELL, I DON'T DISLIKE HER...
SO THEN, DO YOU KISS THE BIG-BIG SISTER?

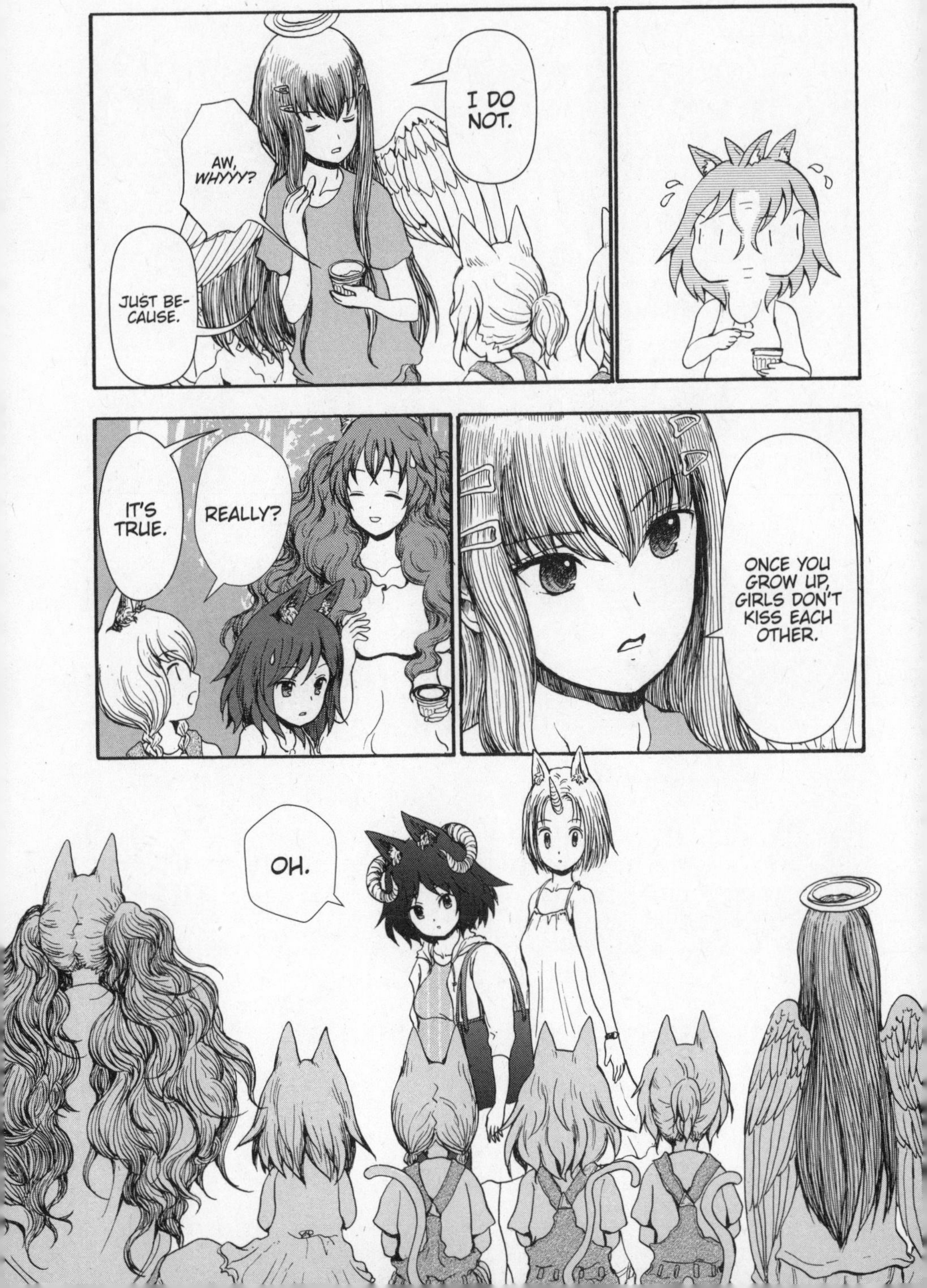
I DO NOT.
AW, WHYYY?
JUST BE-CAUSE.
ONCE YOU GROW UP, GIRLS DON'T KISS EACH OTHER.
REALLY?
IT'S TRUE.
OH.

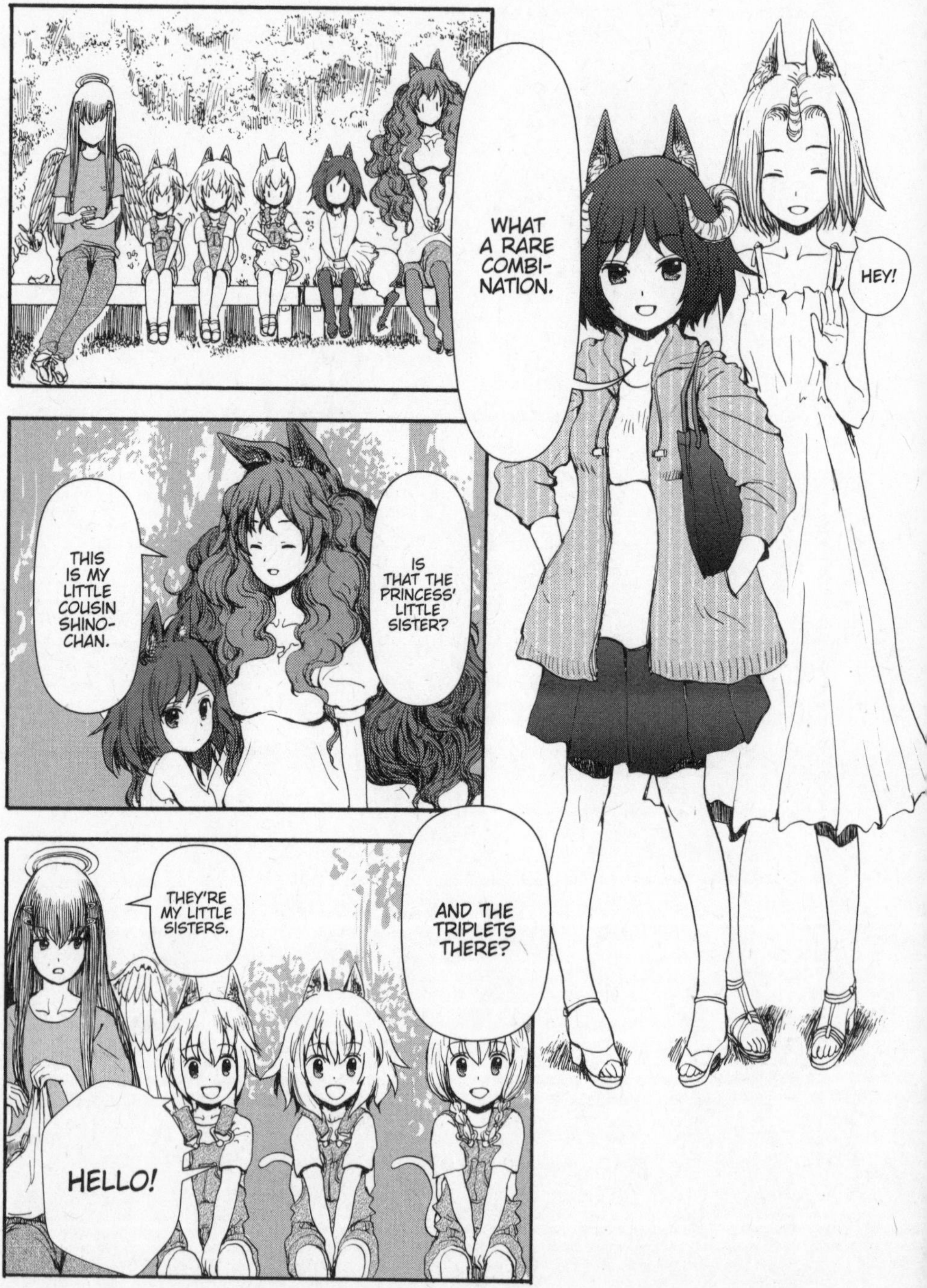
HEY!
WHAT A RARE COMBINATION.
IS THAT THE PRINCESS' LITTLE SISTER?
THIS IS MY LITTLE COUSIN SHINO-CHAN.
AND THE TRIPLETS THERE?
THEY'RE MY LITTLE SISTERS.
HELLO!

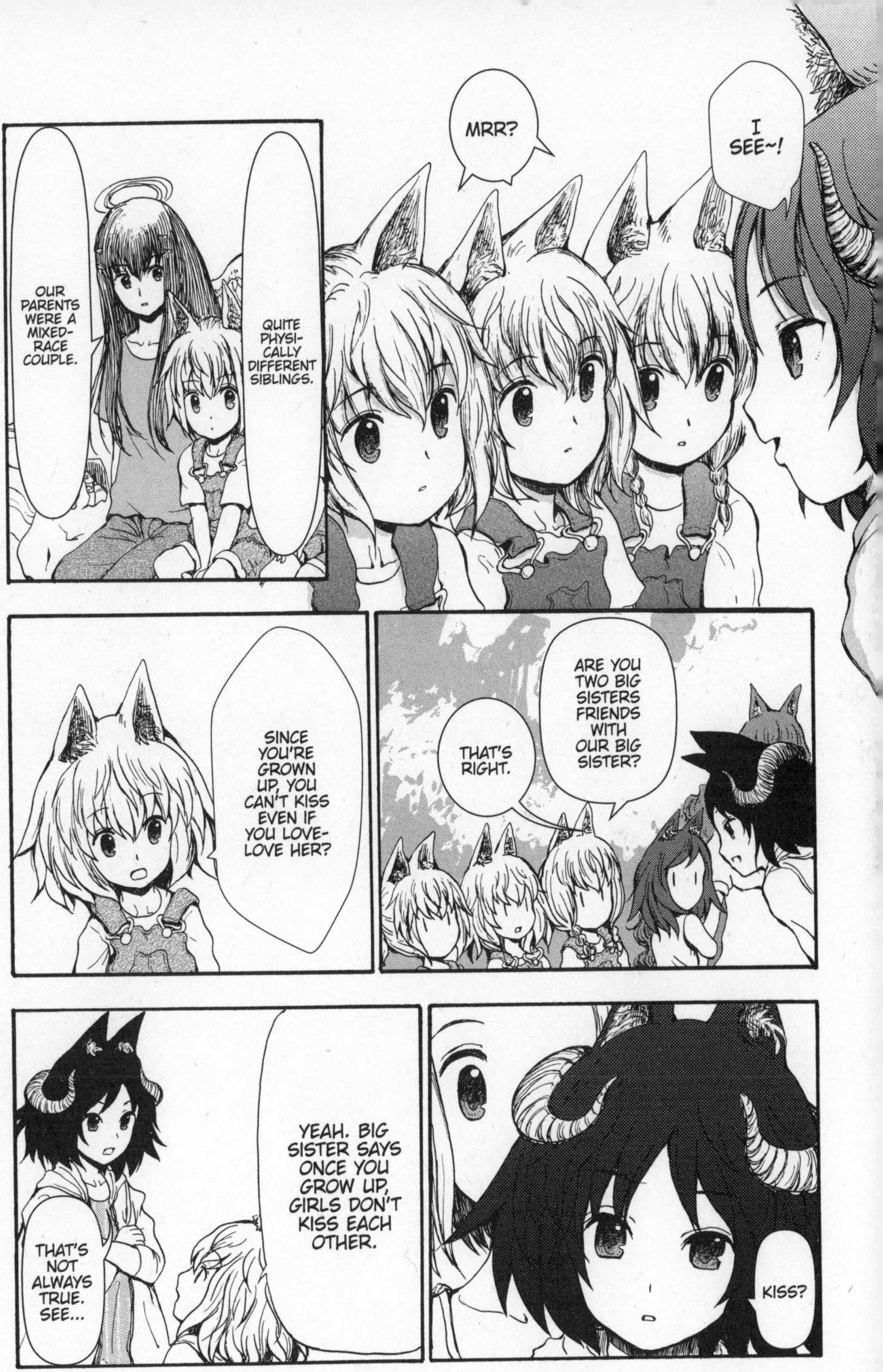
I SEE~!
MRR?
QUITE PHYSICALLY DIFFERENT SIBLINGS.
OUR PARENTS WERE A MIXED-RACE COUPLE.
ARE YOU TWO BIG SISTERS FRIENDS WITH OUR BIG SISTER?
THAT'S RIGHT.
SINCE YOU'RE GROWN UP, YOU CAN'T KISS EVEN IF YOU LOVE-LOVE HER?
KISS?
YEAH. BIG SISTER SAYS ONCE YOU GROW UP, GIRLS DON'T KISS EACH OTHER.
THAT'S NOT ALWAYS TRUE. SEE...

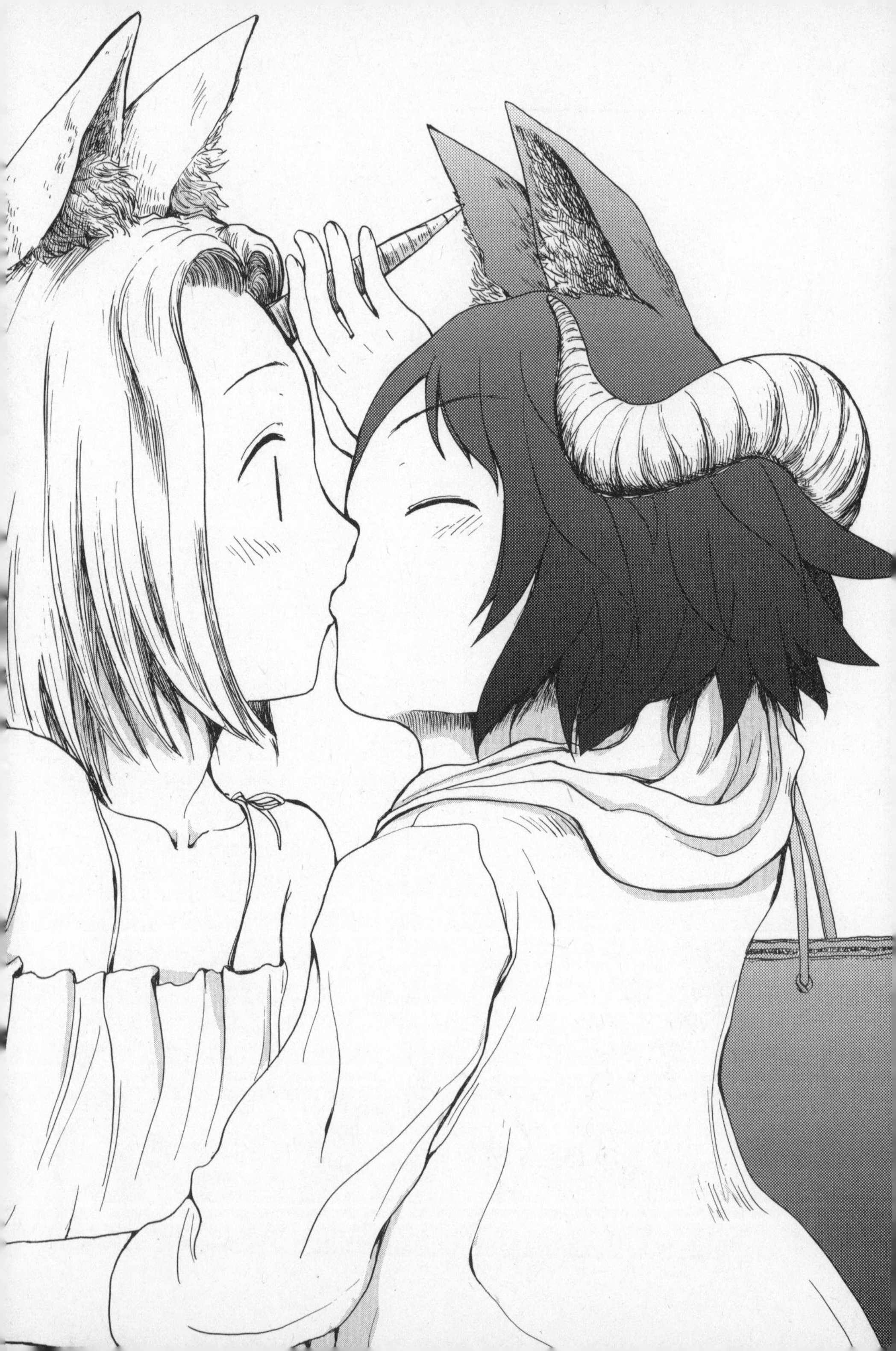

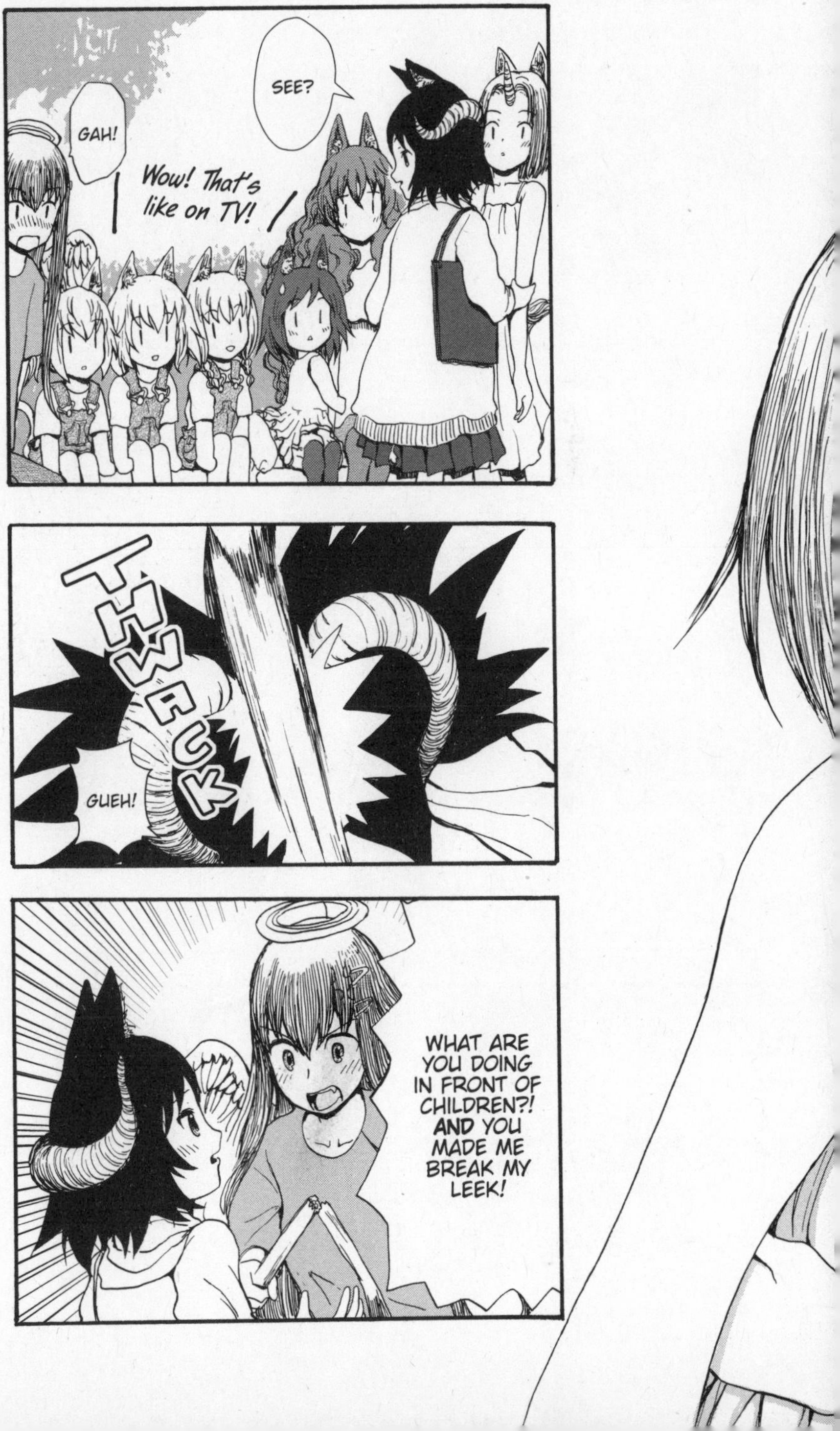
SEE?
Wow! That's like on TV!
GAH!
THWACK
GUEH!
WHAT ARE YOU DOING IN FRONT OF CHILDREN?! AND YOU MADE ME BREAK MY LEEK!

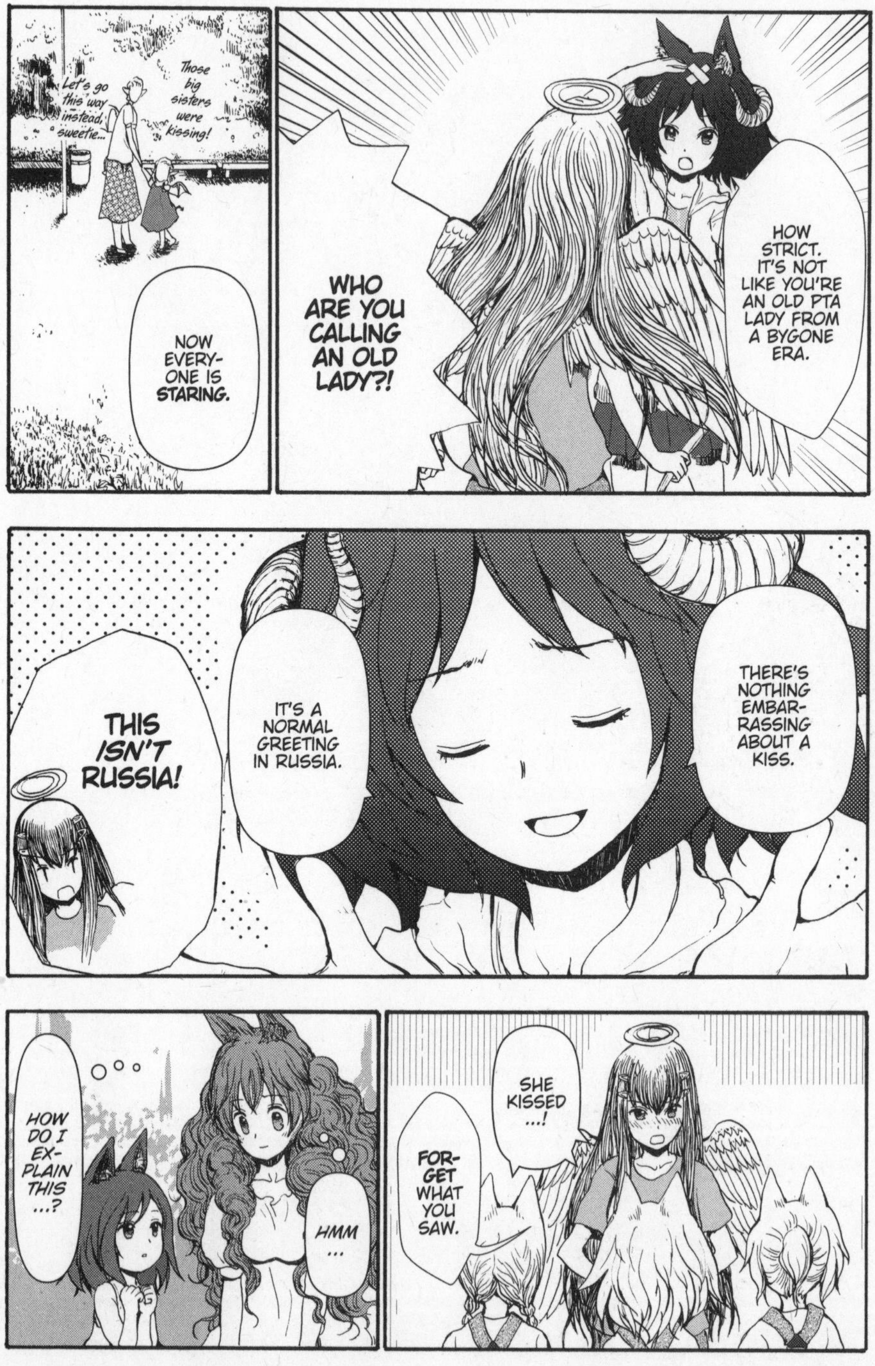
HOW STRICT. IT'S NOT LIKE YOU'RE AN OLD PTA LADY FROM A BYGONE ERA.
WHO ARE YOU CALLING AN OLD LADY?!
Those big sisters were kissing!
Let's go this way instead, sweetie...
NOW EVERY-ONE IS STARING.
THERE'S NOTHING EMBAR-RASSING ABOUT A KISS.
IT'S A NORMAL GREETING IN RUSSIA.
THIS ISN'T RUSSIA!
SHE KISSED ...!
FOR-GET WHAT YOU SAW.
HMM ...
HOW DO I EX-PLAIN THIS ...?

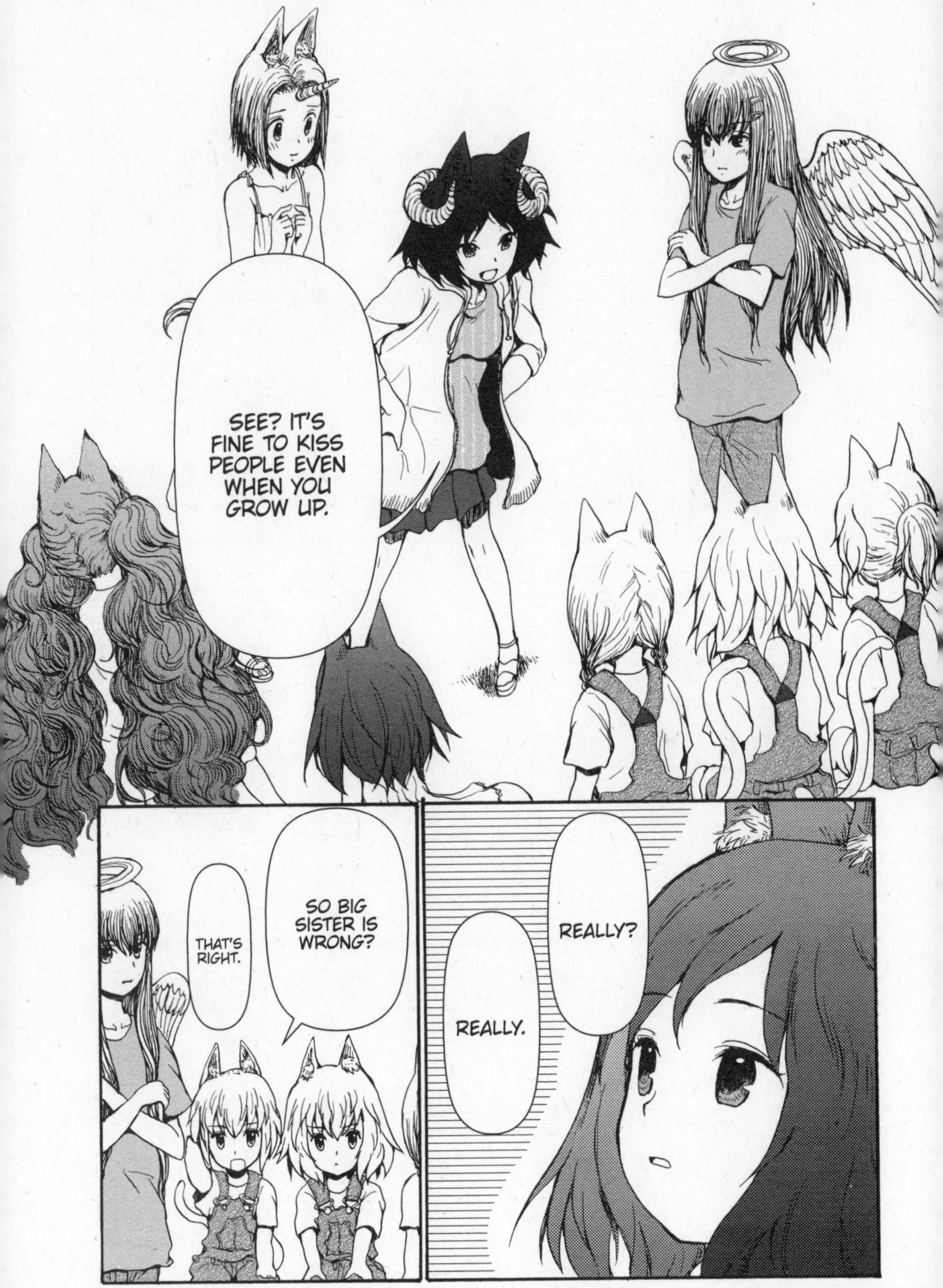
SEE? IT'S FINE TO KISS PEOPLE EVEN WHEN YOU GROW UP.
REALLY?
REALLY.
SO BIG SISTER IS WRONG?
THAT'S RIGHT.

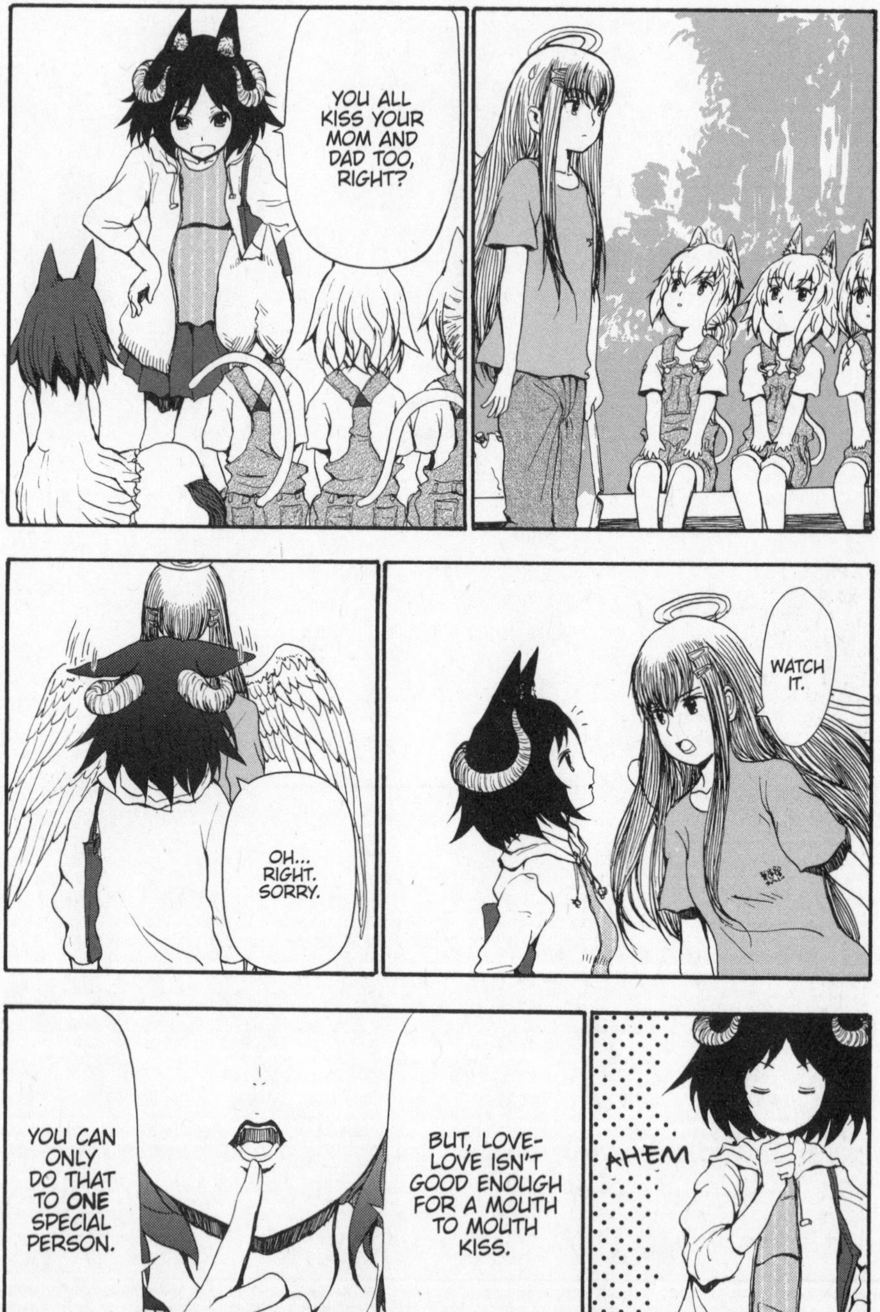
YOU ALL KISS YOUR MOM AND DAD TOO, RIGHT?
WATCH IT.
OH... RIGHT. SORRY.
AHEM
BUT, LOVE-LOVE ISN'T GOOD ENOUGH FOR A MOUTH TO MOUTH KISS.
YOU CAN ONLY DO THAT TO ONE SPECIAL PERSON.

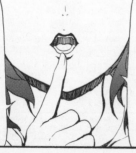

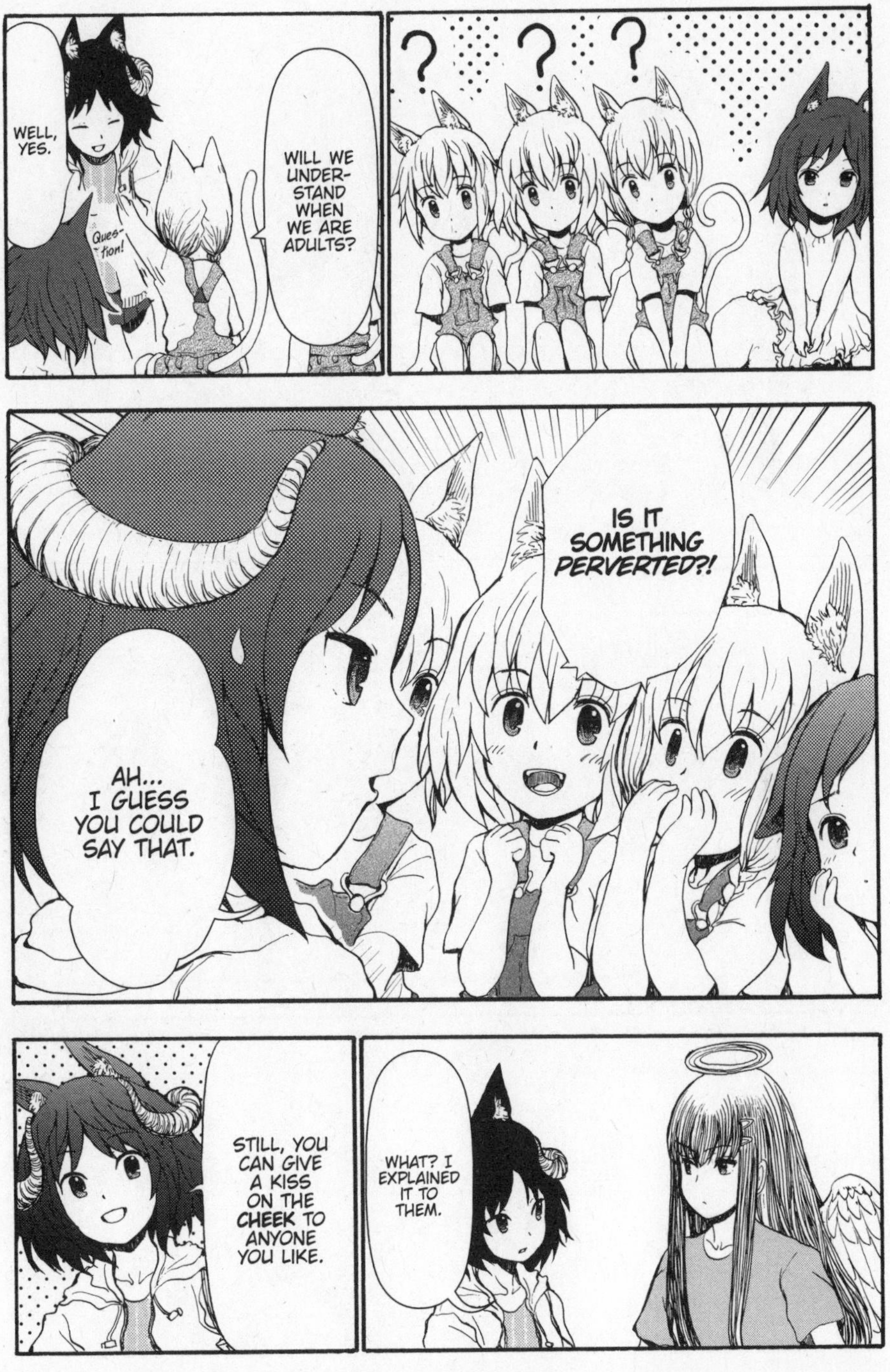
?
?
?
WILL WE UNDER-STAND WHEN WE ARE ADULTS?
Ques-tion!
WELL, YES.
IS IT SOMETHING *PERVERTED?!*
AH... I GUESS YOU COULD SAY THAT.
WHAT? I EXPLAINED IT TO THEM.
STILL, YOU CAN GIVE A KISS ON THE **CHEEK** TO ANYONE YOU LIKE.

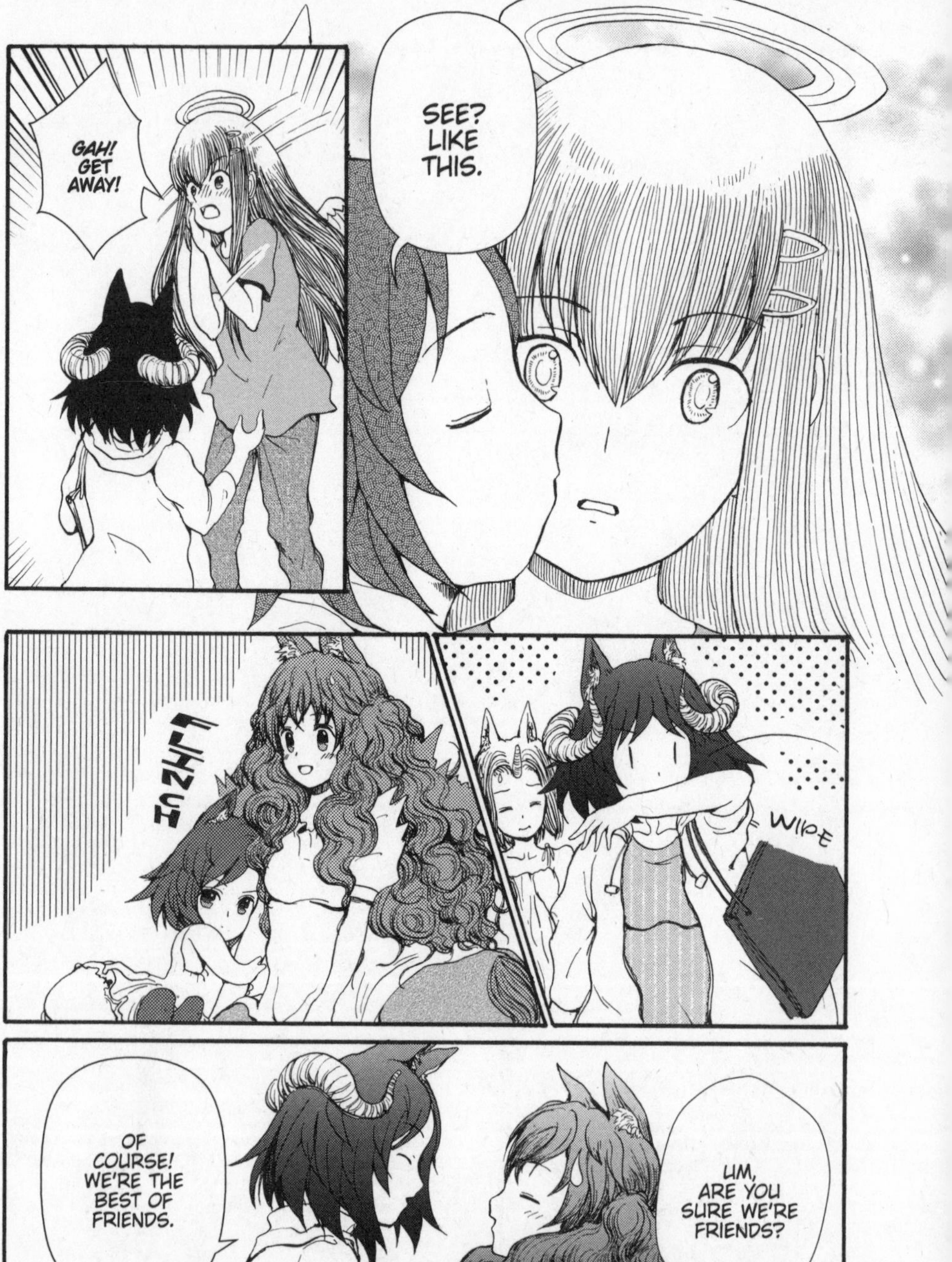
SEE? LIKE THIS.
GAH! GET AWAY!
WIPE
FLINCH
UM, ARE YOU SURE WE'RE FRIENDS?
OF COURSE! WE'RE THE BEST OF FRIENDS.

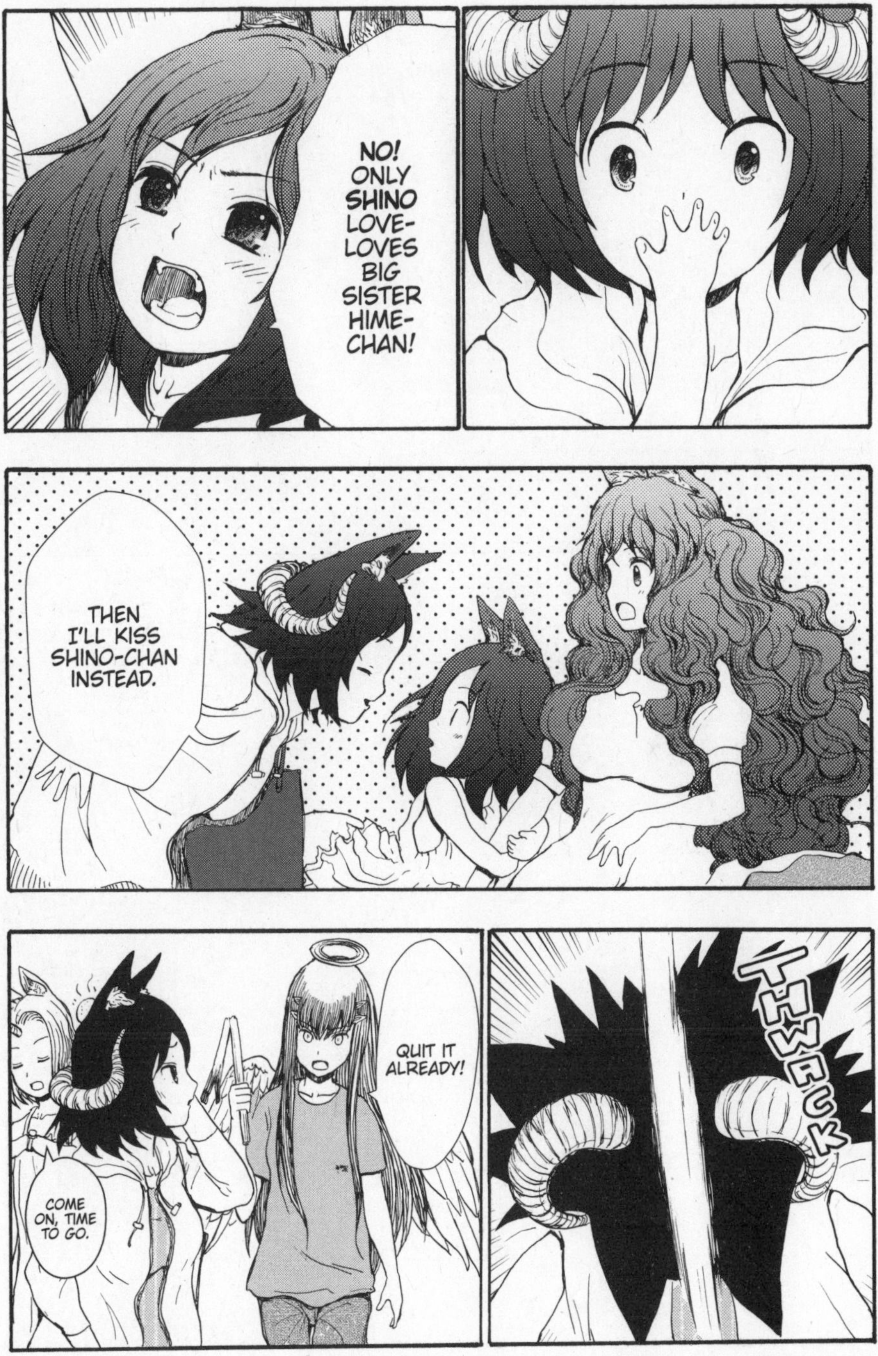
NO! ONLY SHINO LOVE-LOVES BIG SISTER HIME-CHAN!
THEN I'LL KISS SHINO-CHAN INSTEAD.
THWACK
QUIT IT ALREADY!
COME ON, TIME TO GO.

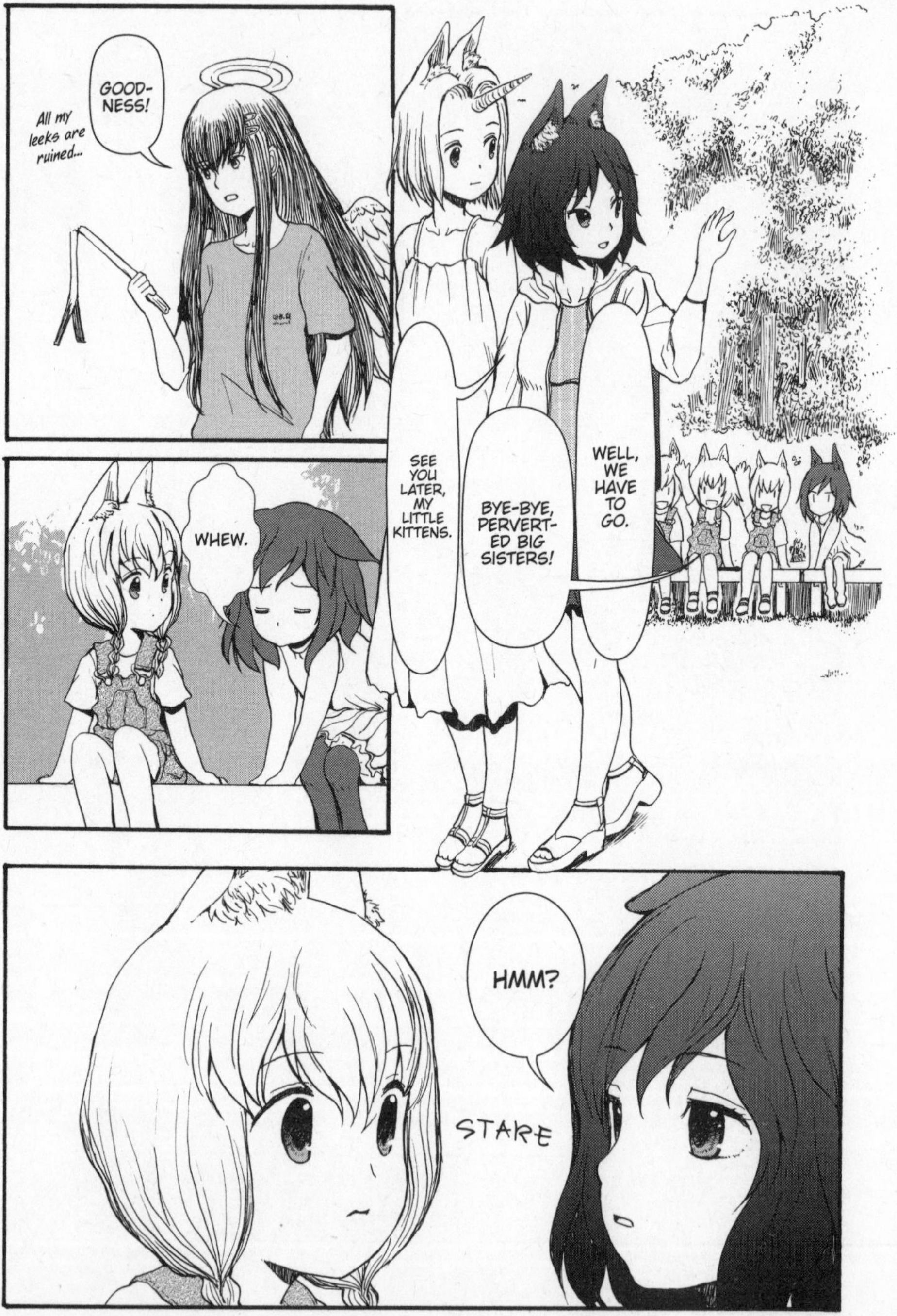
WELL, WE HAVE TO GO.
BYE-BYE, PERVERT-ED BIG SISTERS!
SEE YOU LATER, MY LITTLE KITTENS.
GOOD-NESS!
All my leeks are ruined...
WHEW.
HMM?
STARE

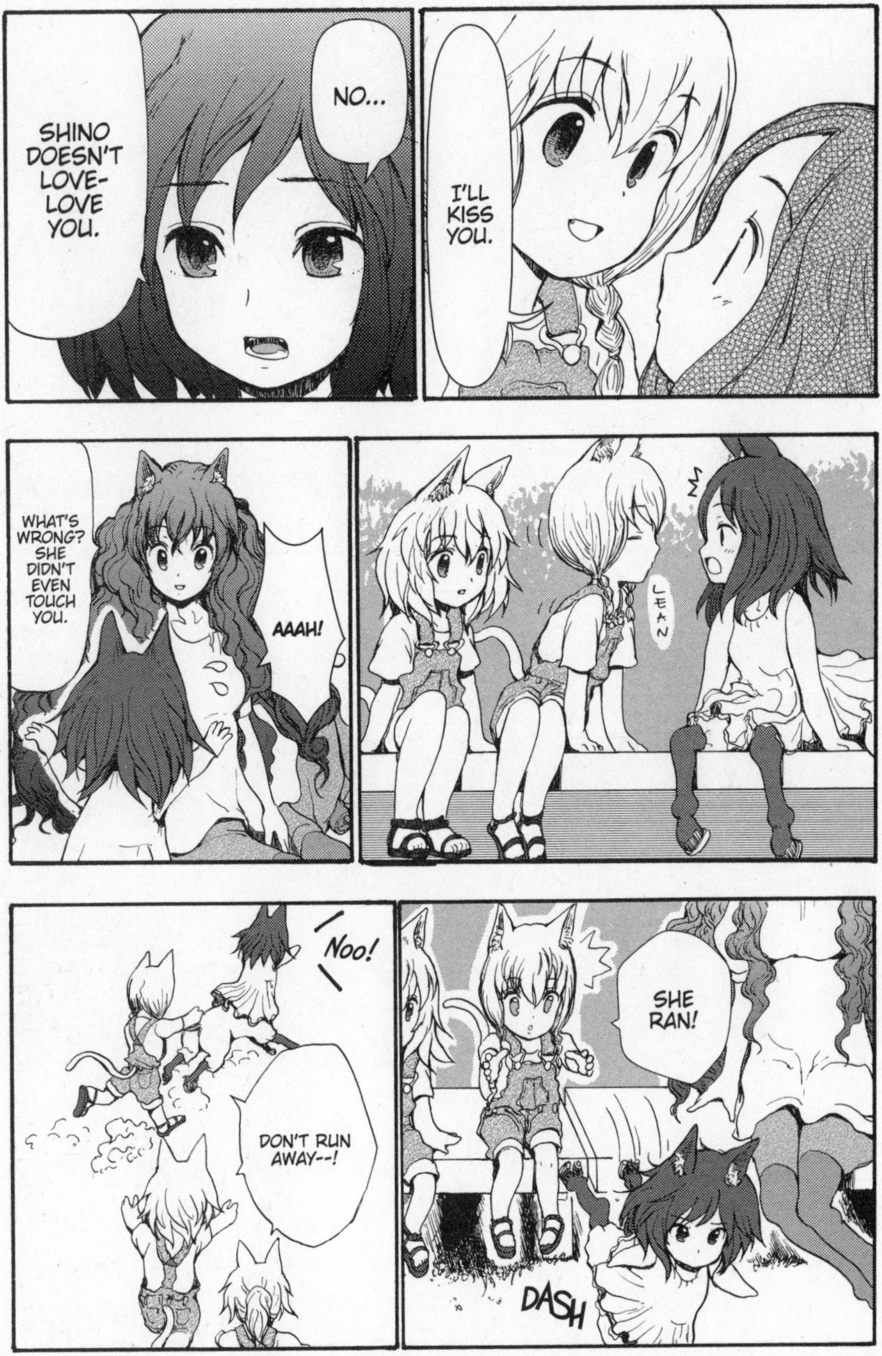
I'LL KISS YOU.
NO...
SHINO DOESN'T LOVE-LOVE YOU.
LEAN
AAAH!
WHAT'S WRONG? SHE DIDN'T EVEN TOUCH YOU.
SHE RAN!
DASH
Noo!
DON'T RUN AWAY--!

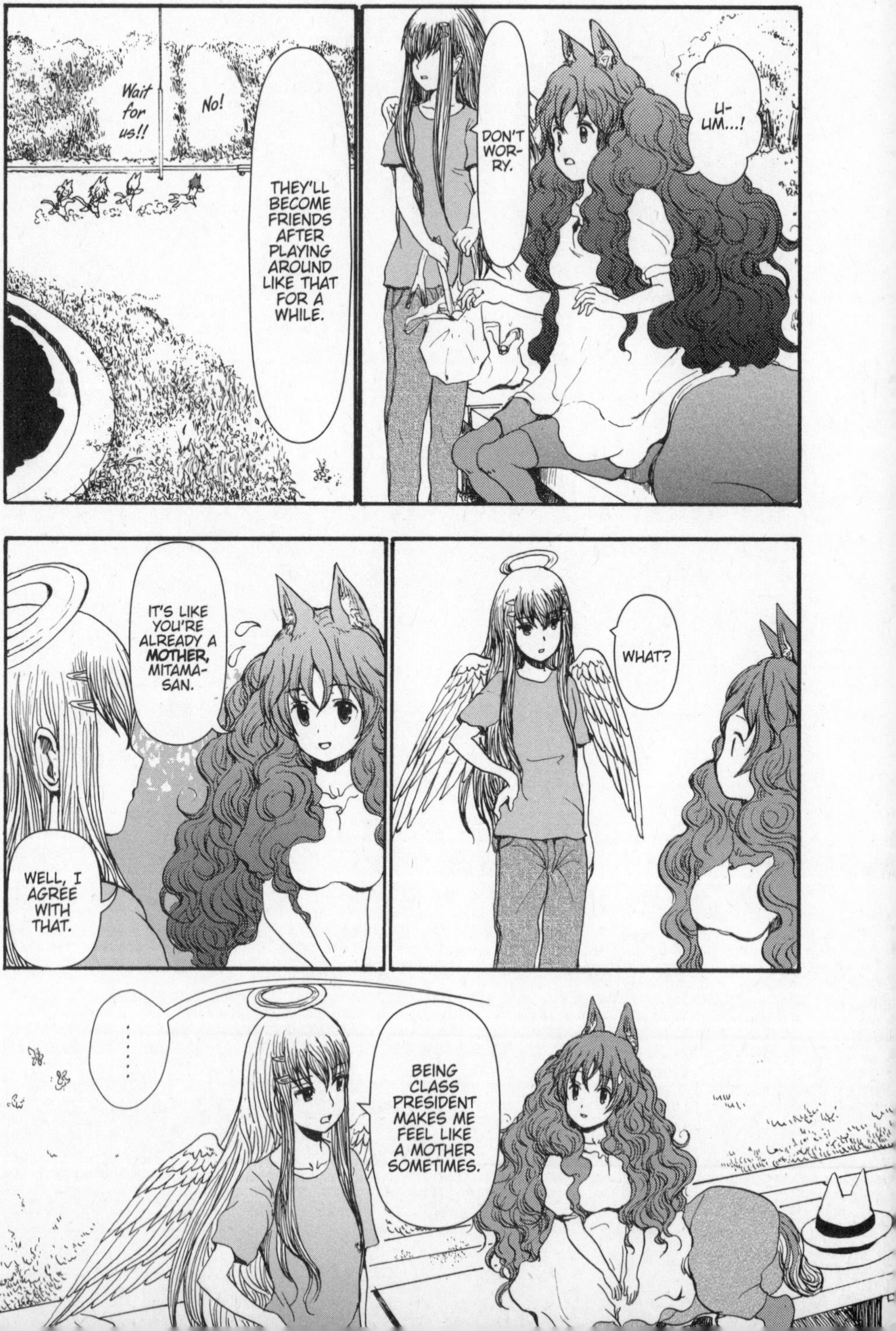
U-UM...!
DON'T WORRY.
THEY'LL BECOME FRIENDS AFTER PLAYING AROUND LIKE THAT FOR A WHILE.
No!
Wait for us!!
WHAT?
IT'S LIKE YOU'RE ALREADY A **MOTHER,** MITAMA-SAN.
WELL, I AGREE WITH THAT.
BEING CLASS PRESIDENT MAKES ME FEEL LIKE A MOTHER SOMETIMES.
......

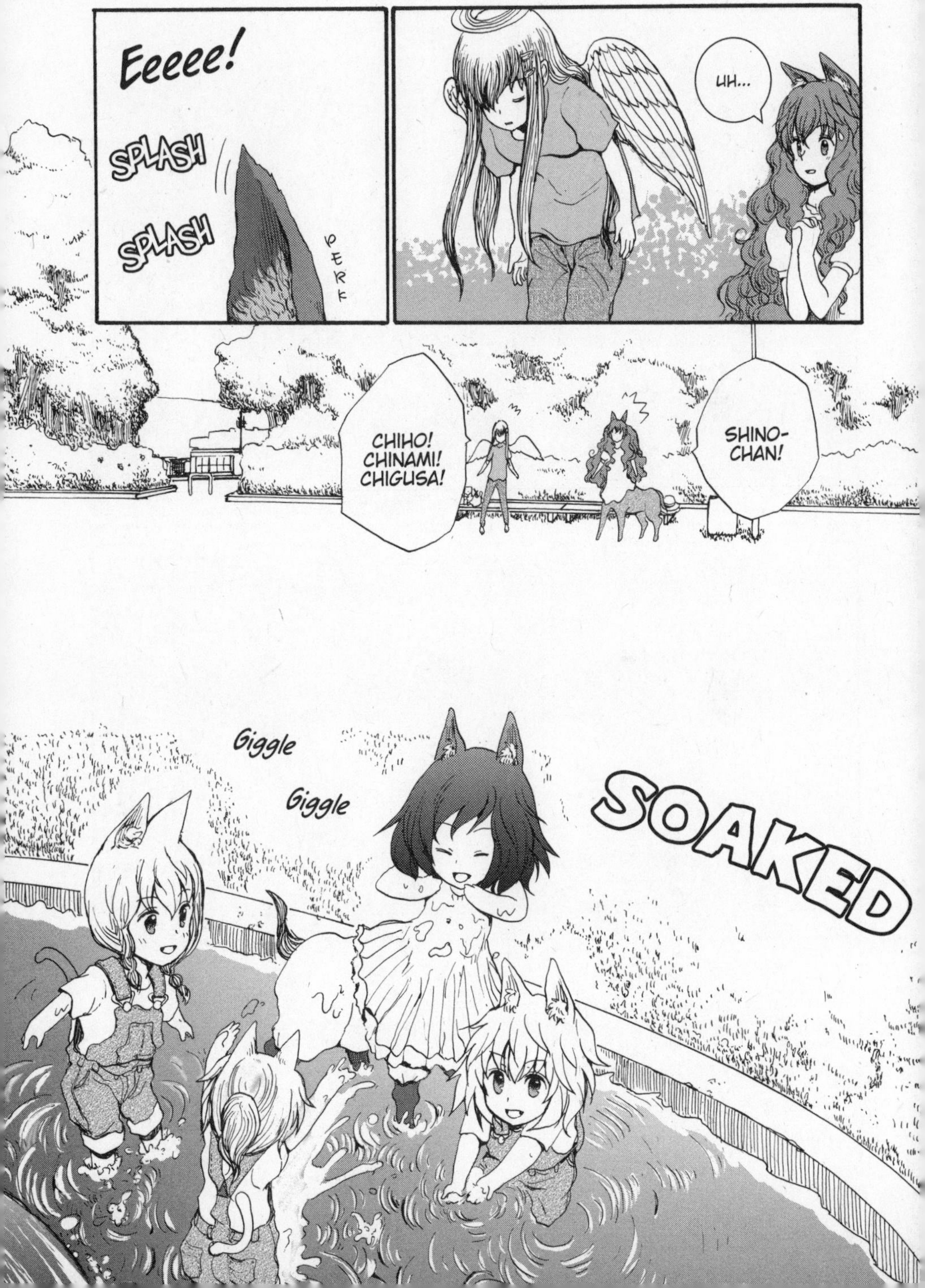
UH...
Eeeee!
SPLASH
SPLASH
PERK
SHINO-CHAN!
CHIHO! CHINAMI! CHIGUSA!
SOAKED
Giggle
Giggle

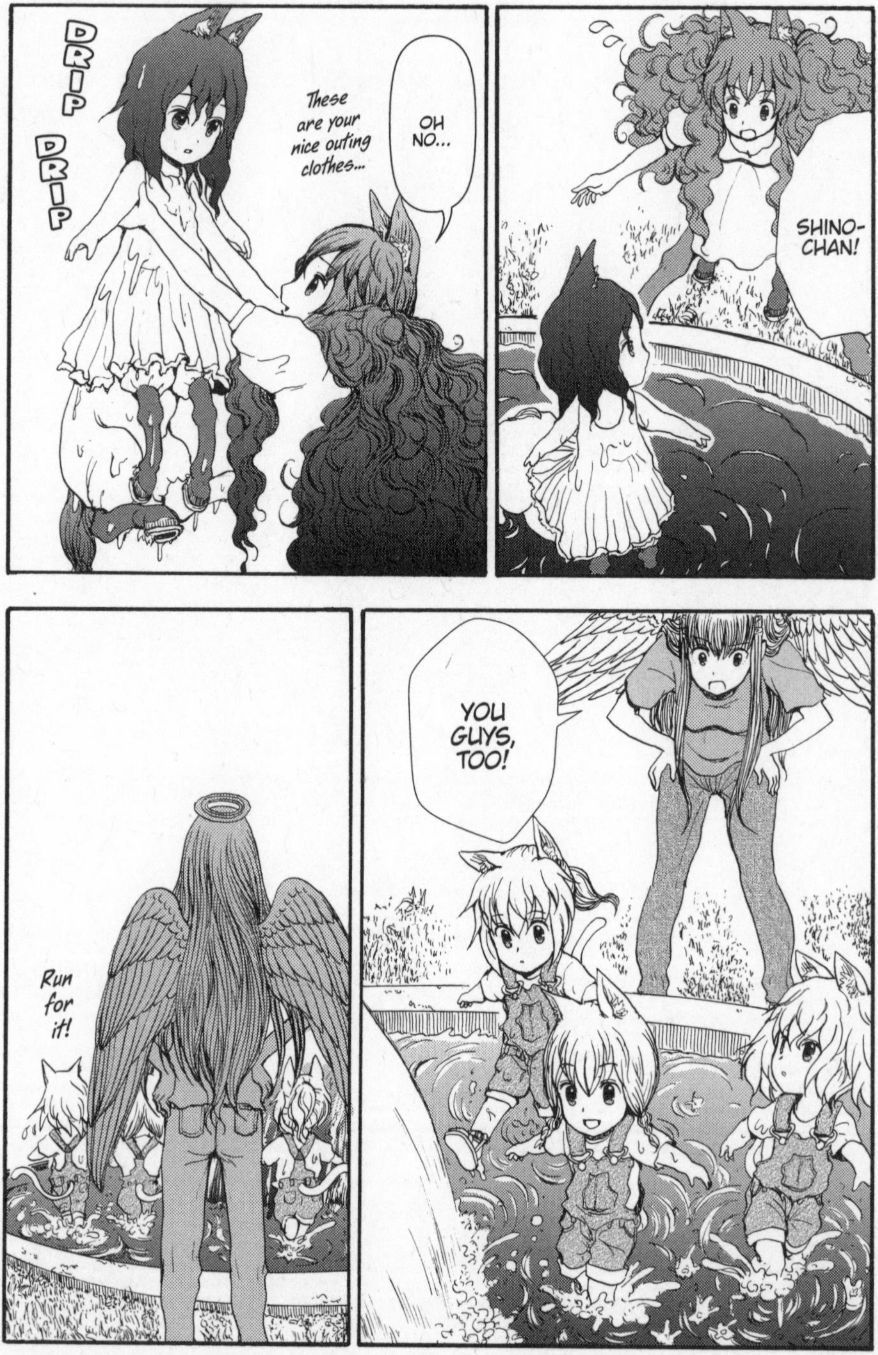
SHINO-CHAN!
OH NO...
These are your nice outing clothes...
DRIP DRIP
YOU GUYS, TOO!
Run for it!

No--!

SNATCH

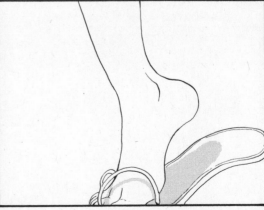

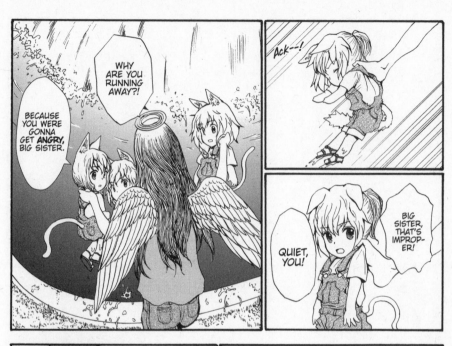

Ack--!
BIG SISTER, THAT'S IMPROPER!
QUIET, YOU!
WHY ARE YOU RUNNING AWAY?!
BECAUSE YOU WERE GONNA GET **ANGRY,** BIG SISTER.
WHEN YOU DEAL WITH LITTLE CHILDREN YOU COME TO UNDERSTAND THE TRIBULATIONS OF ALL THE MOTHERS IN THE WORLD.
I... I SEE WHAT YOU MEAN.
ARE YOU MAD?
NO, I'M NOT MAD.

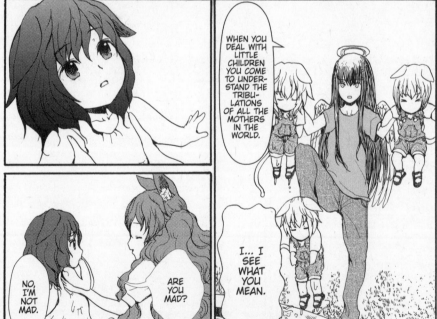

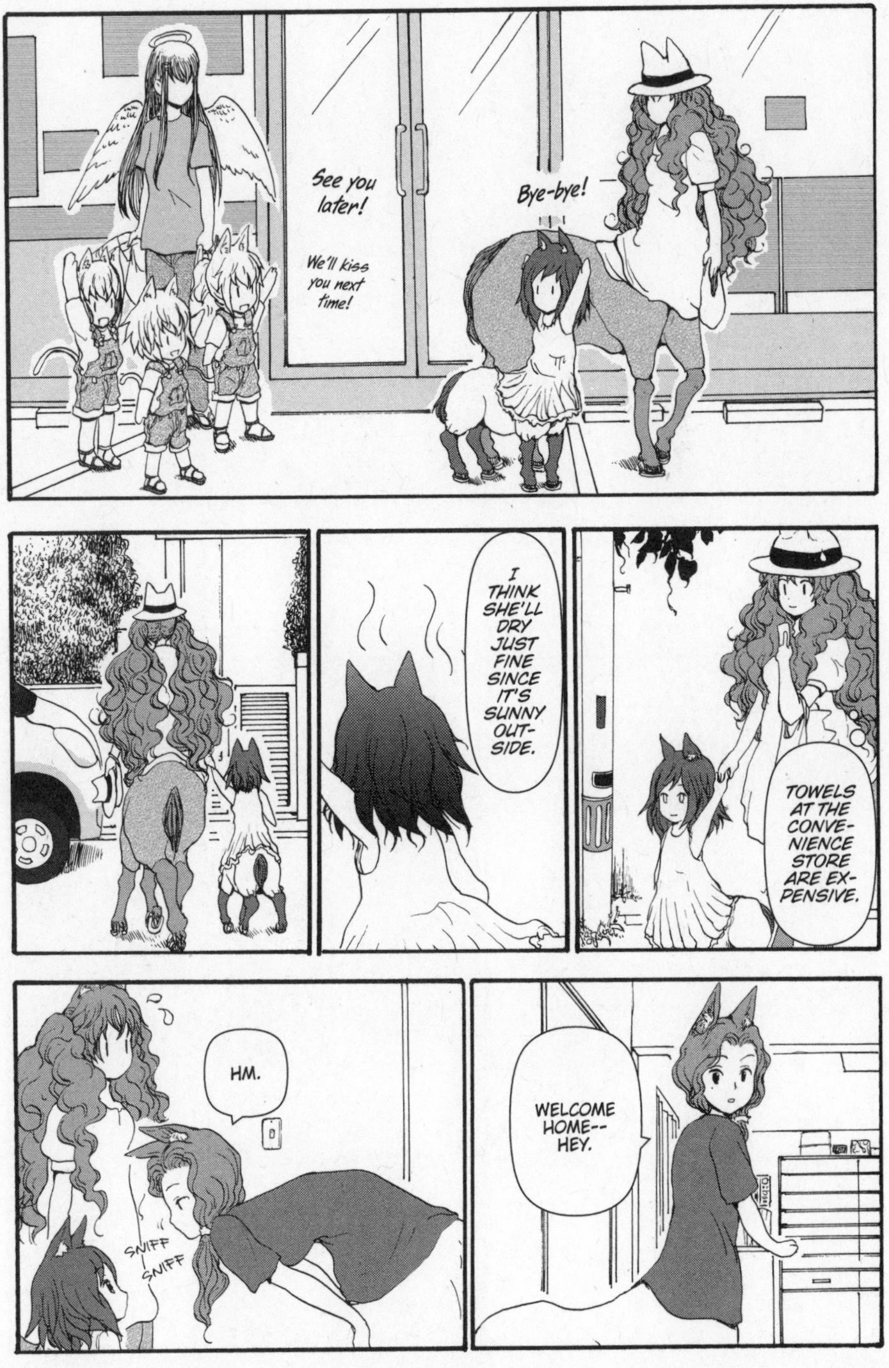
Bye-bye!
See you later!
We'll kiss you next time!
TOWELS AT THE CONVENIENCE STORE ARE EXPENSIVE.
I THINK SHE'LL DRY JUST FINE SINCE IT'S SUNNY OUTSIDE.
WELCOME HOME-- HEY.
HM.
SNIFF SNIFF

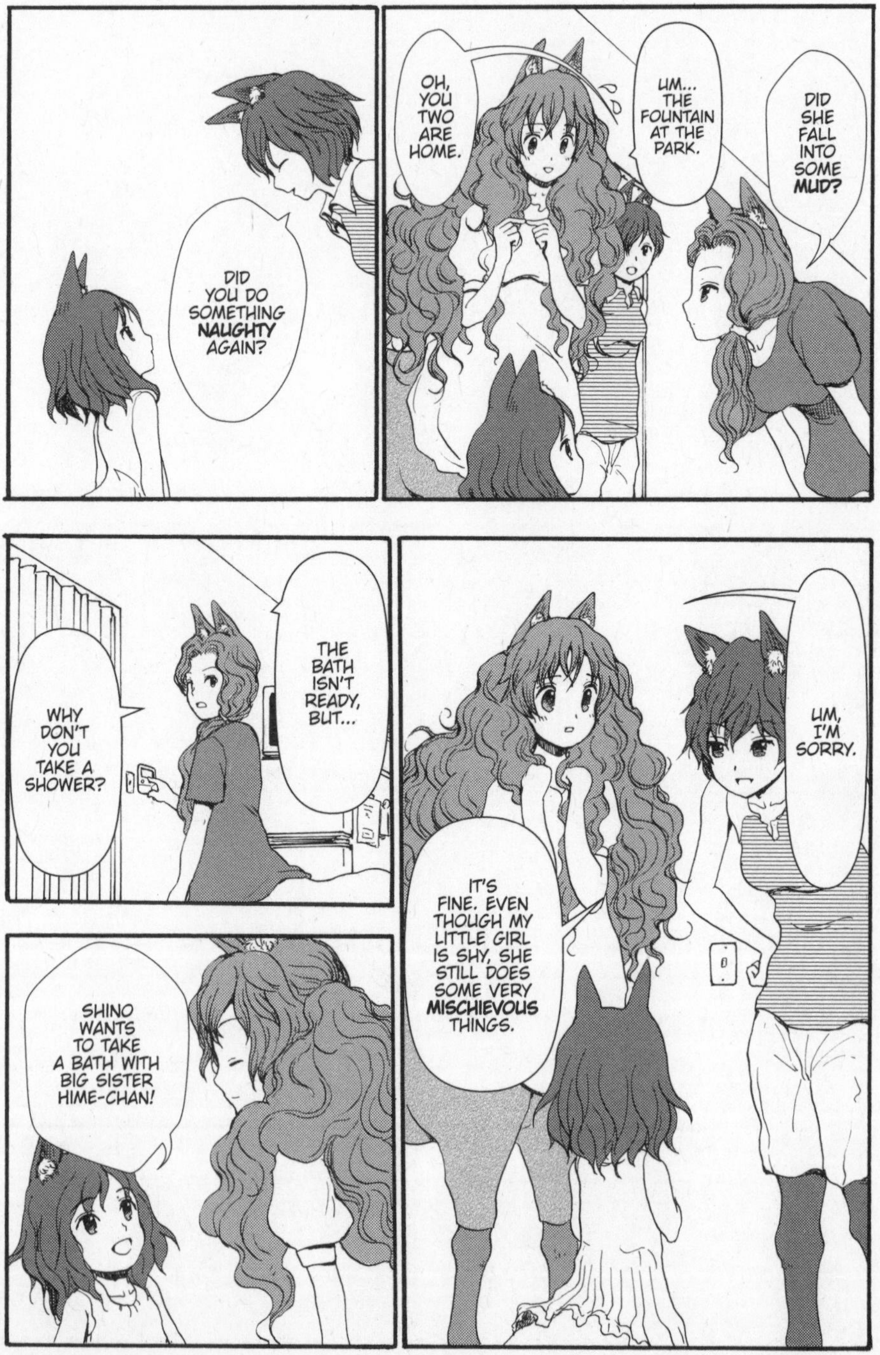
DID SHE FALL INTO SOME MUD?
UM... THE FOUNTAIN AT THE PARK.
OH, YOU TWO ARE HOME.
DID YOU DO SOMETHING NAUGHTY AGAIN?
UM, I'M SORRY.
IT'S FINE. EVEN THOUGH MY LITTLE GIRL IS SHY, SHE STILL DOES SOME VERY MISCHIEVOUS THINGS.
THE BATH ISN'T READY, BUT...
WHY DON'T YOU TAKE A SHOWER?
SHINO WANTS TO TAKE A BATH WITH BIG SISTER HIME-CHAN!

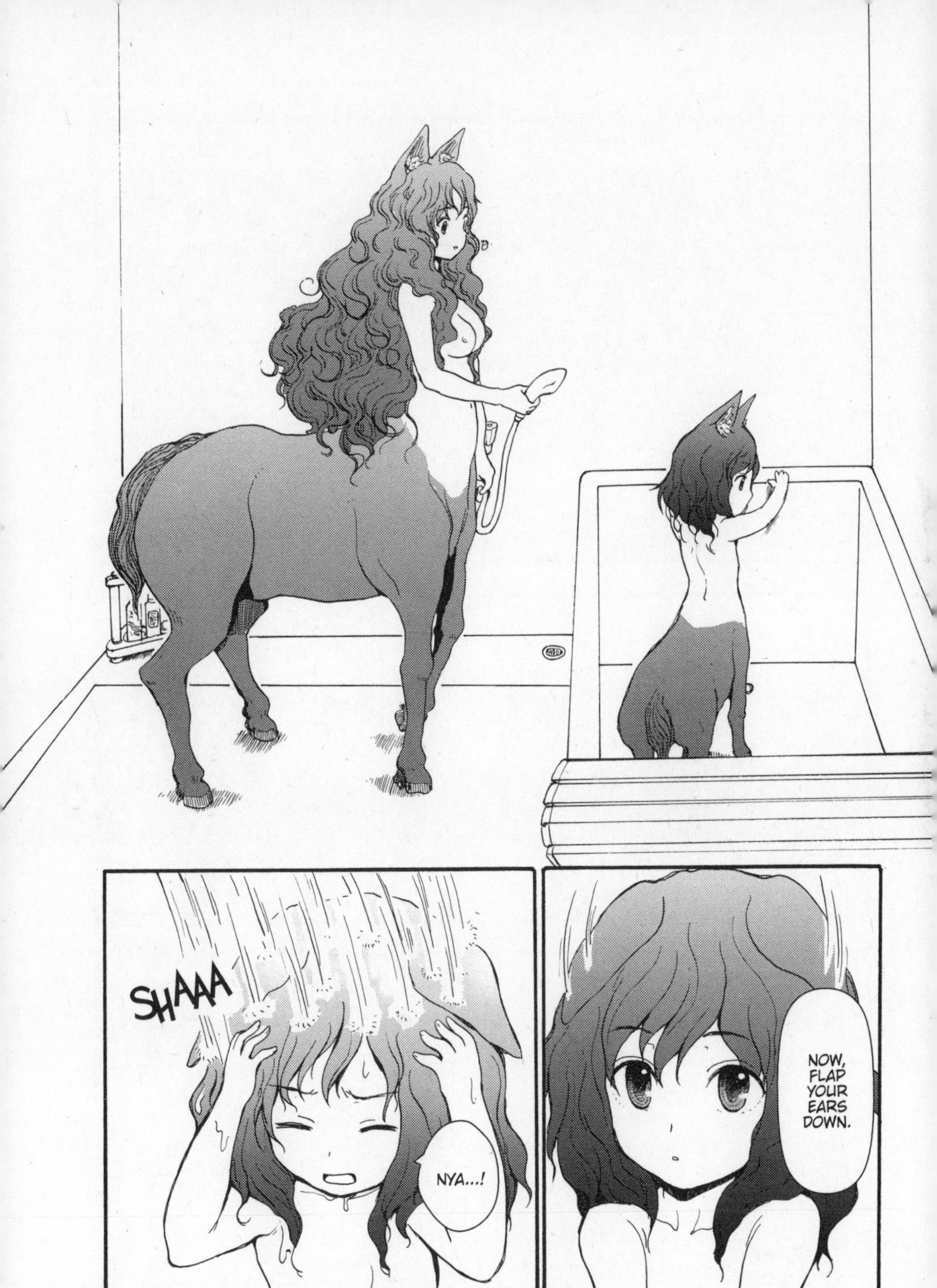
NOW, FLAP YOUR EARS DOWN.
SHAAA
NYA...!

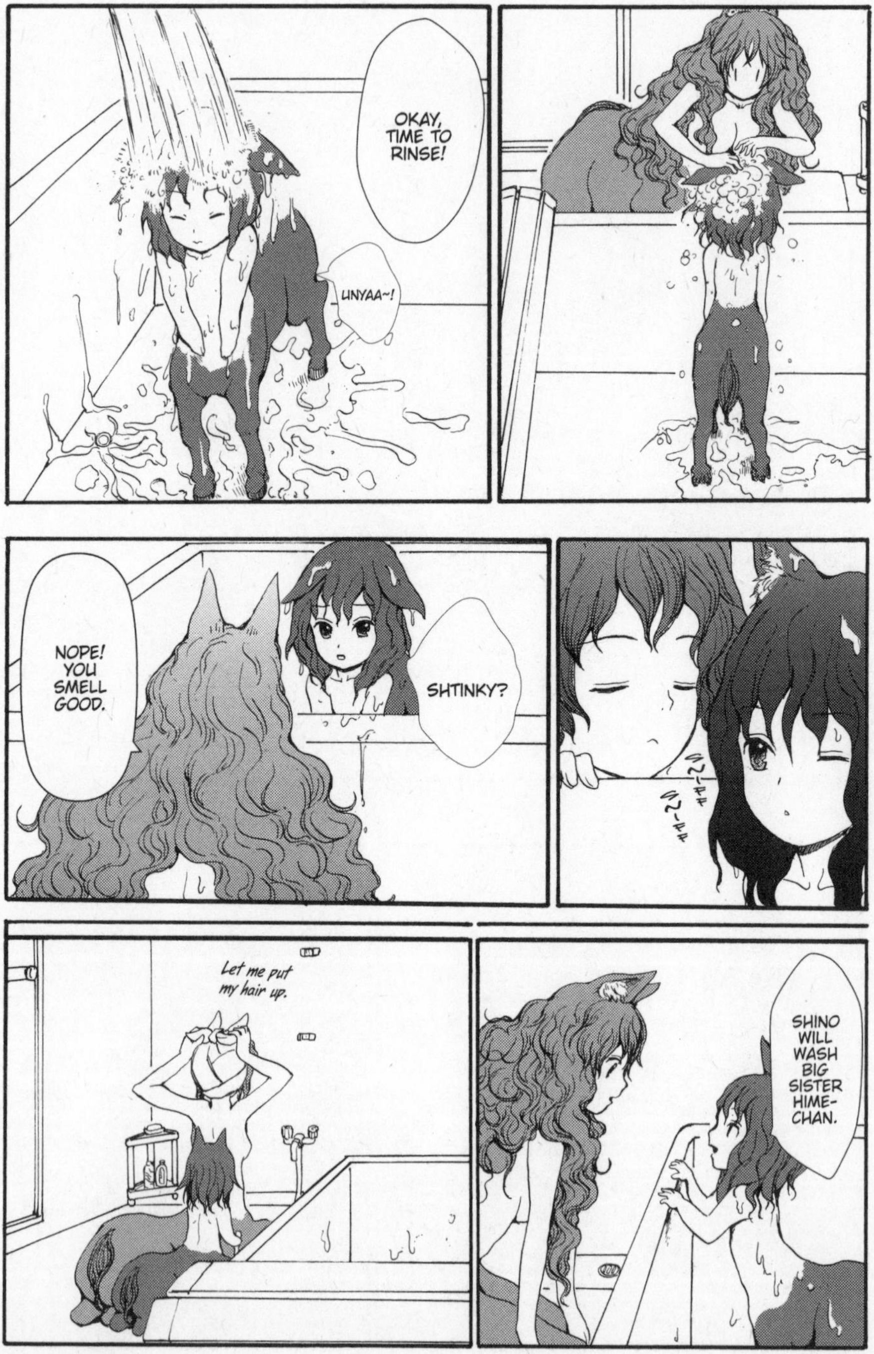
OKAY, TIME TO RINSE!
UNYAA~!
SNIFF
SNIFF
SHTINKY?
NOPE! YOU SMELL GOOD.
SHINO WILL WASH BIG SISTER HIME-CHAN.
Let me put my hair up.

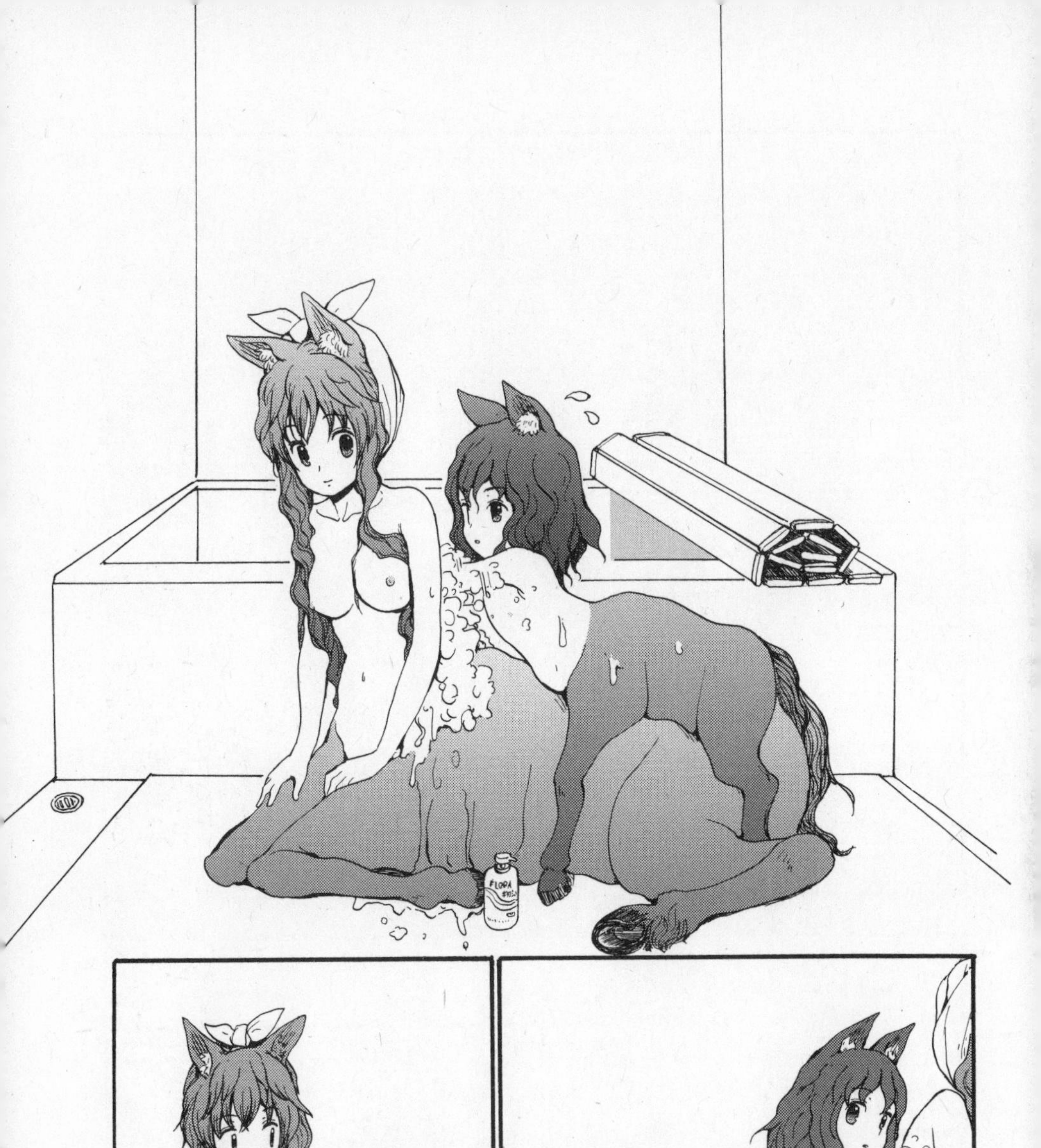
FLORA
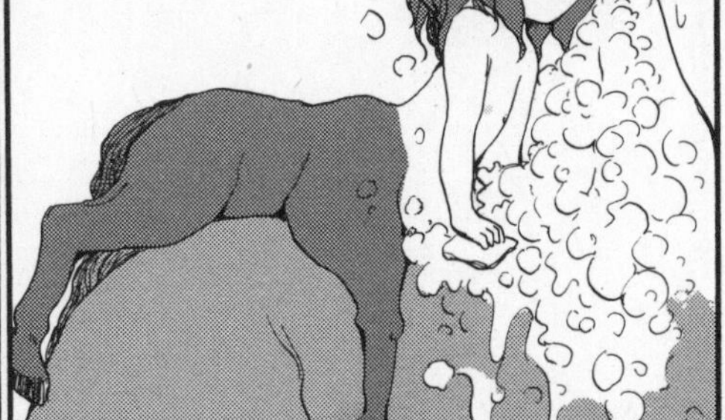
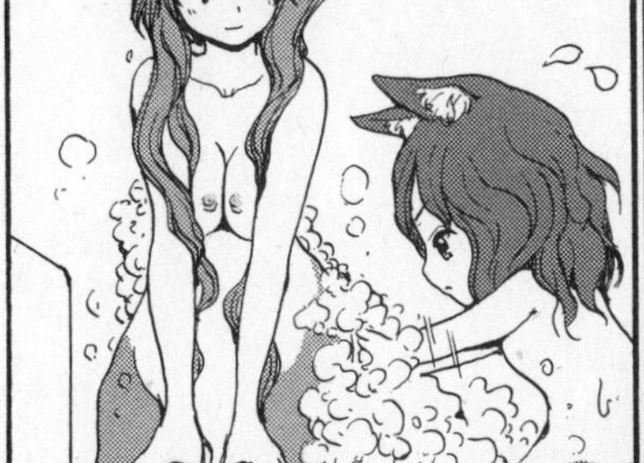

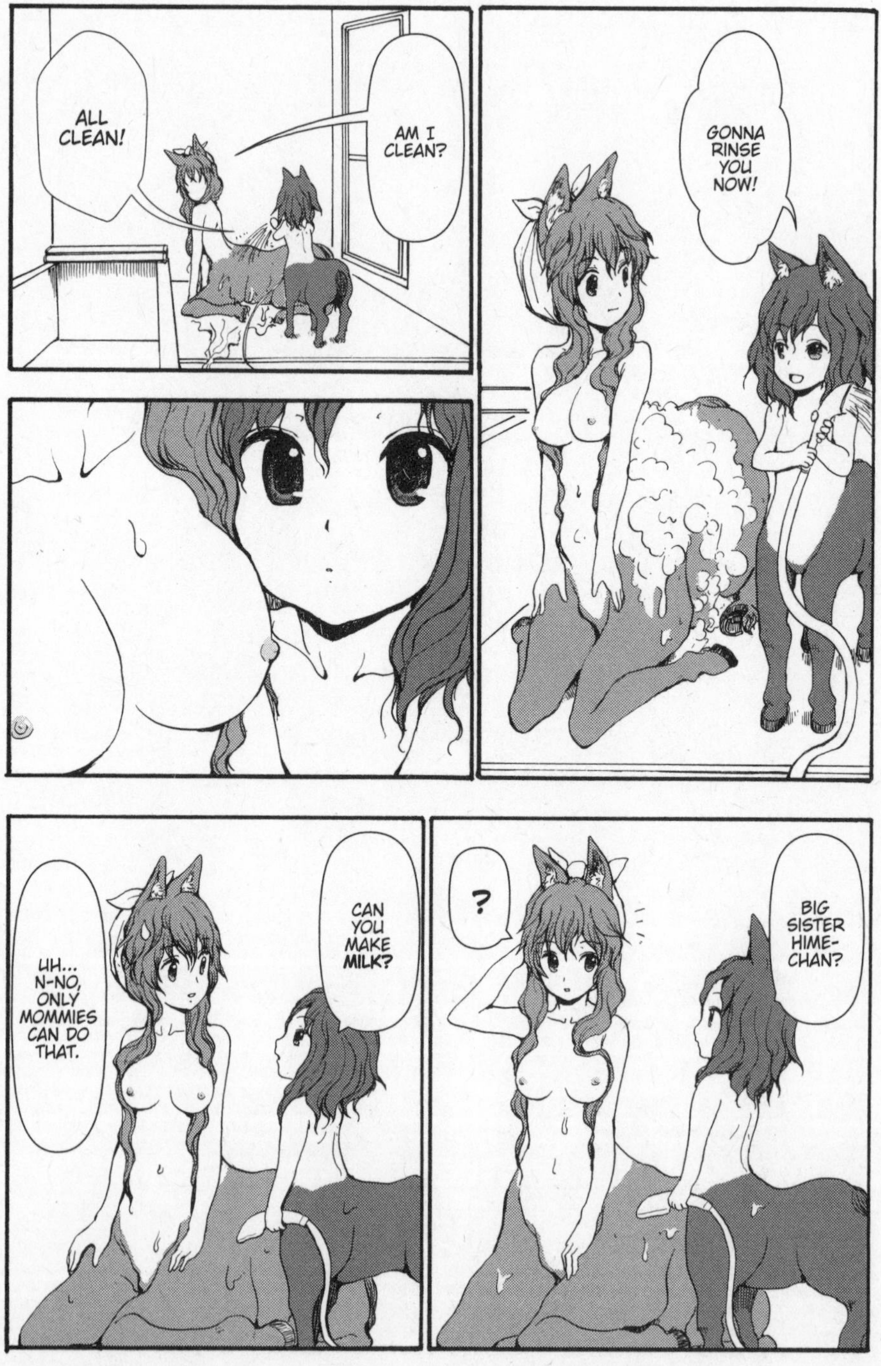
GONNA RINSE YOU NOW!
AM I CLEAN?
ALL CLEAN!
BIG SISTER HIME-CHAN?
?
CAN YOU MAKE MILK?
UH... N-NO, ONLY MOMMIES CAN DO THAT.

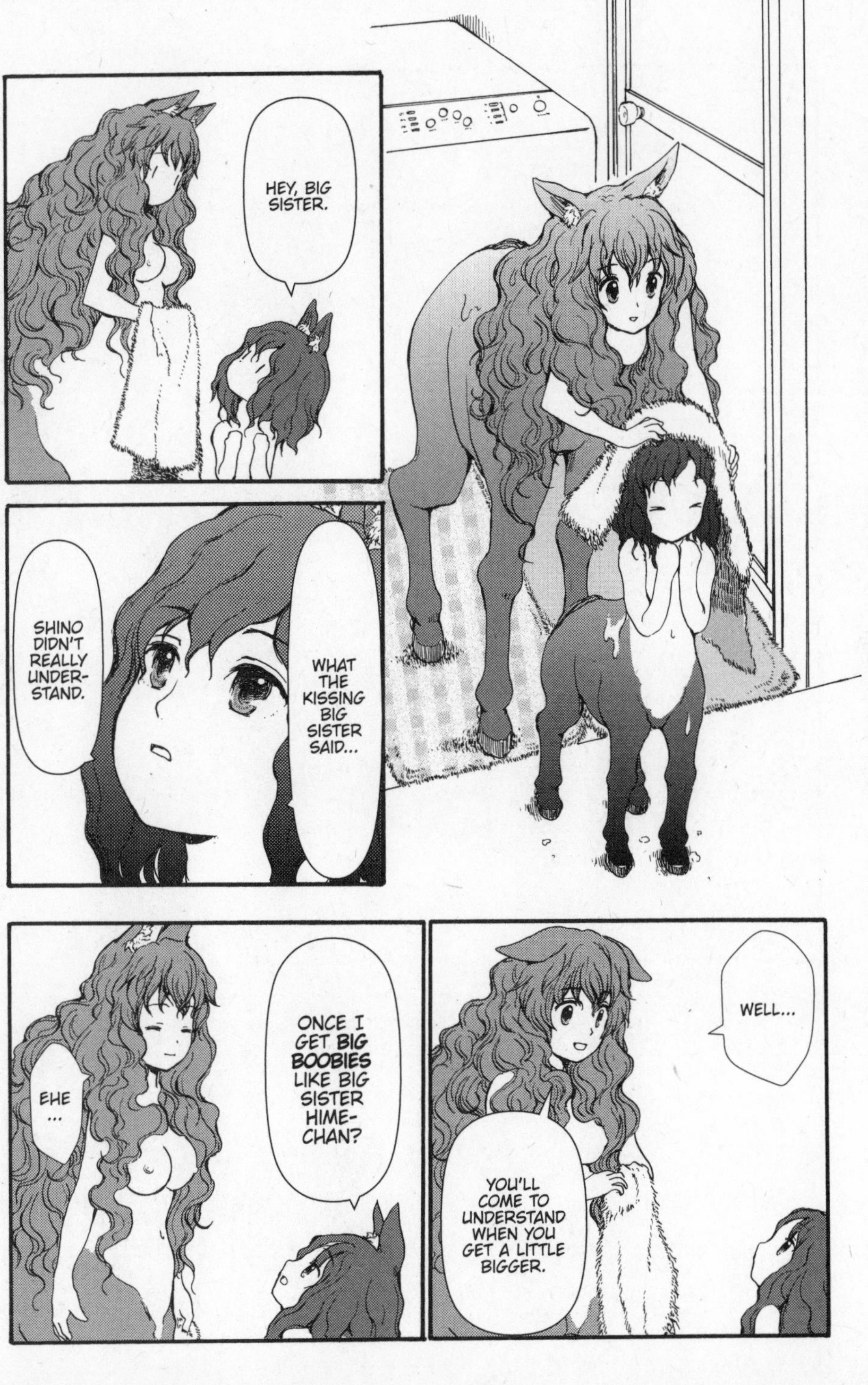
HEY, BIG SISTER.
WHAT THE KISSING BIG SISTER SAID...
SHINO DIDN'T REALLY UNDER-STAND.
WELL...
YOU'LL COME TO UNDERSTAND WHEN YOU GET A LITTLE BIGGER.
ONCE I GET **BIG BOOBIES** LIKE BIG SISTER HIME-CHAN?
EHE ...

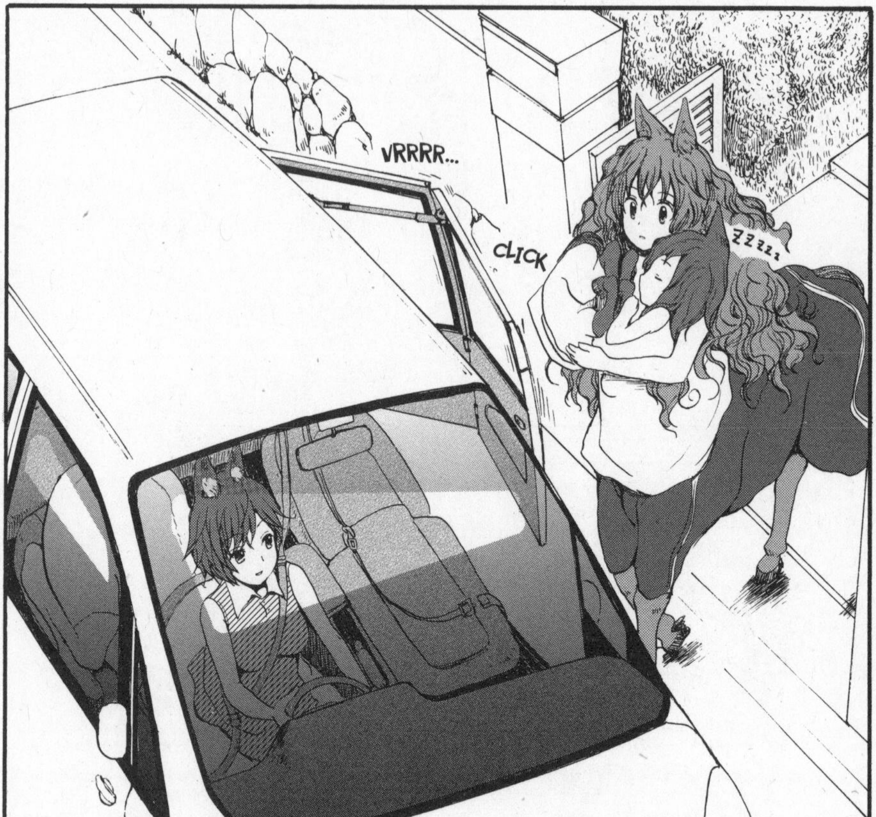
VRRRR...
CLICK
ZZZzzz

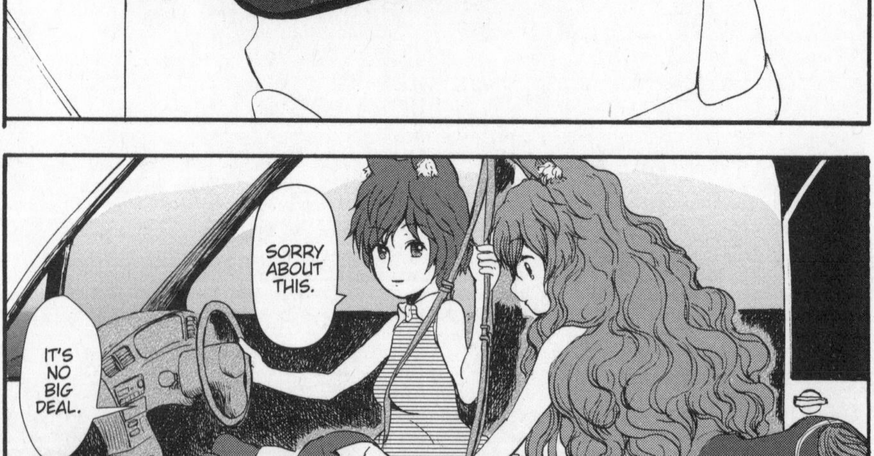
SORRY ABOUT THIS.
IT'S NO BIG DEAL.

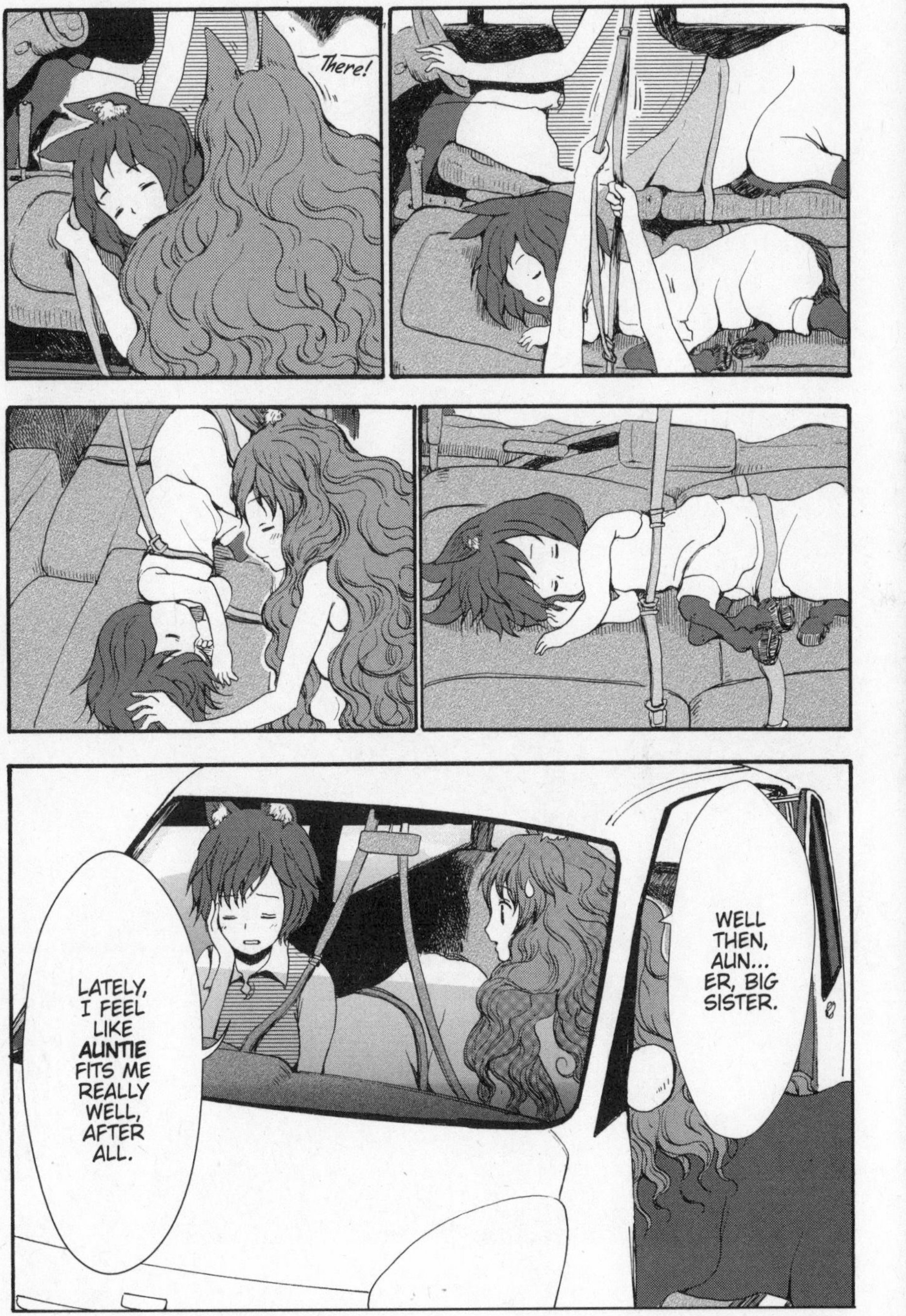
There!
WELL THEN, AUN... ER, BIG SISTER.
LATELY, I FEEL LIKE **AUNTIE** FITS ME REALLY WELL, AFTER ALL.

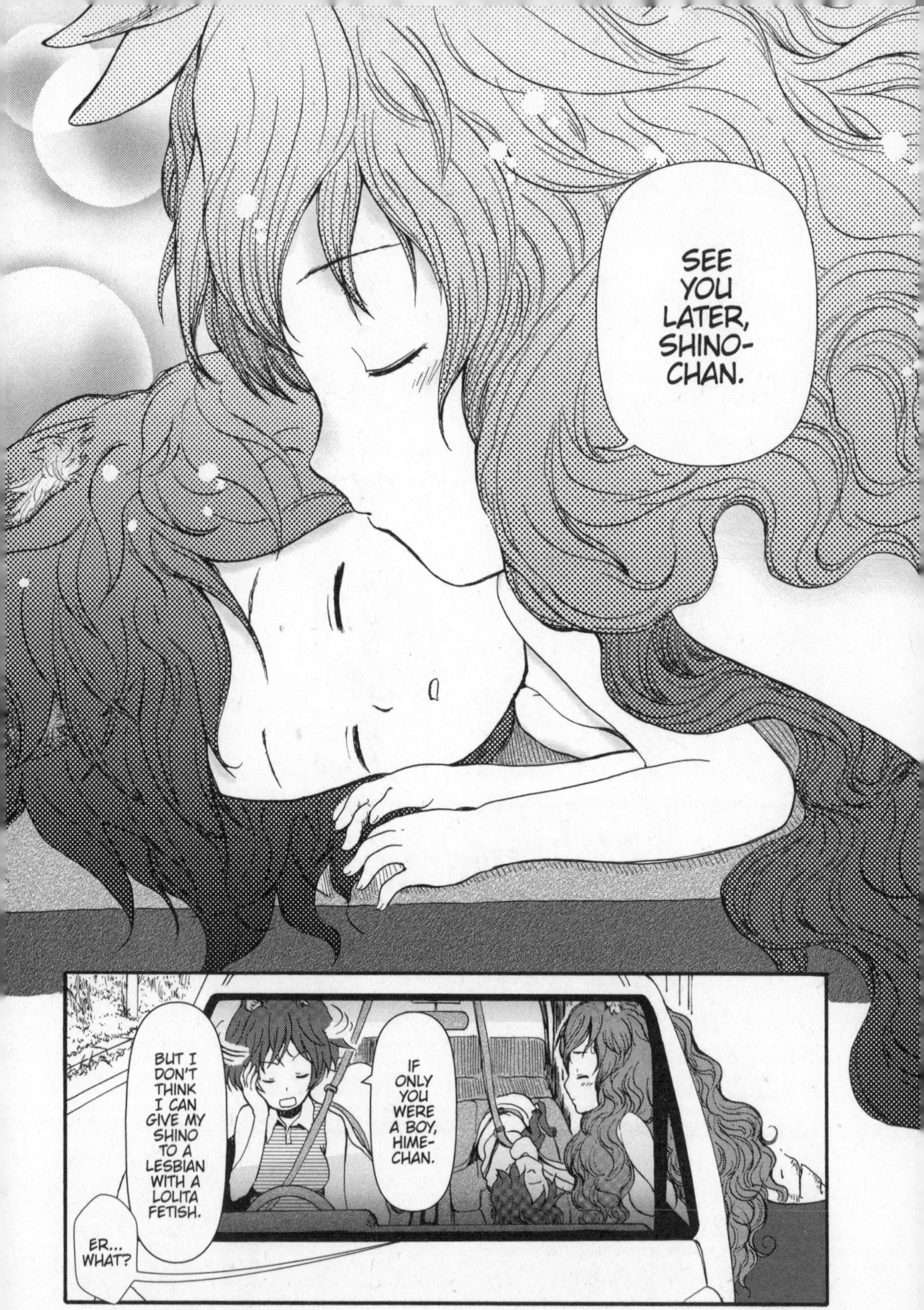
SEE YOU LATER, SHINO-CHAN.
IF ONLY YOU WERE A BOY, HIME-CHAN.
BUT I DON'T THINK I CAN GIVE MY SHINO TO A LESBIAN WITH A LOLITA FETISH.
ER... WHAT?

A Centaur's Life

CANINES

ORDER *CARNIVORA*, FAMILY *CANIDAE*. IT IS BELIEVED
THAT THE GRAY WOLVES OF TRIBE *CANINI* ("TRUE DOGS")
WERE THE ANCESTORS OF MODERN DOMESTIC DOGS
(*CANIS LUPUS FAMILIARIS*). ALTHOUGH THERE ARE MANY
BREEDS OF MODERN DOGS (SUCH AS SHIBA INU,
POMERANIAN, ST. BERNARD, ETC), THEY ALL BELONG
TO THE SAME SUBSPECIES AND CAN BE INTERBRED. THEY
CAN ALSO PROCREATE WITH FELLOW MEMBERS OF THE
GENUS *CANIS* IN TRIBE *CANINI*. FAMILY *CANIDAE* ALSO
INCLUDES TRIBE *VULPINI*, OR "TRUE FOXES."

THE MIDDLE LIMBS ARE A NOT A UNIQUE FEATURE FOR
CANINES. MANY MAMMALS USE THESE EXTRA LEGS
FOR TRAVELING LONG DISTANCES. THEY ARE A
GENETICALLY DOMINANT TRAIT, SO IT IS UNCOMMON
FOR A POPULATION TO LOSE THEIR MIDDLE LIMBS
UNLESS THE SPECIES UNDERGOES REGULAR MUTATION.
THIS FEATURE IS PRESENT REGARDLESS OF
SPECIES, HUNTING STYLE, OR DOMESTICATION.

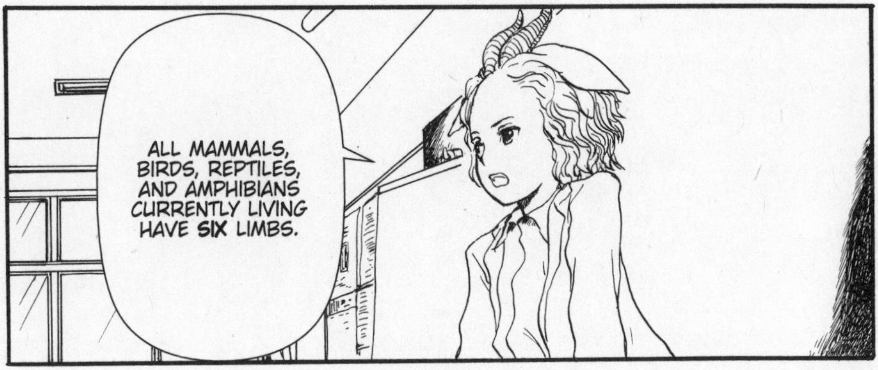
ALL MAMMALS, BIRDS, REPTILES, AND AMPHIBIANS CURRENTLY LIVING HAVE SIX LIMBS.

CENTAUR'S SECRET
~LECTURE ON BIOLOGY AND GENETICS~

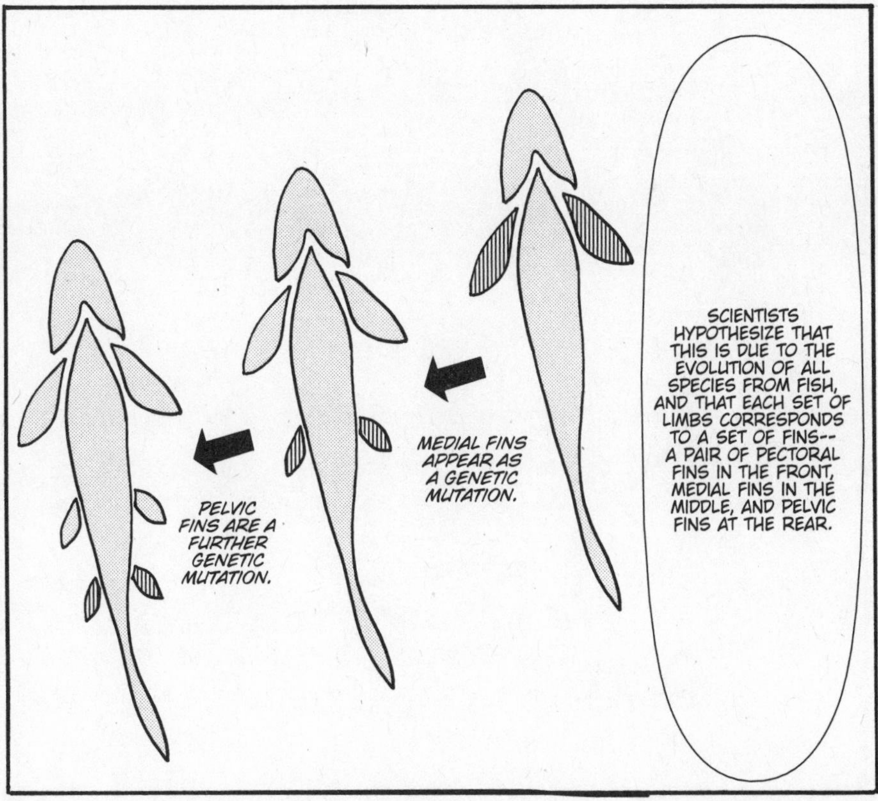
SCIENTISTS HYPOTHESIZE THAT THIS IS DUE TO THE EVOLUTION OF ALL SPECIES FROM FISH, AND THAT EACH SET OF LIMBS CORRESPONDS TO A SET OF FINS-- A PAIR OF PECTORAL FINS IN THE FRONT, MEDIAL FINS IN THE MIDDLE, AND PELVIC FINS AT THE REAR.
MEDIAL FINS APPEAR AS A GENETIC MUTATION.
PELVIC FINS ARE A FURTHER GENETIC MUTATION.

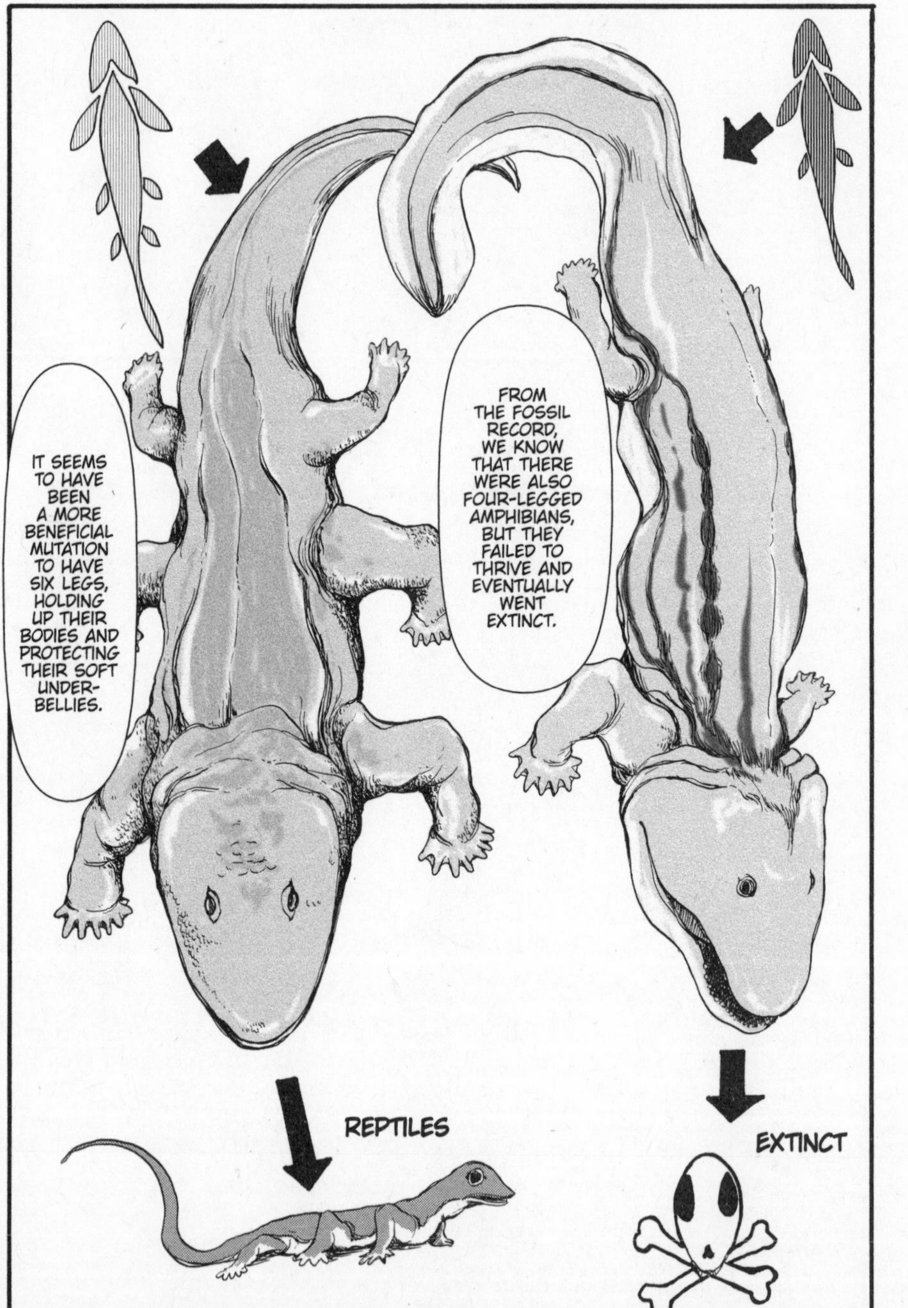

FROM THE FOSSIL RECORD, WE KNOW THAT THERE WERE ALSO FOUR-LEGGED AMPHIBIANS, BUT THEY FAILED TO THRIVE AND EVENTUALLY WENT EXTINCT.
IT SEEMS TO HAVE BEEN A MORE BENEFICIAL MUTATION TO HAVE SIX LEGS, HOLDING UP THEIR BODIES AND PROTECTING THEIR SOFT UNDER-BELLIES.
EXTINCT
REPTILES

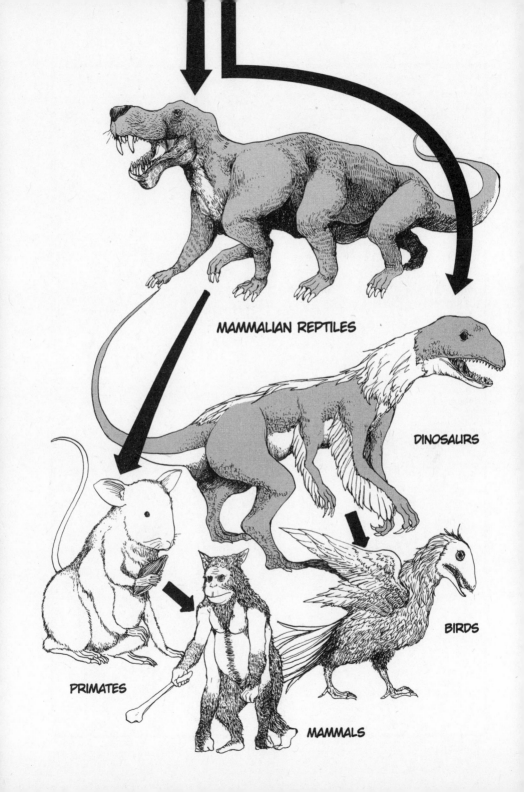

MAMMALIAN REPTILES

DINOSAURS

PRIMATES

BIRDS

MAMMALS

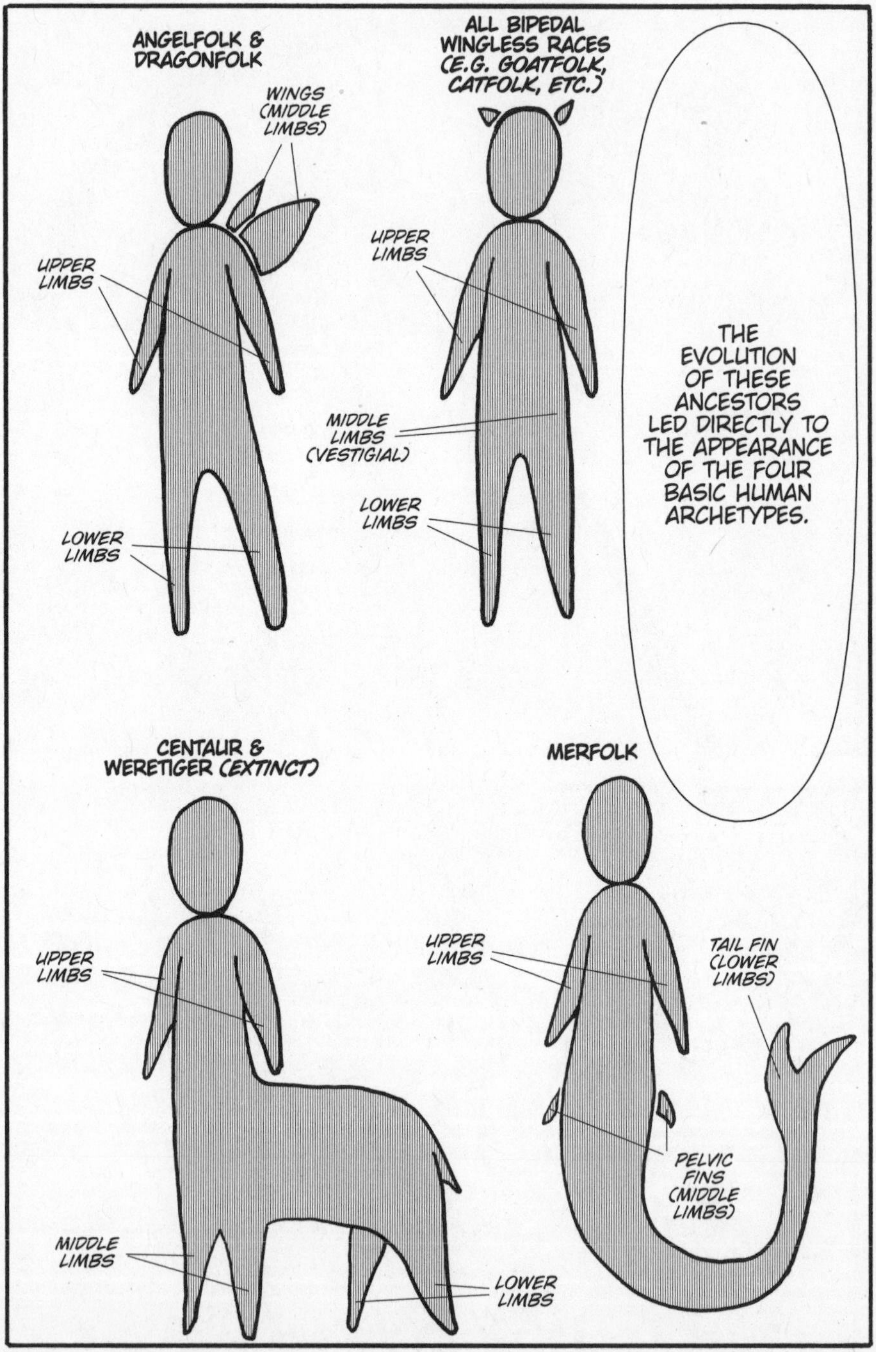
THE EVOLUTION OF THESE ANCESTORS LED DIRECTLY TO THE APPEARANCE OF THE FOUR BASIC HUMAN ARCHETYPES.
ALL BIPEDAL WINGLESS RACES (E.G. GOATFOLK, CATFOLK, ETC.)
UPPER LIMBS
MIDDLE LIMBS (VESTIGIAL)
LOWER LIMBS
ANGELFOLK & DRAGONFOLK
WINGS (MIDDLE LIMBS)
UPPER LIMBS
LOWER LIMBS
MERFOLK
UPPER LIMBS
TAIL FIN (LOWER LIMBS)
PELVIC FINS (MIDDLE LIMBS)
CENTAUR & WERETIGER (EXTINCT)
UPPER LIMBS
MIDDLE LIMBS
LOWER LIMBS

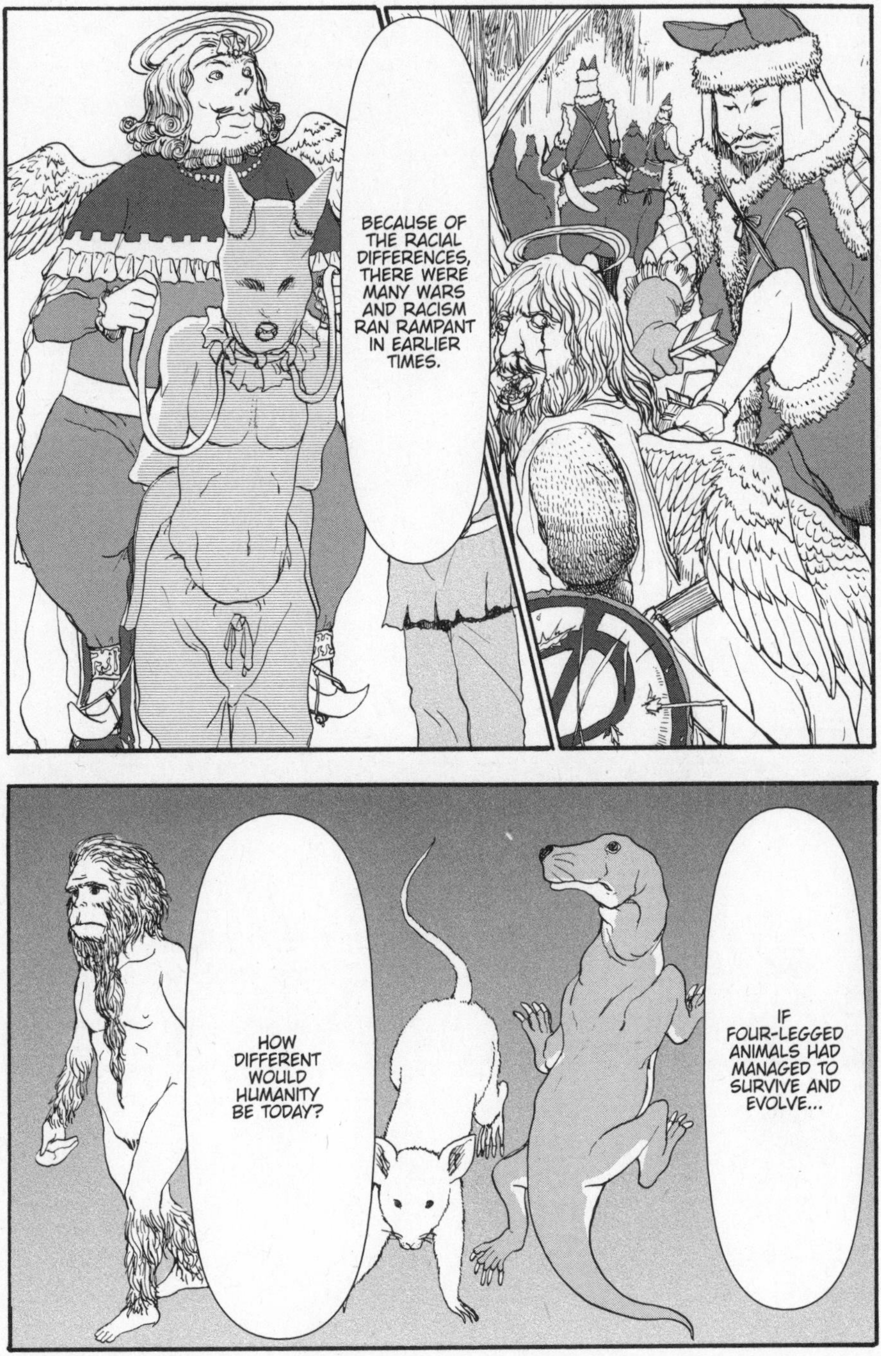
BECAUSE OF THE RACIAL DIFFERENCES, THERE WERE MANY WARS AND RACISM RAN RAMPANT IN EARLIER TIMES.
IF FOUR-LEGGED ANIMALS HAD MANAGED TO SURVIVE AND EVOLVE...
HOW DIFFERENT WOULD HUMANITY BE TODAY?

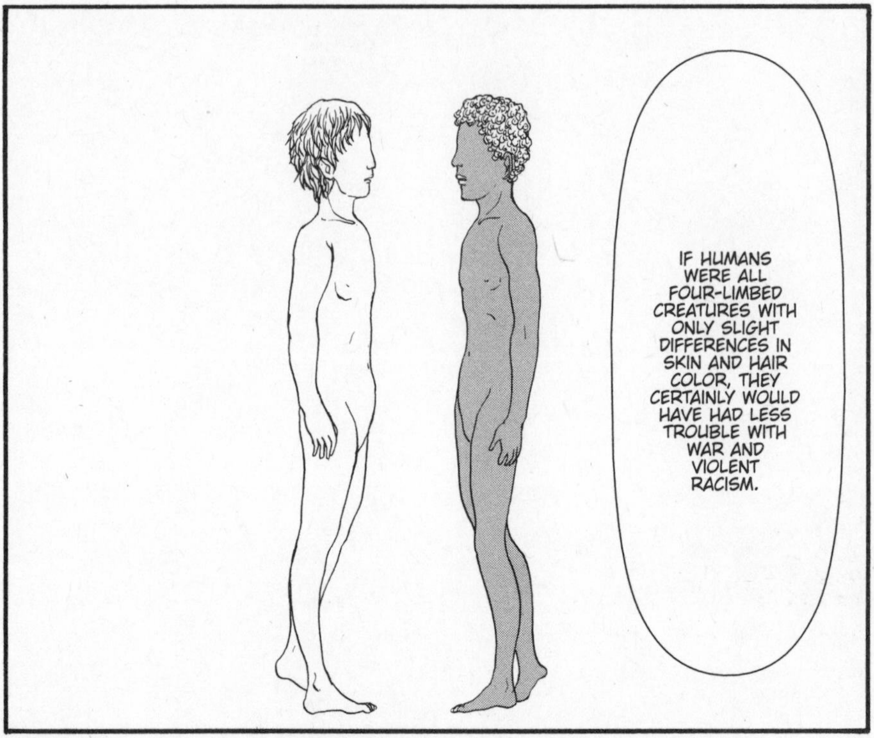
IF HUMANS WERE ALL FOUR-LIMBED CREATURES WITH ONLY SLIGHT DIFFERENCES IN SKIN AND HAIR COLOR, THEY CERTAINLY WOULD HAVE HAD LESS TROUBLE WITH WAR AND VIOLENT RACISM.

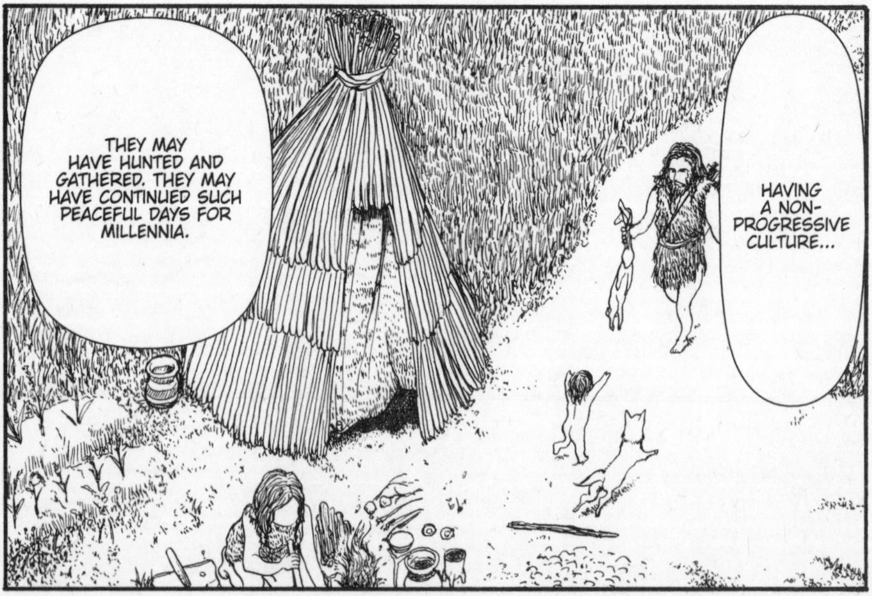
HAVING A NON-PROGRESSIVE CULTURE...
THEY MAY HAVE HUNTED AND GATHERED. THEY MAY HAVE CONTINUED SUCH PEACEFUL DAYS FOR MILLENNIA.

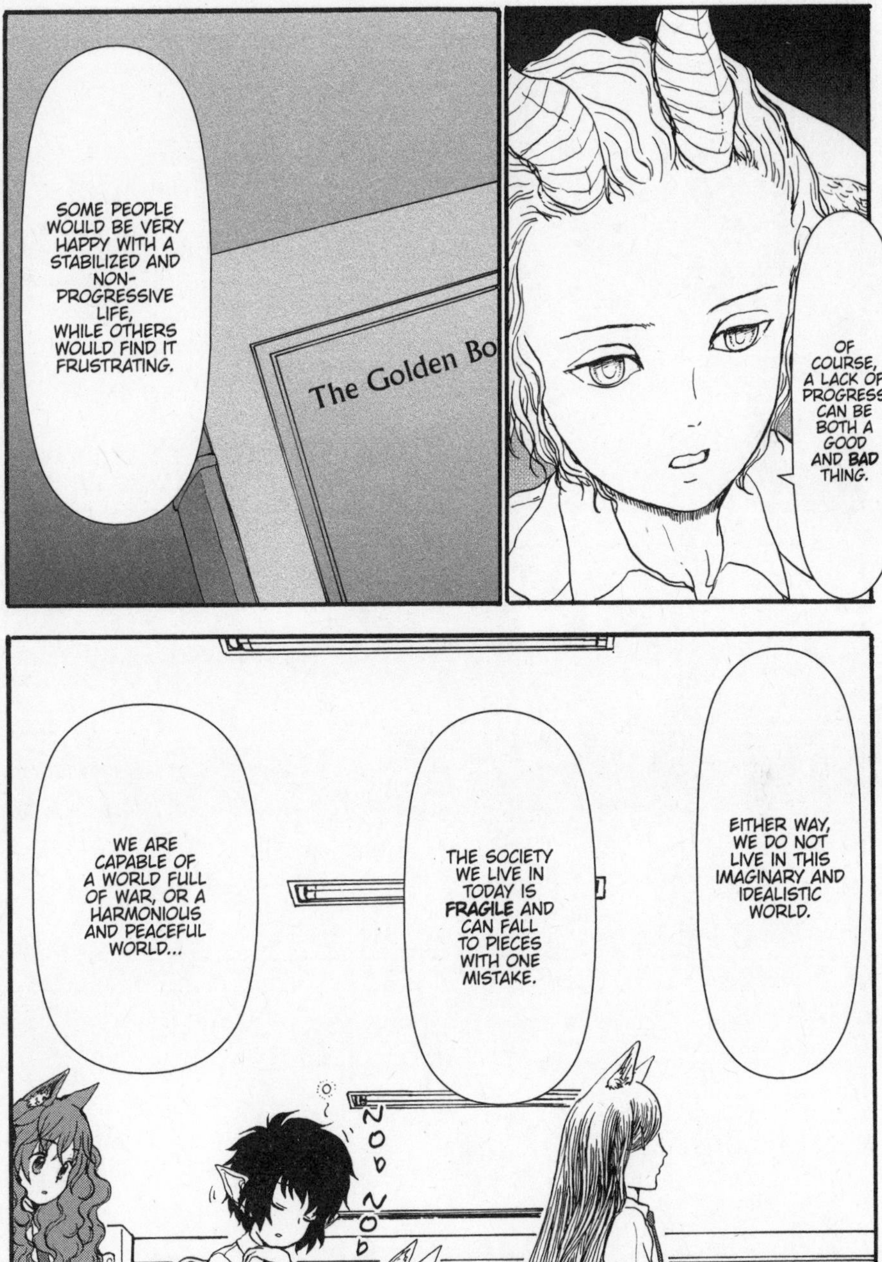
OF COURSE, A LACK OF PROGRESS CAN BE BOTH A GOOD AND **BAD** THING.
SOME PEOPLE WOULD BE VERY HAPPY WITH A STABILIZED AND NON-PROGRESSIVE LIFE, WHILE OTHERS WOULD FIND IT FRUSTRATING.
The Golden Bo
EITHER WAY, WE DO NOT LIVE IN THIS IMAGINARY AND IDEALISTIC WORLD.
THE SOCIETY WE LIVE IN TODAY IS **FRAGILE** AND CAN FALL TO PIECES WITH ONE MISTAKE.
WE ARE CAPABLE OF A WORLD FULL OF WAR, OR A HARMONIOUS AND PEACEFUL WORLD...
NOD NOD

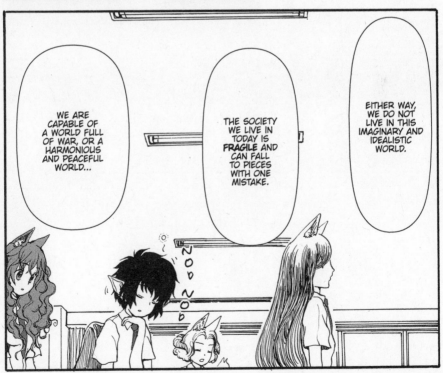

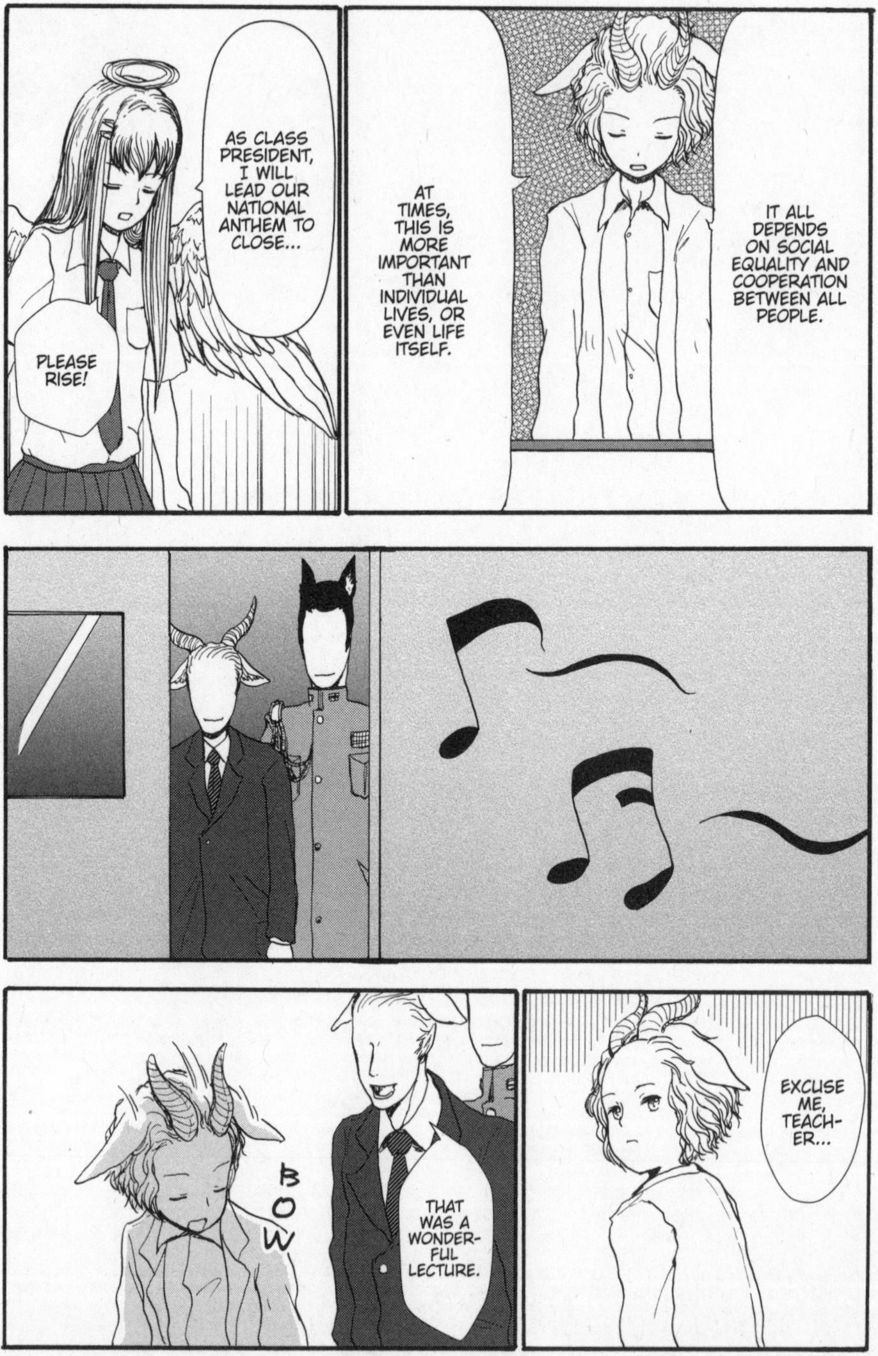
IT ALL DEPENDS ON SOCIAL EQUALITY AND COOPERATION BETWEEN ALL PEOPLE.
AT TIMES, THIS IS MORE IMPORTANT THAN INDIVIDUAL LIVES, OR EVEN LIFE ITSELF.
AS CLASS PRESIDENT, I WILL LEAD OUR NATIONAL ANTHEM TO CLOSE...
PLEASE RISE!
EXCUSE ME, TEACHER...
BOW
THAT WAS A WONDERFUL LECTURE.

A Centaur's Life

TIGER

FELINES

ORDER *CARNIVORA*, FAMILY *FELIDAE*. AS WITH THE
DOMESTIC DOG FROM FAMILY *CANIDAE*, THE DOMESTIC
HOUSECAT (*FELIS SYLVESTRIS CATUS*) IS AN ICONIC PET.
IT IS BELIEVED THAT THEY WERE DOMESTICATED FROM
WILDCATS (*FELIS SYVESTRIS*), SUPPORTED BY DNA TEST
RESULTS SHOWING HIGH PROBABILITY THAT MODERN
HOUSECATS ARE CLOSE DESCENDANTS OF THE WILDCAT.
SUBFAMILY *FELINAE* INCLUDES SMALL CATS SUCH
AS HOUSECATS AND WILDCATS AS WELL AS SOME
MEDIUM-SIZED CATS SUCH AS THE LYNX AND COUGAR.
SUBFAMILY *PANTHERINAE* INCLUDES LARGER CATS
SUCH AS THE TIGER, LION, LEOPARD, AND JAGUAR.

MOST MEMBERS OF FAMILY *FELIDAE* HAVE LOST THEIR
MIDDLE LIMBS OR HAVE EVOLVED THEM FOR OTHER USES
THAN WALKING. FOR INSTANCE, THE TIGER (*PANTHERA TIGRIS*)
ONLY HAS VESTIGIAL REMNANTS OF THEIR MIDDLE LIMBS
WHICH ARE EASY TO MISS AT FIRST GLANCE. IT IS BELIEVED
THAT THIS IS AN ADAPTATION TO THEIR POUNCING STYLE OF
HUNTING. MANY PUREBRED HOUSECATS HAVE SUBSTANTIAL
WINGS, BUT THIS IS A RESULT OF HUMAN BREEDING FOR
DESIRABLE TRAITS. WING SIZE DECREASES IN NON-PUREBRED
OFFSPRING. WILDCATS HAVE VERY SMALL WINGS.

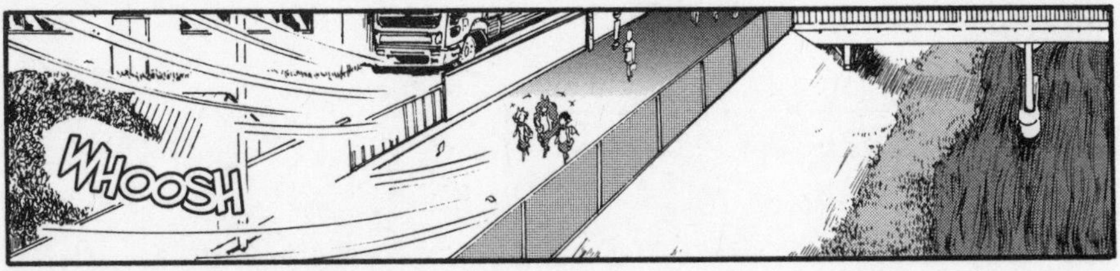
WHOOSH

CHAPTER 6

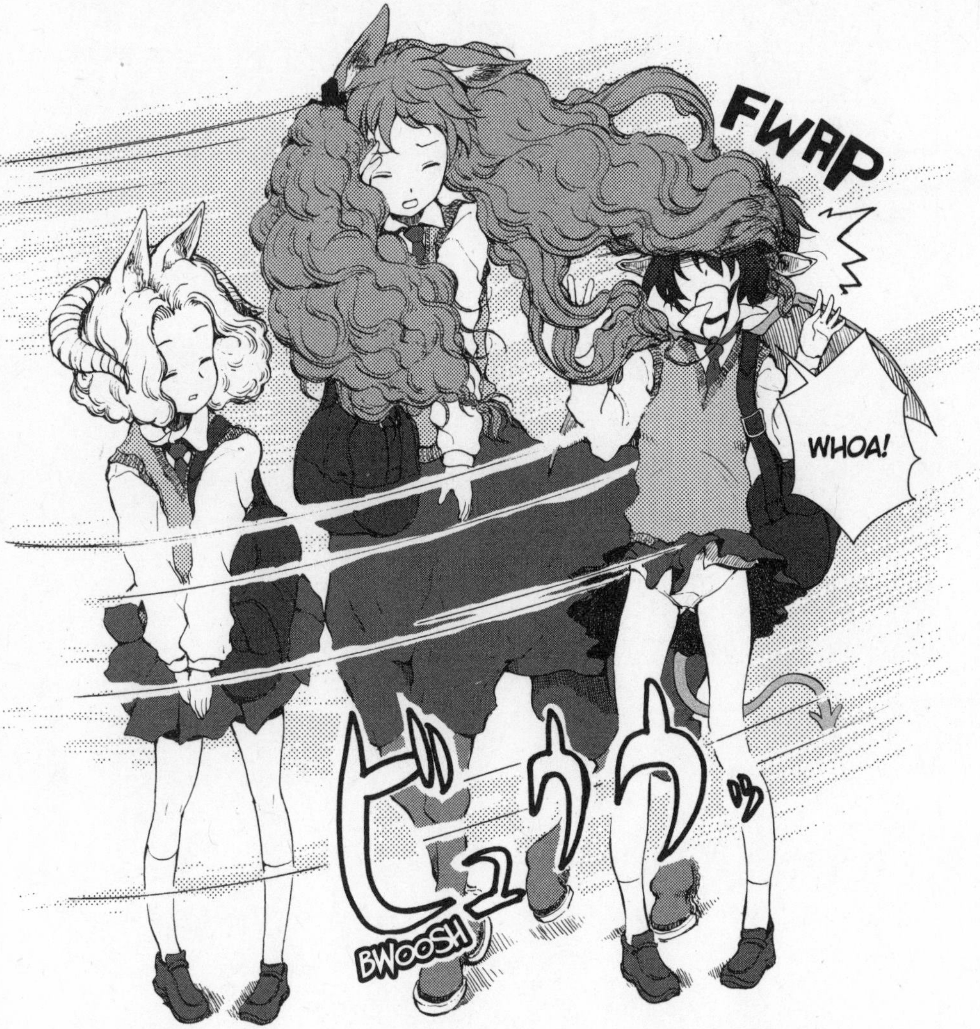
FWAP
WHOA!
BWOOSH

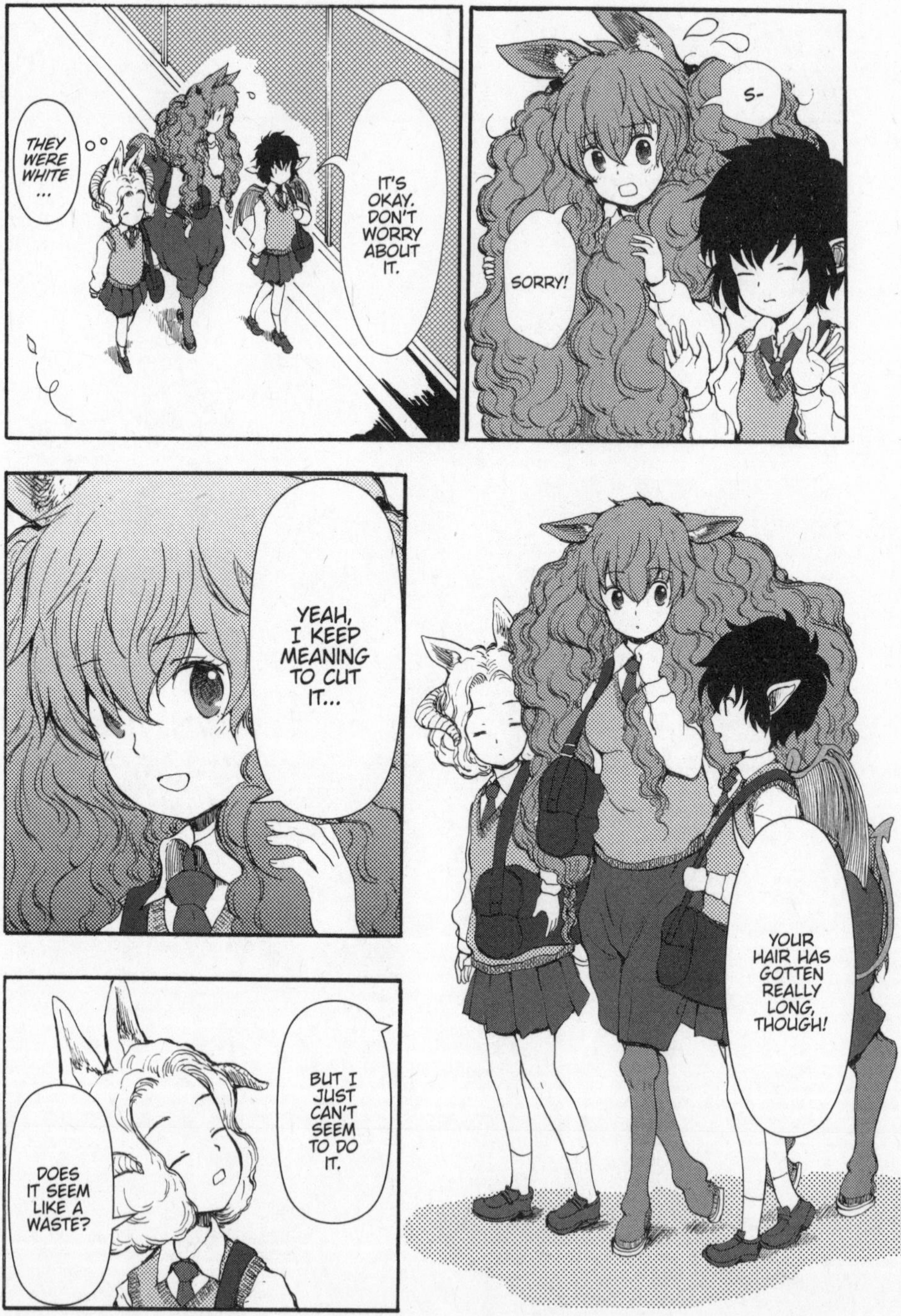
S-
SORRY!
IT'S OKAY. DON'T WORRY ABOUT IT.
THEY WERE WHITE ...
YOUR HAIR HAS GOTTEN REALLY LONG, THOUGH!
YEAH, I KEEP MEANING TO CUT IT...
BUT I JUST CAN'T SEEM TO DO IT.
DOES IT SEEM LIKE A WASTE?

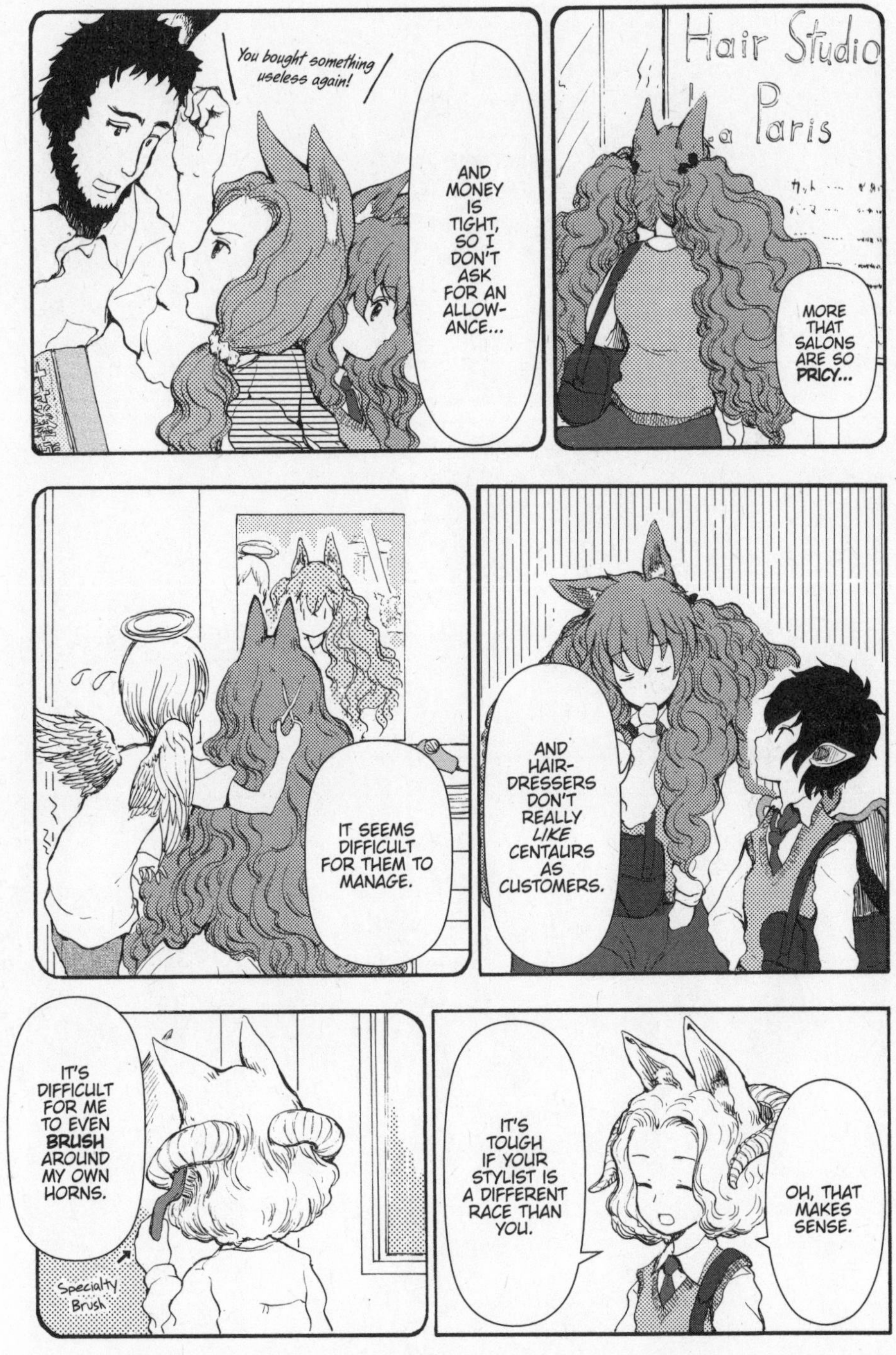
Hair Studio
a Paris
MORE THAT SALONS ARE SO **PRICY...**
AND MONEY IS TIGHT, SO I DON'T ASK FOR AN ALLOW-ANCE...
You bought something useless again!
AND HAIR-DRESSERS DON'T REALLY *LIKE* CENTAURS AS CUSTOMERS.
IT SEEMS DIFFICULT FOR THEM TO MANAGE.
OH, THAT MAKES SENSE.
IT'S TOUGH IF YOUR STYLIST IS A DIFFERENT RACE THAN YOU.
IT'S DIFFICULT FOR ME TO EVEN **BRUSH** AROUND MY OWN HORNS.
Specialty Brush

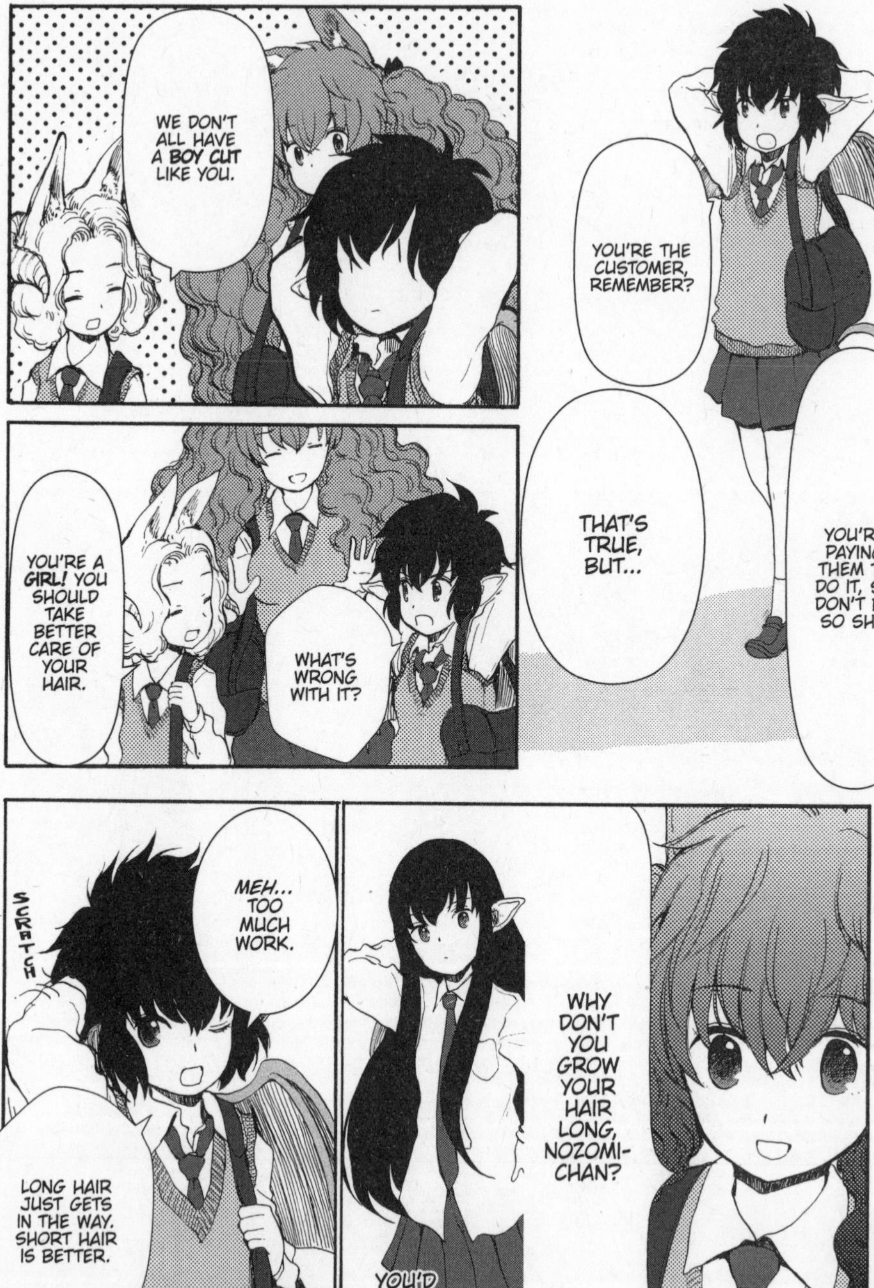
YOU'RE THE CUSTOMER, REMEMBER?
YOU'RE PAYING THEM TO DO IT, SO DON'T BE SO SHY.
THAT'S TRUE, BUT...
WE DON'T ALL HAVE A **BOY CUT** LIKE YOU.
YOU'RE A **GIRL!** YOU SHOULD TAKE BETTER CARE OF YOUR HAIR.
WHAT'S WRONG WITH IT?
WHY DON'T YOU GROW YOUR HAIR LONG, NOZOMI-CHAN?
YOU'D LOOK SO PRETTY.
MEH... TOO MUCH WORK.
SCRATCH
LONG HAIR JUST GETS IN THE WAY. SHORT HAIR IS BETTER.

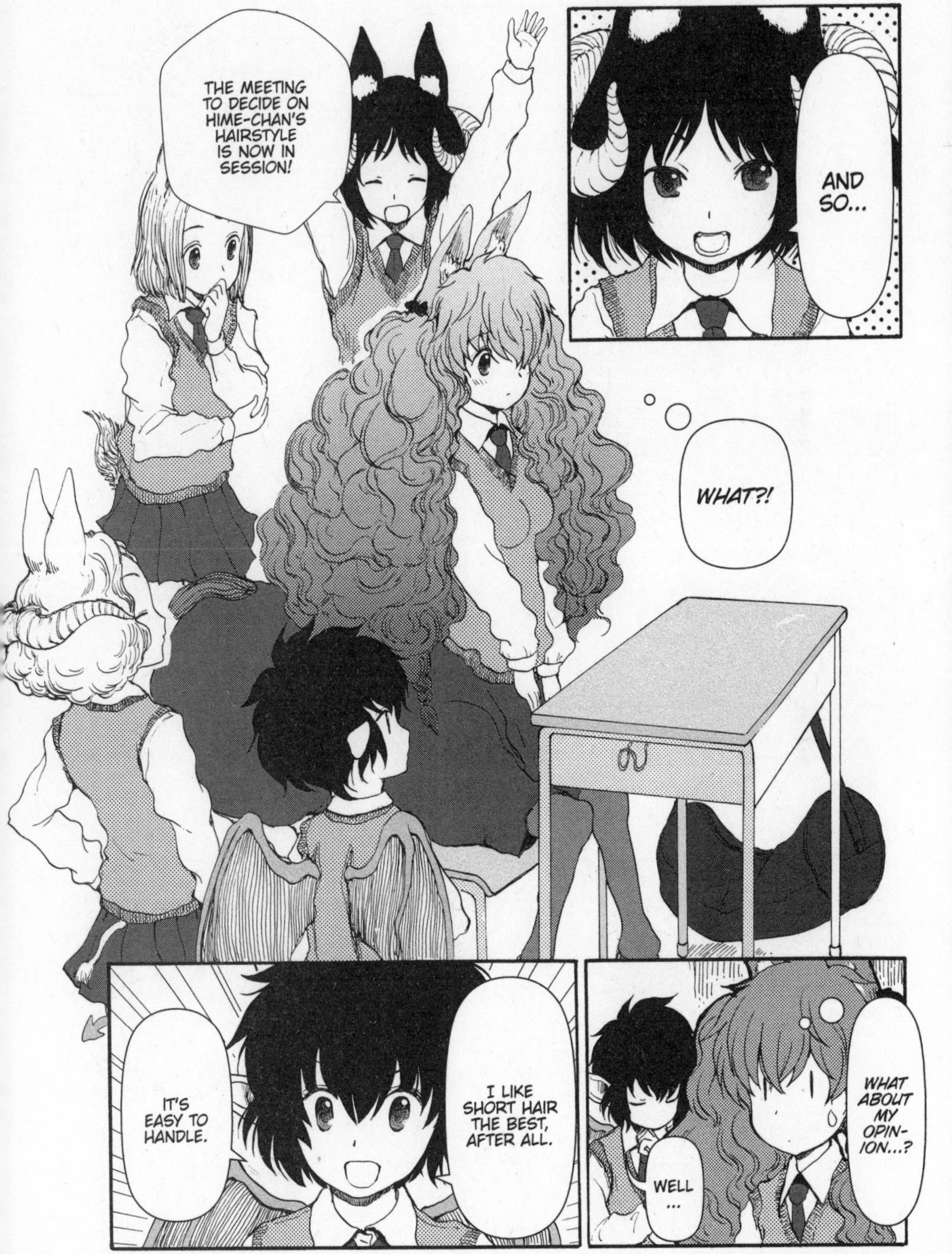
AND SO...
THE MEETING TO DECIDE ON HIME-CHAN'S HAIRSTYLE IS NOW IN SESSION!
WHAT?!
WHAT ABOUT MY OPIN-ION...?
WELL ...
I LIKE SHORT HAIR THE BEST, AFTER ALL.
IT'S EASY TO HANDLE.

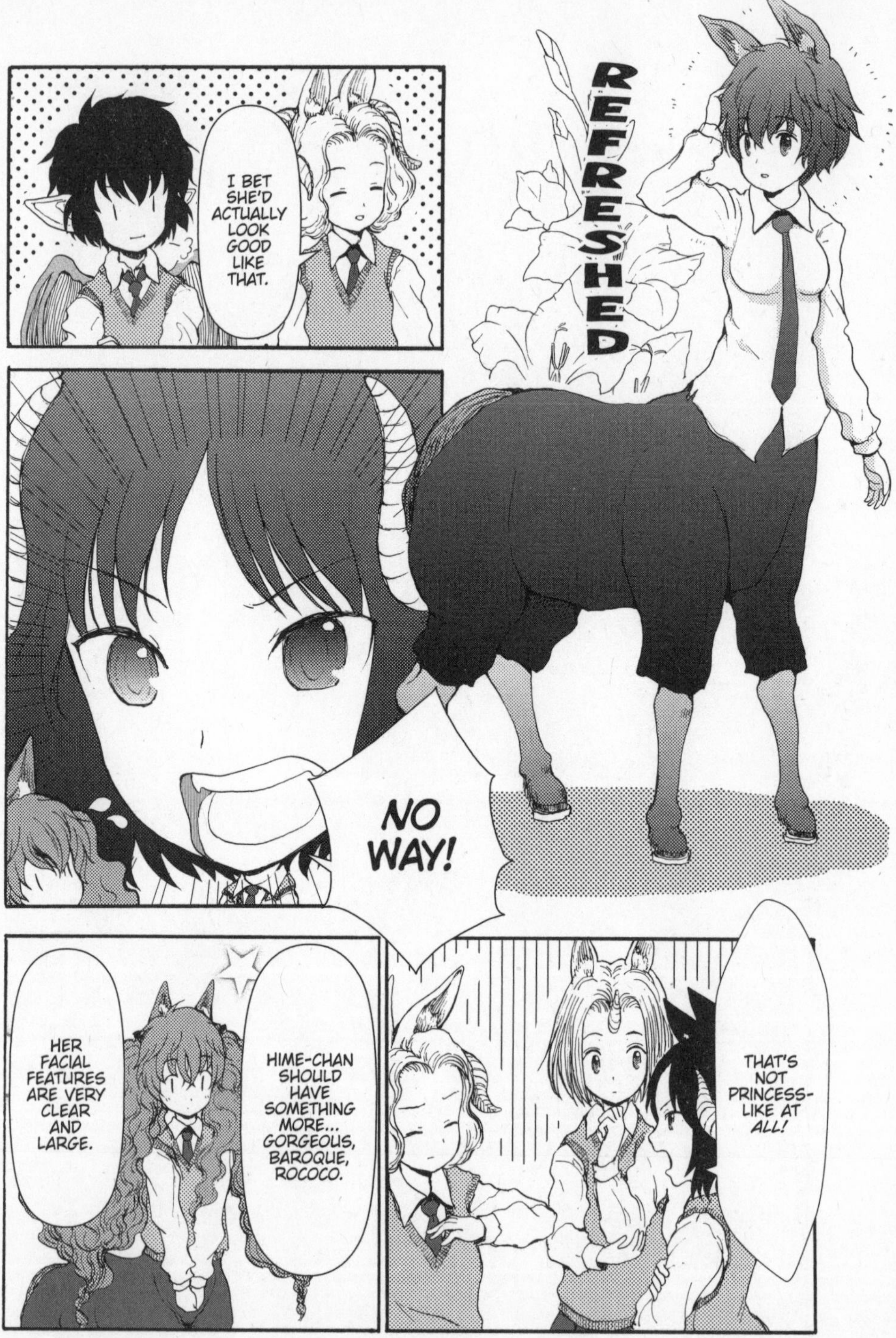
REFRESHED
I BET SHE'D ACTUALLY LOOK GOOD LIKE THAT.
NO WAY!
THAT'S NOT PRINCESS-LIKE AT *ALL*!
HIME-CHAN SHOULD HAVE SOMETHING MORE... GORGEOUS, BAROQUE, ROCOCO.
HER FACIAL FEATURES ARE VERY CLEAR AND LARGE.

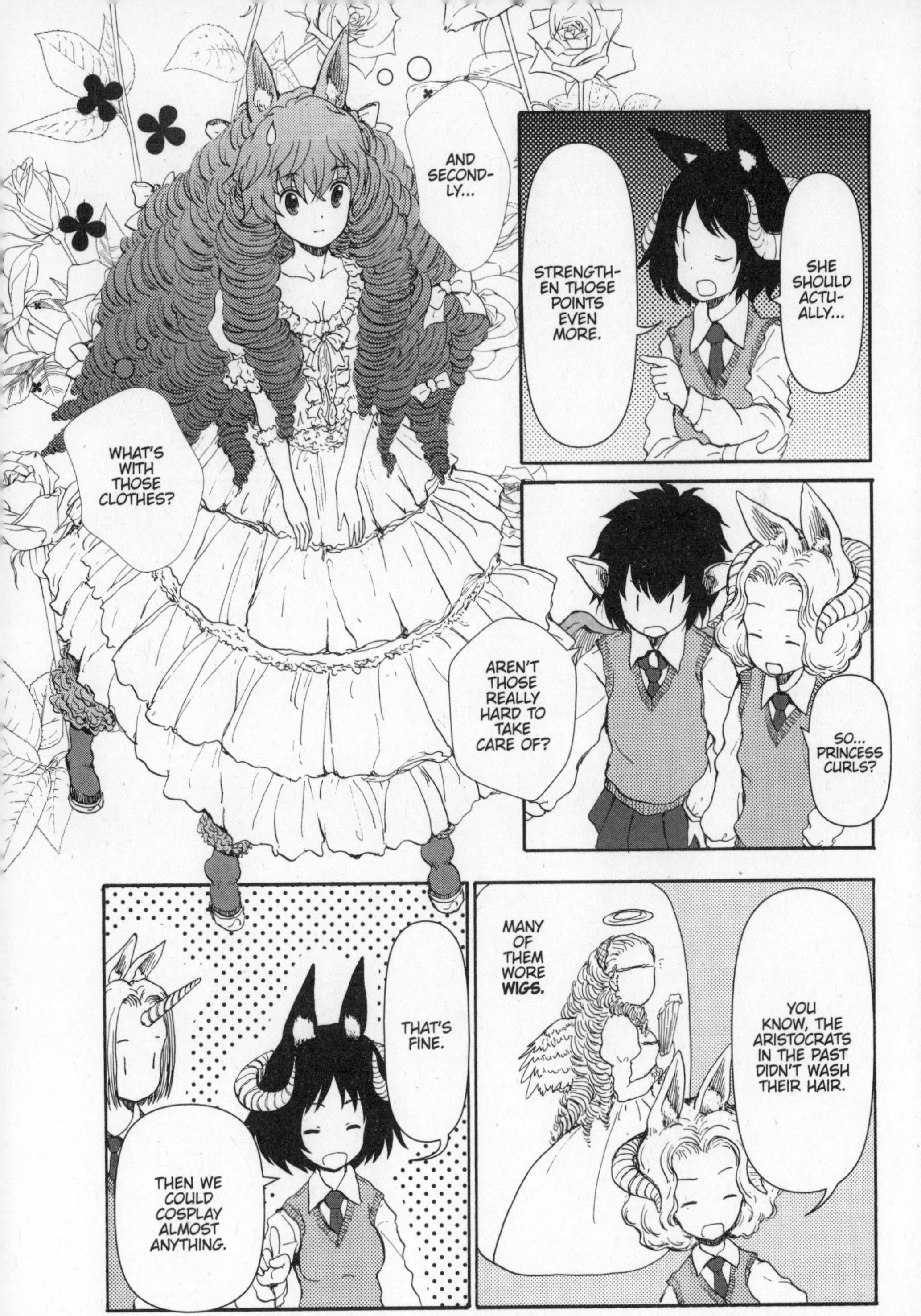
SHE SHOULD ACTU-ALLY...
STRENGTH-EN THOSE POINTS EVEN MORE.
SO... PRINCESS CURLS?
AREN'T THOSE REALLY HARD TO TAKE CARE OF?
AND SECOND-LY...
WHAT'S WITH THOSE CLOTHES?
YOU KNOW, THE ARISTOCRATS IN THE PAST DIDN'T WASH THEIR HAIR.
MANY OF THEM WORE **WIGS.**
THAT'S FINE.
THEN WE COULD COSPLAY ALMOST ANYTHING.

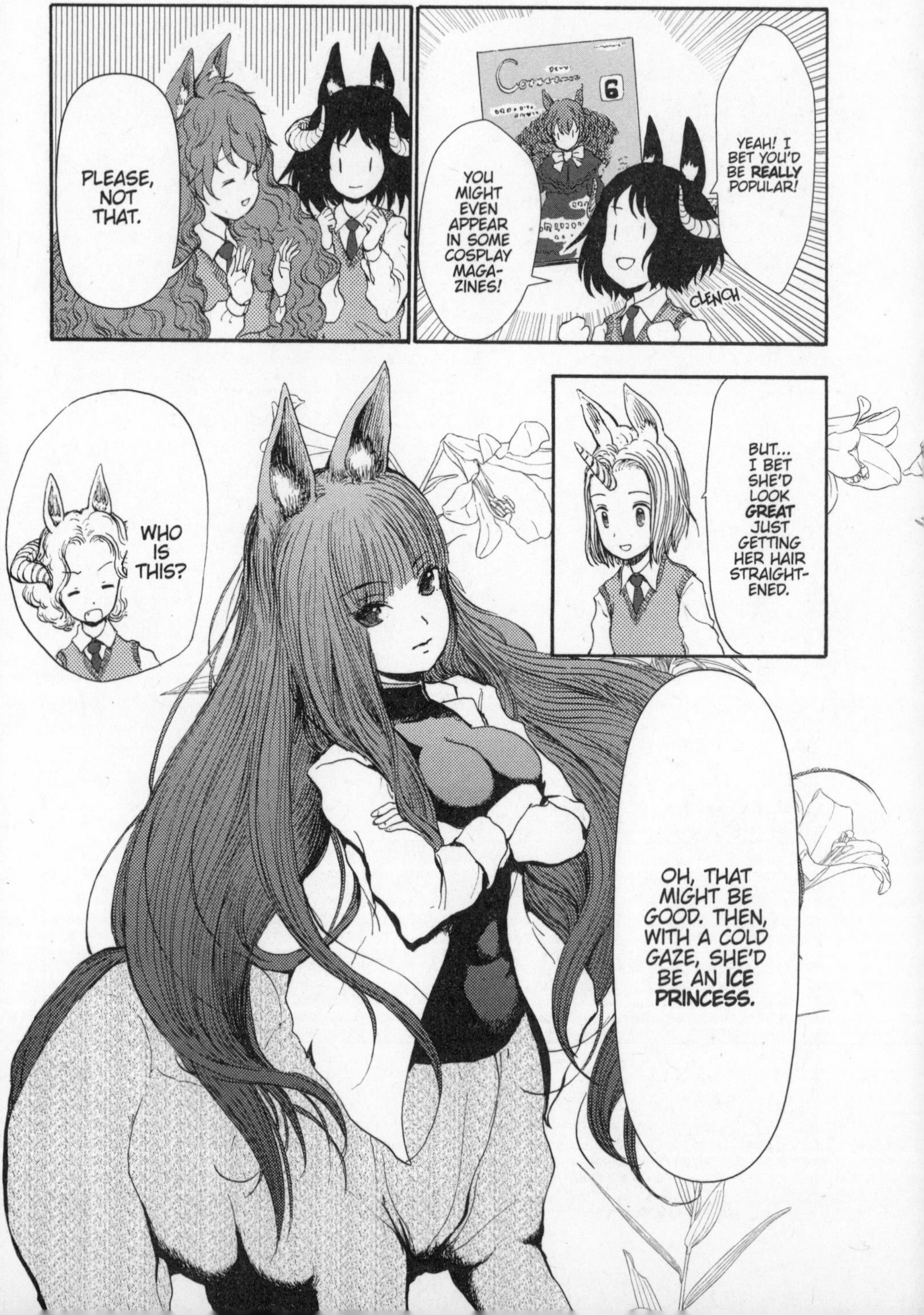
YEAH! I BET YOU'D BE **REALLY** POPULAR!
YOU MIGHT EVEN APPEAR IN SOME COSPLAY MAGA-ZINES!
CLENCH
PLEASE, NOT THAT.
BUT... I BET SHE'D LOOK **GREAT** JUST GETTING HER HAIR STRAIGHT-ENED.
WHO IS THIS?
OH, THAT MIGHT BE GOOD. THEN, WITH A COLD GAZE, SHE'D BE AN ICE **PRINCESS.**

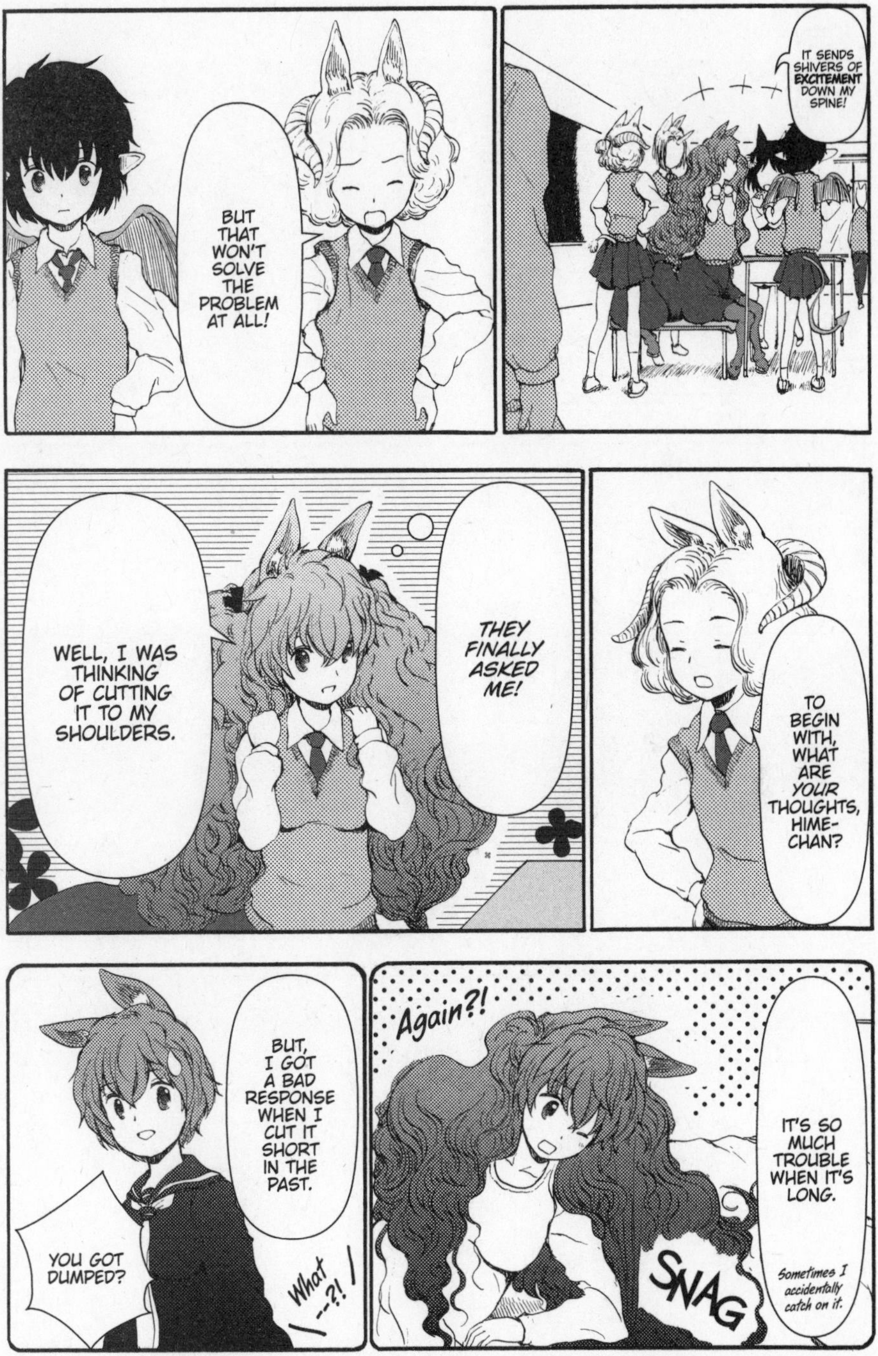
IT SENDS SHIVERS OF EXCITEMENT DOWN MY SPINE!
BUT THAT WON'T SOLVE THE PROBLEM AT ALL!
TO BEGIN WITH, WHAT ARE YOUR THOUGHTS, HIME-CHAN?
THEY FINALLY ASKED ME!
WELL, I WAS THINKING OF CUTTING IT TO MY SHOULDERS.
IT'S SO MUCH TROUBLE WHEN IT'S LONG.
Again?!
SNAG
Sometimes I accidentally catch on it.
BUT, I GOT A BAD RESPONSE WHEN I CUT IT SHORT IN THE PAST.
What--?!
YOU GOT DUMPED?

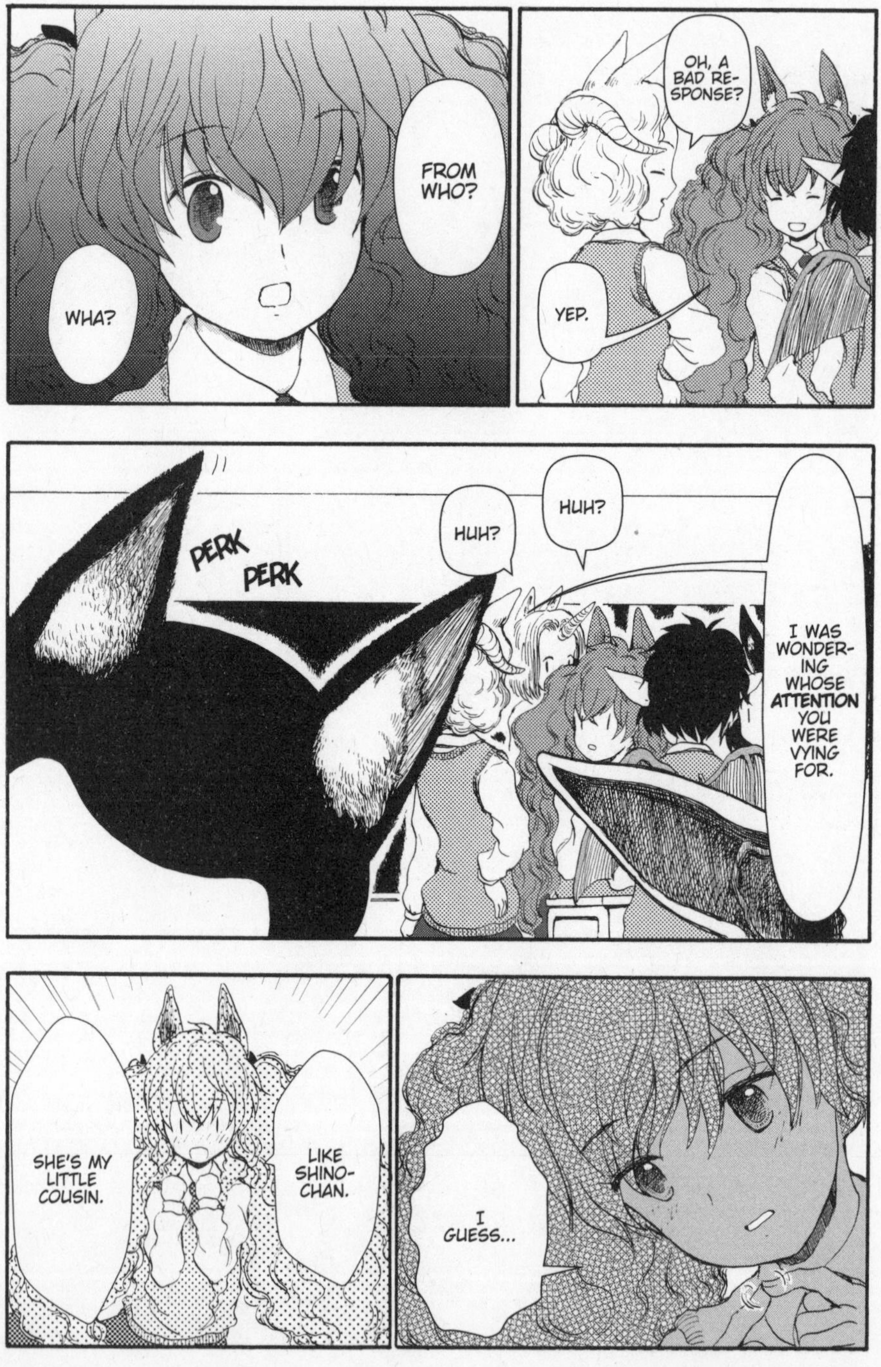
OH, A BAD RE-SPONSE?
YEP.
FROM WHO?
WHA?
I WAS WONDER-ING WHOSE **ATTENTION** YOU WERE VYING FOR.
HUH?
HUH?
PERK PERK
I GUESS...
LIKE SHINO-CHAN.
SHE'S MY LITTLE COUSIN.

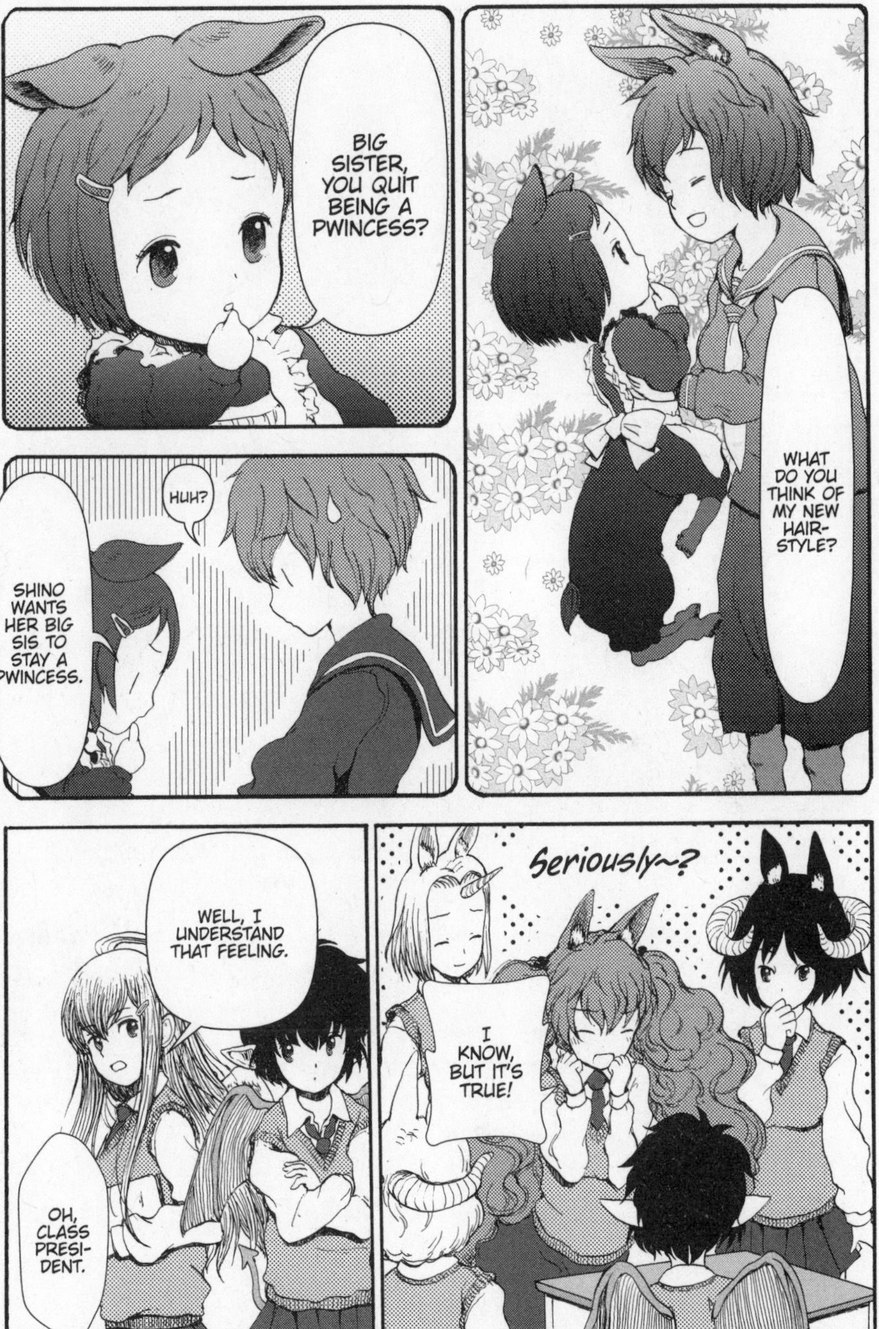
WHAT DO YOU THINK OF MY NEW HAIR-STYLE?
BIG SISTER, YOU QUIT BEING A PWINCESS?
HUH?
SHINO WANTS HER BIG SIS TO STAY A PWINCESS.
Seriously~?
I KNOW, BUT IT'S TRUE!
WELL, I UNDERSTAND THAT FEELING.
OH, CLASS PRESIDENT.

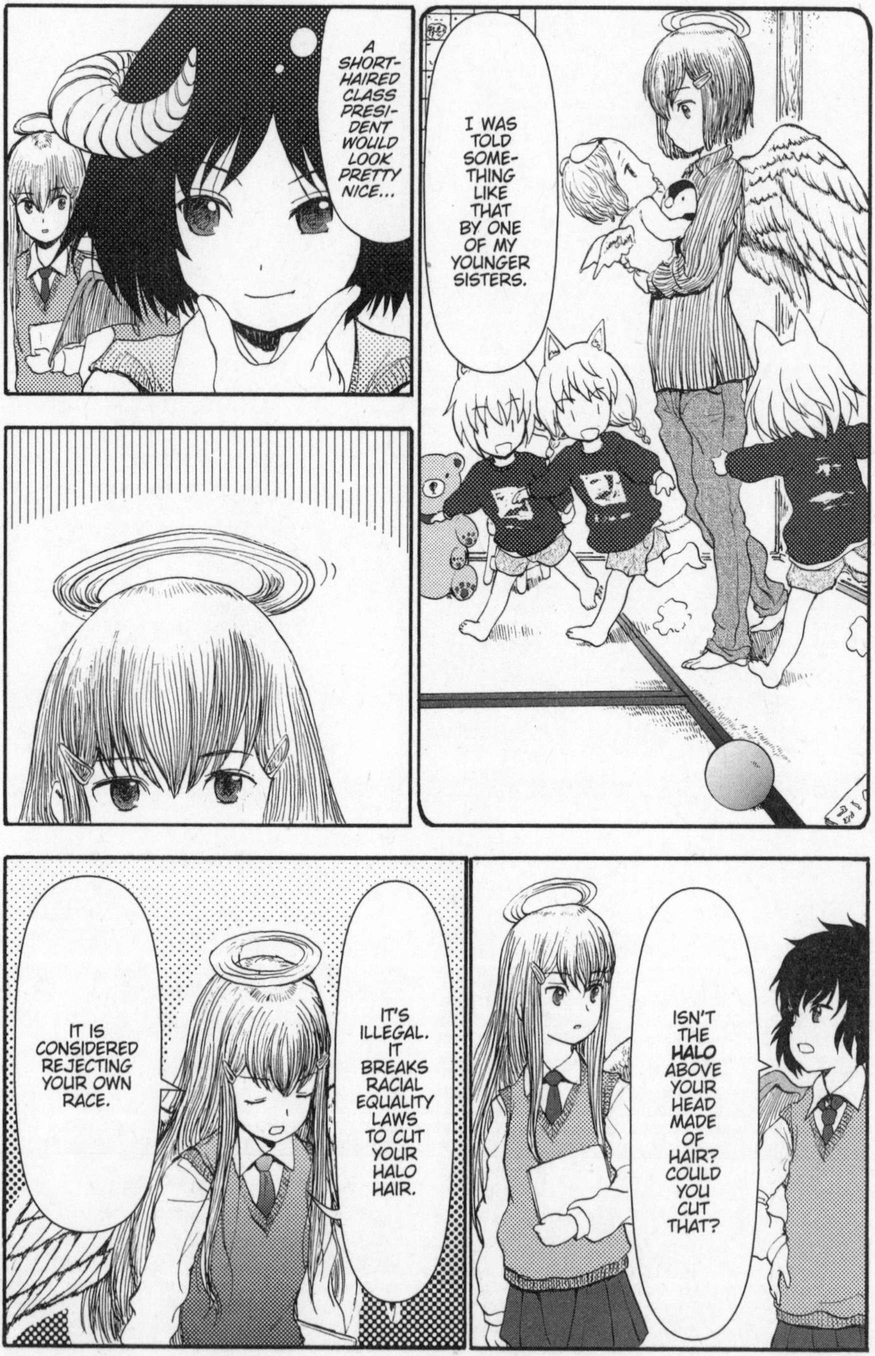
I WAS TOLD SOMETHING LIKE THAT BY ONE OF MY YOUNGER SISTERS.
A SHORT-HAIRED CLASS PRESIDENT WOULD LOOK PRETTY NICE...
ISN'T THE HALO ABOVE YOUR HEAD MADE OF HAIR? COULD YOU CUT THAT?
IT'S ILLEGAL. IT BREAKS RACIAL EQUALITY LAWS TO CUT YOUR HALO HAIR.
IT IS CONSIDERED REJECTING YOUR OWN RACE.

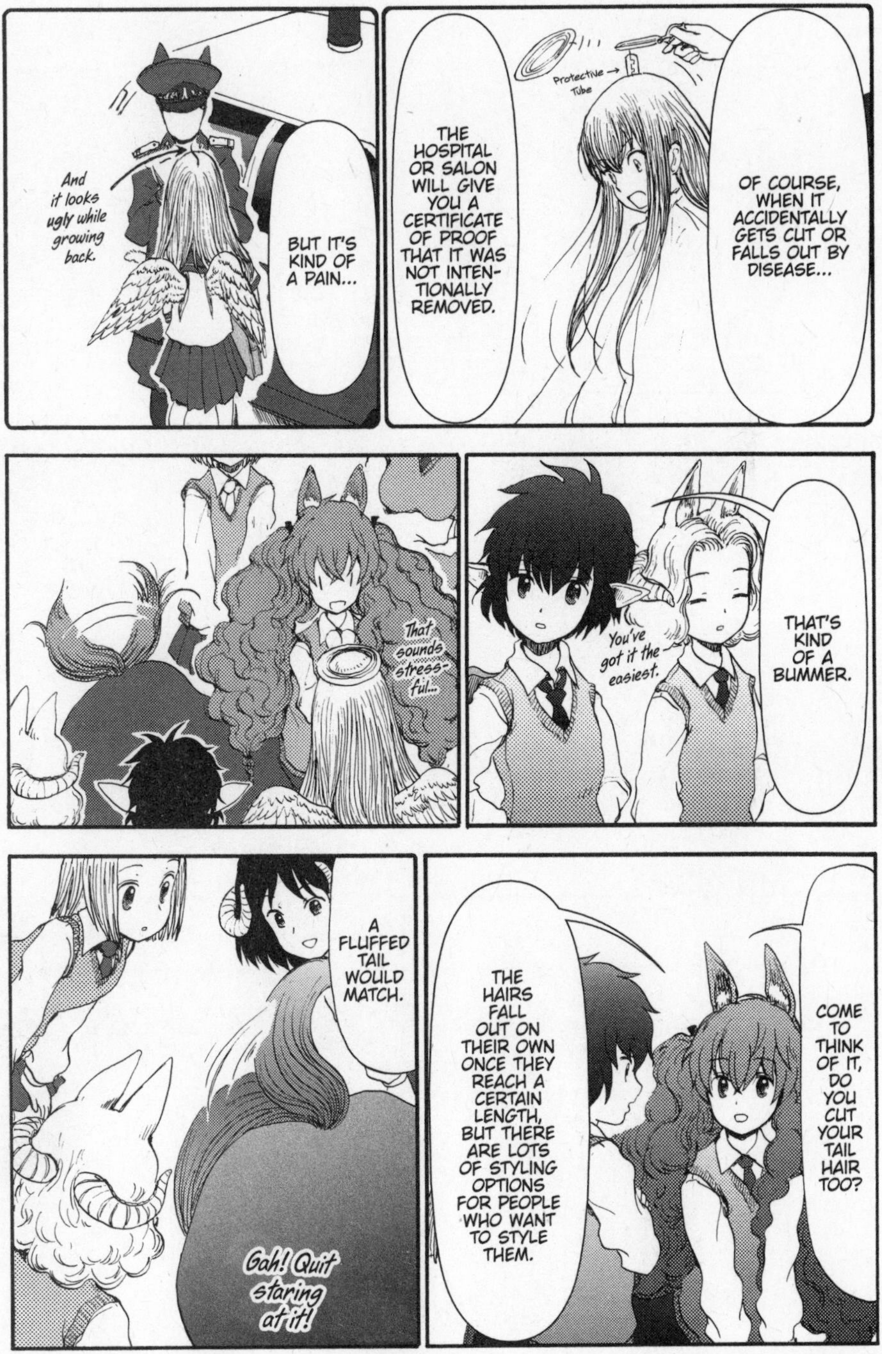
OF COURSE, WHEN IT ACCIDENTALLY GETS CUT OR FALLS OUT BY DISEASE...
Protective Tube
THE HOSPITAL OR SALON WILL GIVE YOU A CERTIFICATE OF PROOF THAT IT WAS NOT INTENTIONALLY REMOVED.
BUT IT'S KIND OF A PAIN...
And it looks ugly while growing back.
THAT'S KIND OF A BUMMER.
You've got it the easiest.
That sounds stressful...
COME TO THINK OF IT, DO YOU CUT YOUR TAIL HAIR TOO?
THE HAIRS FALL OUT ON THEIR OWN ONCE THEY REACH A CERTAIN LENGTH, BUT THERE ARE LOTS OF STYLING OPTIONS FOR PEOPLE WHO WANT TO STYLE THEM.
A FLUFFED TAIL WOULD MATCH.
Gah! Quit staring at it!

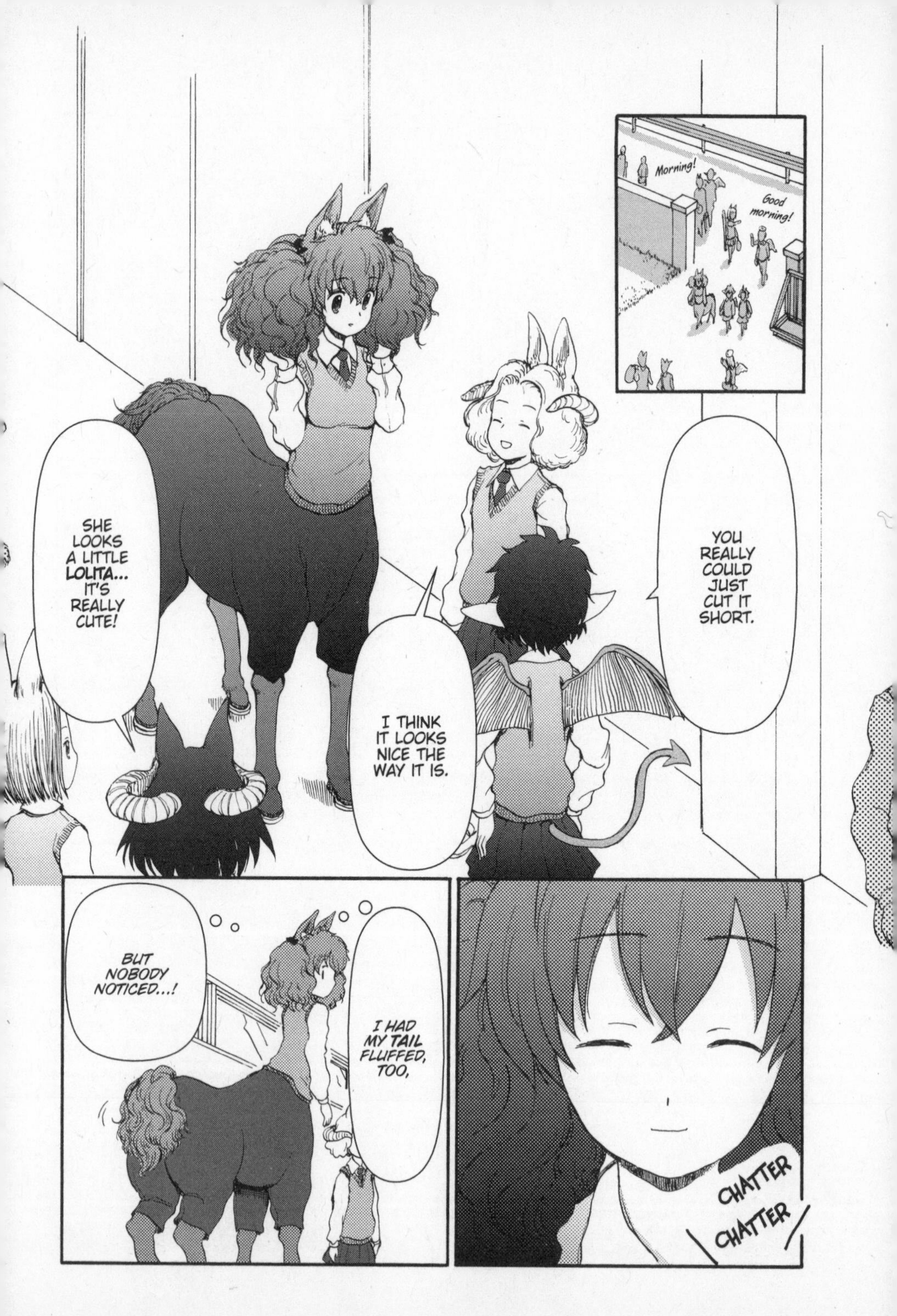
Morning!
Good morning!
YOU REALLY COULD JUST CUT IT SHORT.
I THINK IT LOOKS NICE THE WAY IT IS.
SHE LOOKS A LITTLE LOLITA... IT'S REALLY CUTE!
CHATTER
CHATTER
I HAD MY TAIL FLUFFED, TOO,
BUT NOBODY NOTICED...!

A Centaur's Life

EQUINES

ORDER *PERISSODACTYLA*, FAMILY *EQUIIDAE*. EQUINES SUCH AS
HORSES, DONKEYS, AND MULES ARE ICONIC SPECIES OF LIVESTOCK.

ALL MEMBERS OF ORDER *PERISSODACTYLA* HAVE MIDDLE LIMBS, AND
THE MAJORITY OF THEIR WEIGHT IS ON THEIR THIRD PHALANGES. HORSES
HAVE PUT EMPHASIS ON THEIR THIRD PHALANGES AND THEIR OTHERS HAVE
FADED AWAY. THEIR HOOVES ARE MOSTLY MADE OF KERATIN, THE MATERIAL
THAT MAKES UP HUMAN FINGERNAILS. ALTHOUGH THEY LOOK PHYSICALLY
SIMILAR TO THE LOWER HALF OF THE CENTAUR RACE, IT IS BELIEVED THIS IS
DUE TO CONVERGENT EVOLUTION. THERE ARE MANY VARIANTS THAT
REJECT THE IDEA OF PARALLEL EVOLUTION FROM A COMMON ANCESTOR.

PERISSODACTYLA APPEARED TO HAVE FLOURISHED IN THE TERTIARY PERIOD
OF THE CENOZOIC ERA, BUT UNLIKE THE BOVINES (ORDER *ARTIODACTYLA*,
FAMILY *BOVINAE*) WITH THEIR COMPLEX STOMACHS, IT SEEMS THEY WEREN'T
ABLE TO COMPETE WITH THE CHANGING DIETS. CURRENTLY THERE ARE ONLY
THREE FAMILIES IN EXISTENCE: *EQUIIDAE* (INCLUDES THE HORSE, ZEBRA,
AND ASS), *RHINOCEROTIDAE* (RHINOCEROS), AND *TAPIRIDAE* (TAPIR).

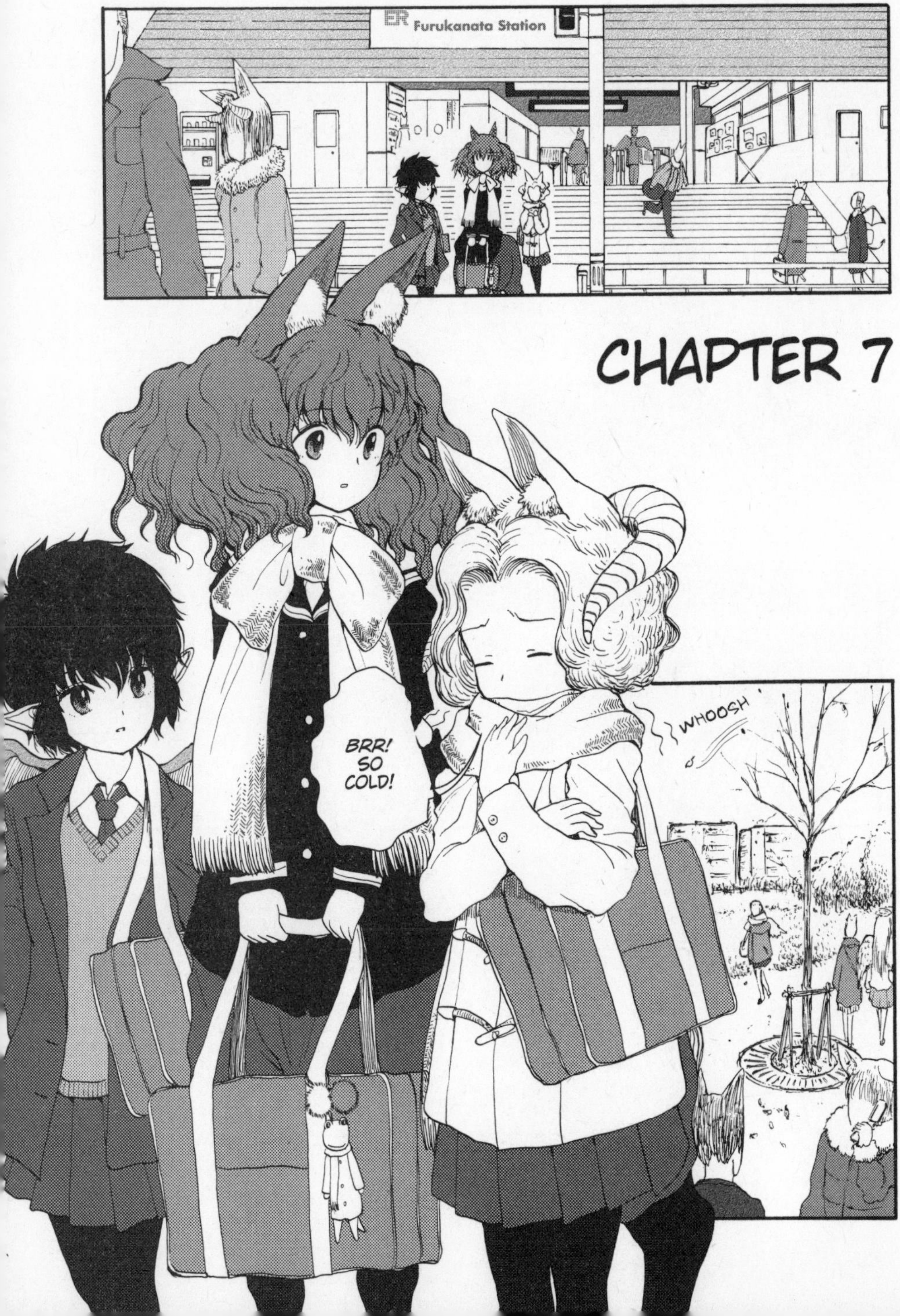
ER Furukanata Station
CHAPTER 7
BRR! SO COLD!
WHOOSH

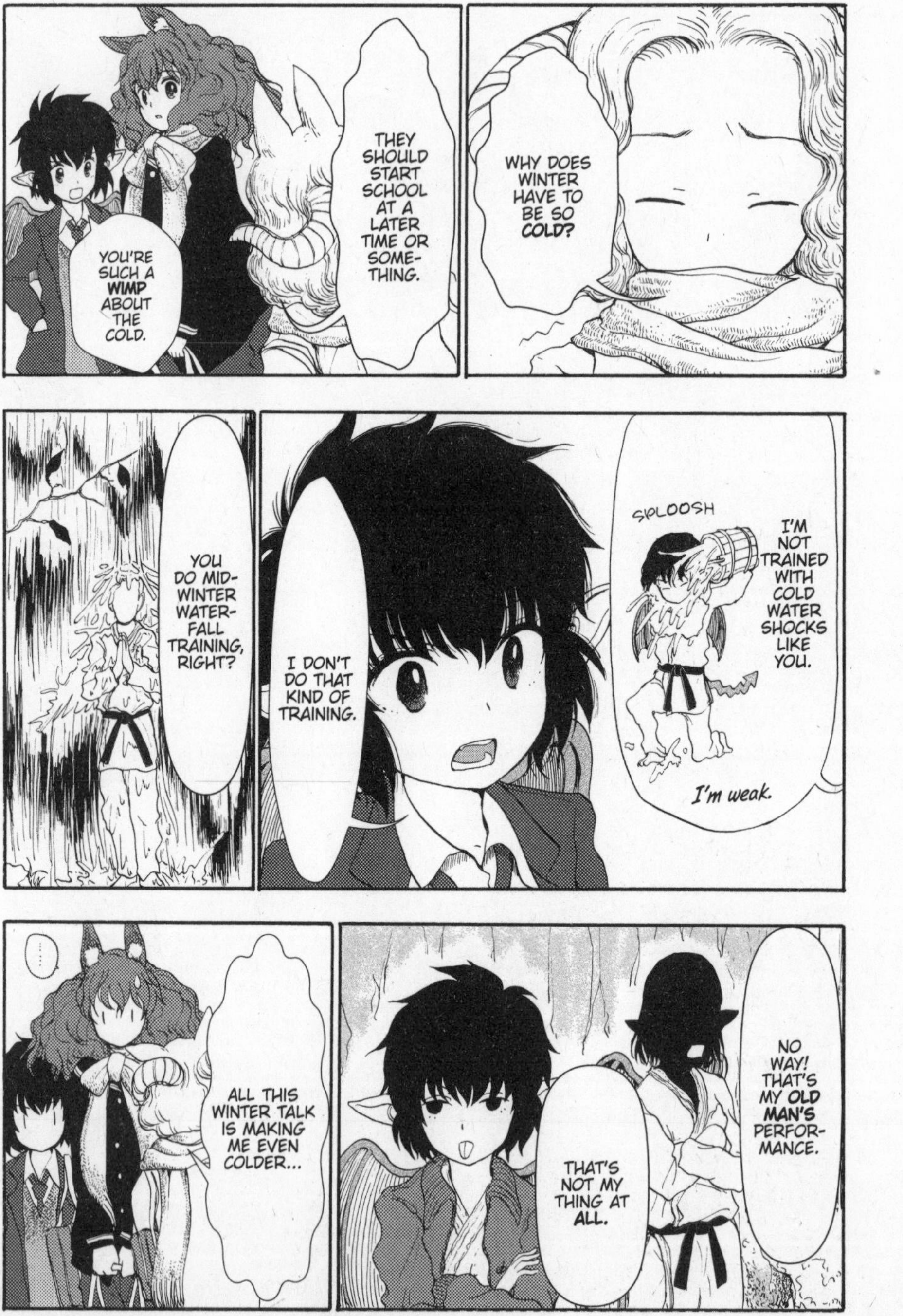
WHY DOES WINTER HAVE TO BE SO **COLD?**
THEY SHOULD START SCHOOL AT A LATER TIME OR SOME-THING.
YOU'RE SUCH A **WIMP** ABOUT THE COLD.
SPLOOSH
I'M NOT TRAINED WITH COLD WATER SHOCKS LIKE YOU.
I'm weak.
I DON'T DO THAT KIND OF TRAINING.
YOU DO MID-WINTER WATER-FALL TRAINING, RIGHT?
NO WAY! THAT'S MY **OLD MAN'S** PERFOR-MANCE.
THAT'S NOT MY THING AT **ALL.**
ALL THIS WINTER TALK IS MAKING ME EVEN COLDER...
......

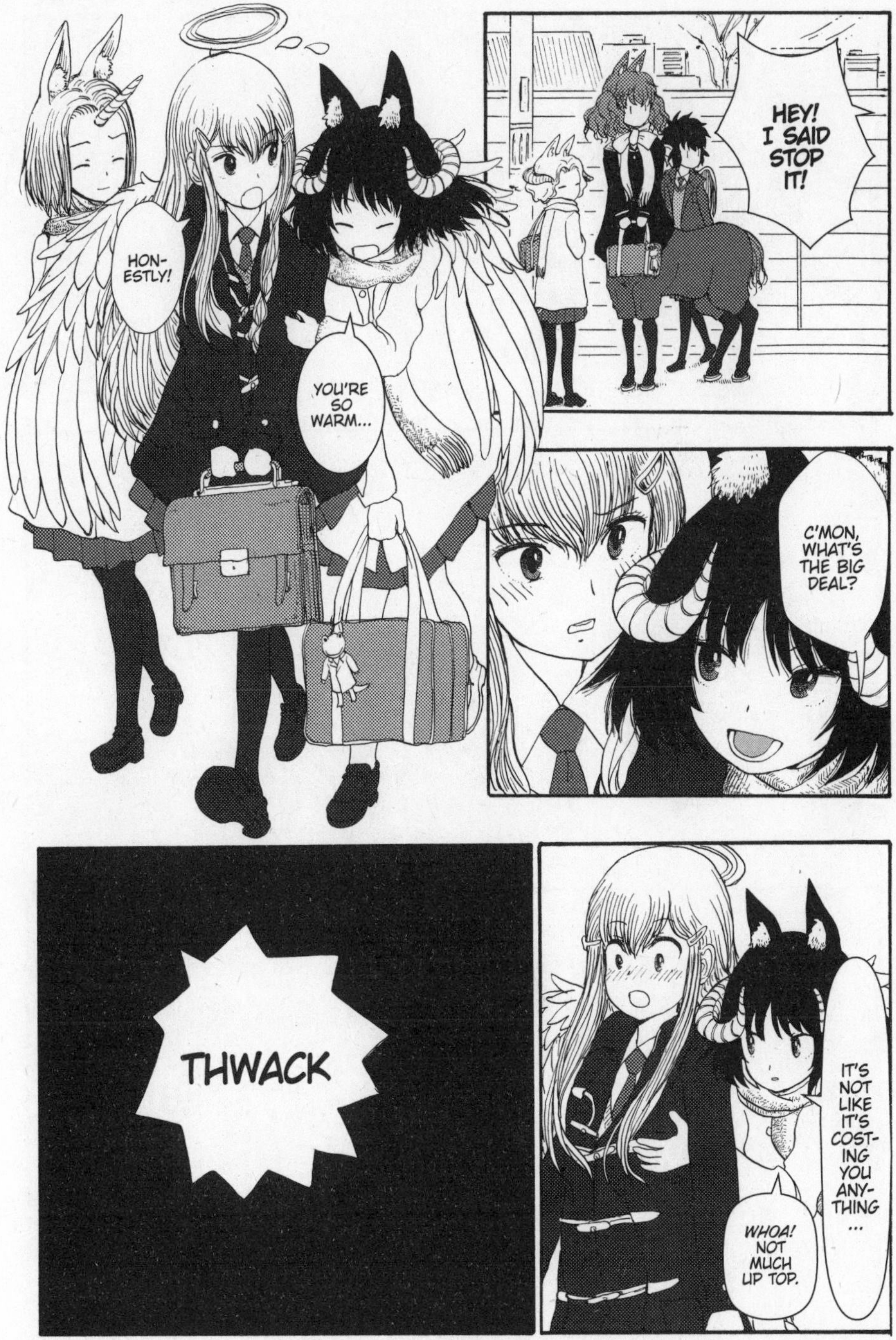
HEY! I SAID STOP IT!
C'MON, WHAT'S THE BIG DEAL?
HON-ESTLY!
YOU'RE SO WARM...
IT'S NOT LIKE IT'S COSTING YOU ANYTHING...
WHOA! NOT MUCH UP TOP.
THWACK

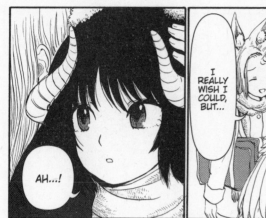

SHE'S YOUR GIRLFRIEND! DO SOMETHING ABOUT HER!
I REALLY WISH I COULD, BUT...
AH...!
Good morning.
GOOD MORNING, YOU THREE.
HEY.
GOOD MORNING.
... MORNING.
HEY...
WHY DON'T YOU ALL JOIN IN AS WELL? IT'S WAAARM....
DON'T INVITE PEOPLE WITHOUT PERMISSION!
WHY NOT? THAT'S WHAT THESE WINGS ARE FOR, RIGHT?
THEY'RE FOR ME!

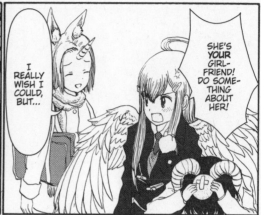

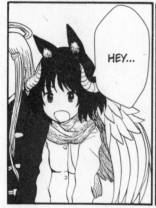

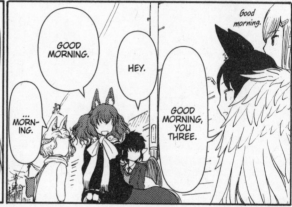

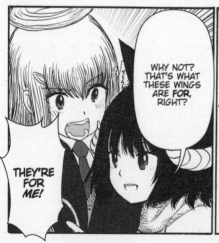

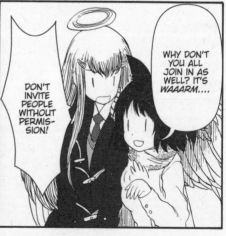

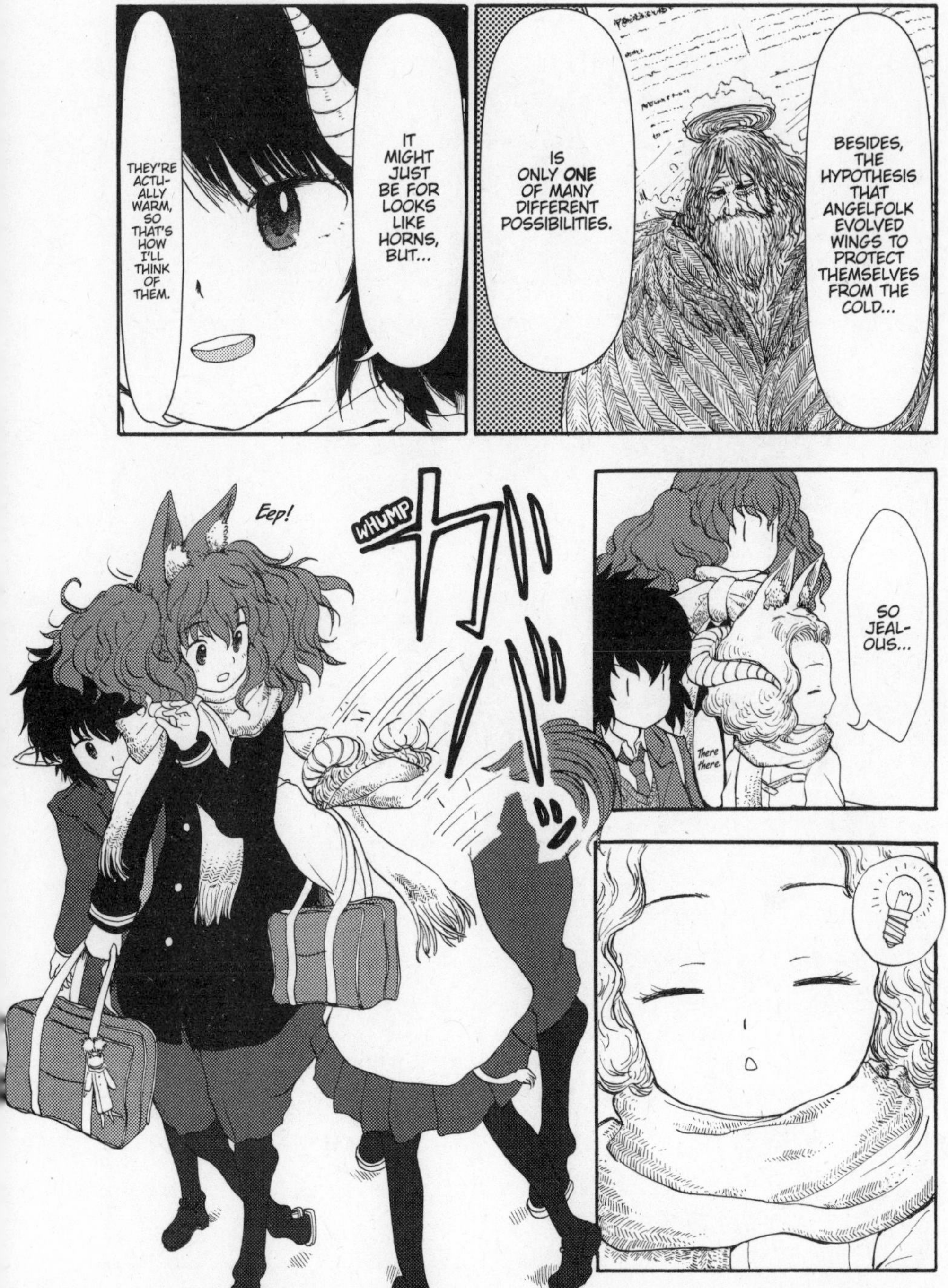
BESIDES, THE HYPOTHESIS THAT ANGELFOLK EVOLVED WINGS TO PROTECT THEMSELVES FROM THE COLD...
IS ONLY ONE OF MANY DIFFERENT POSSIBILITIES.
IT MIGHT JUST BE FOR LOOKS LIKE HORNS, BUT...
THEY'RE ACTU-ALLY WARM, SO THAT'S HOW I'LL THINK OF THEM.
SO JEAL-OUS...
There there.
WHUMP
Eep!

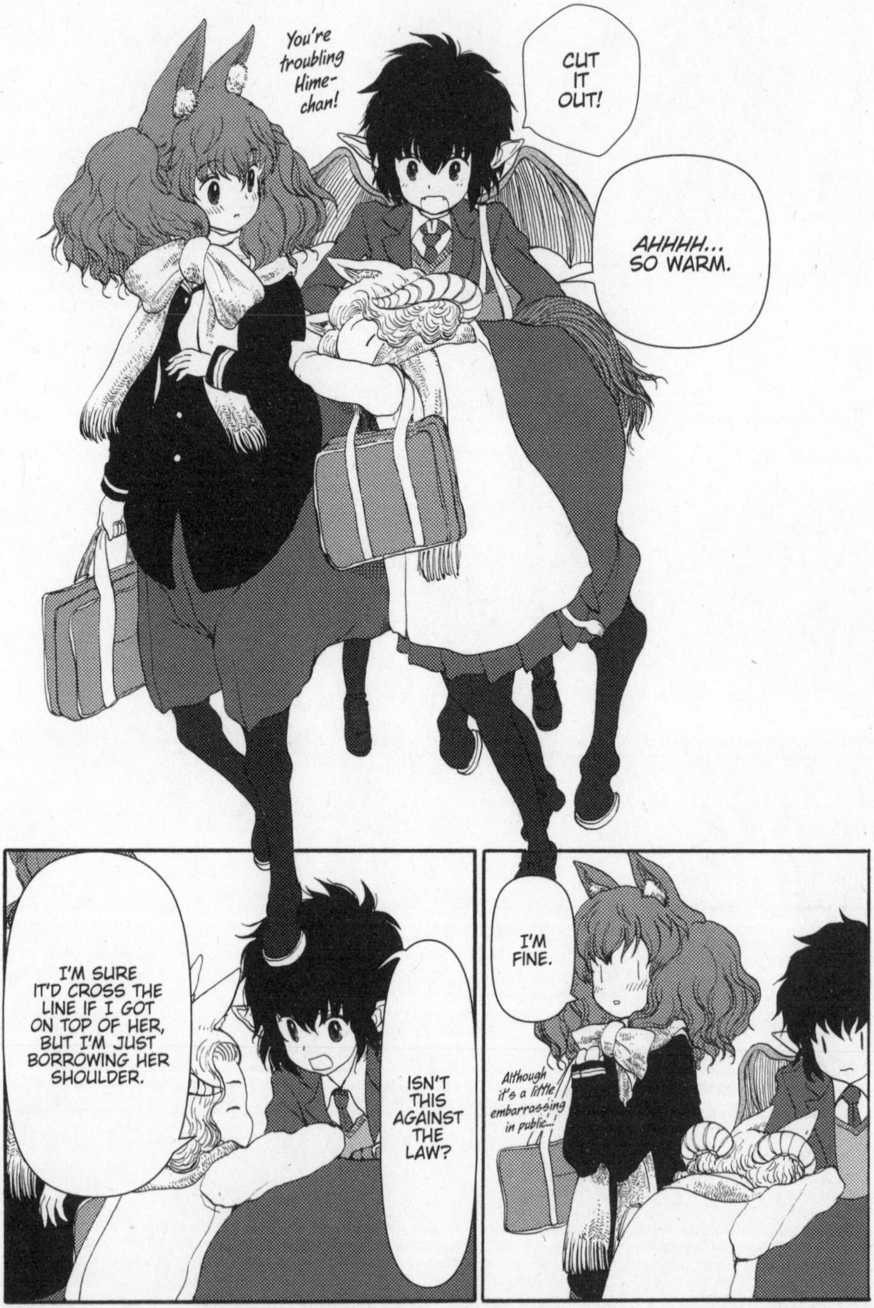
CUT IT OUT!
You're troubling Hime-chan!
AHHHH... SO WARM.
I'M FINE.
Although it's a little embarrassing in public...
ISN'T THIS AGAINST THE LAW?
I'M SURE IT'D CROSS THE LINE IF I GOT ON TOP OF HER, BUT I'M JUST BORROWING HER SHOULDER.

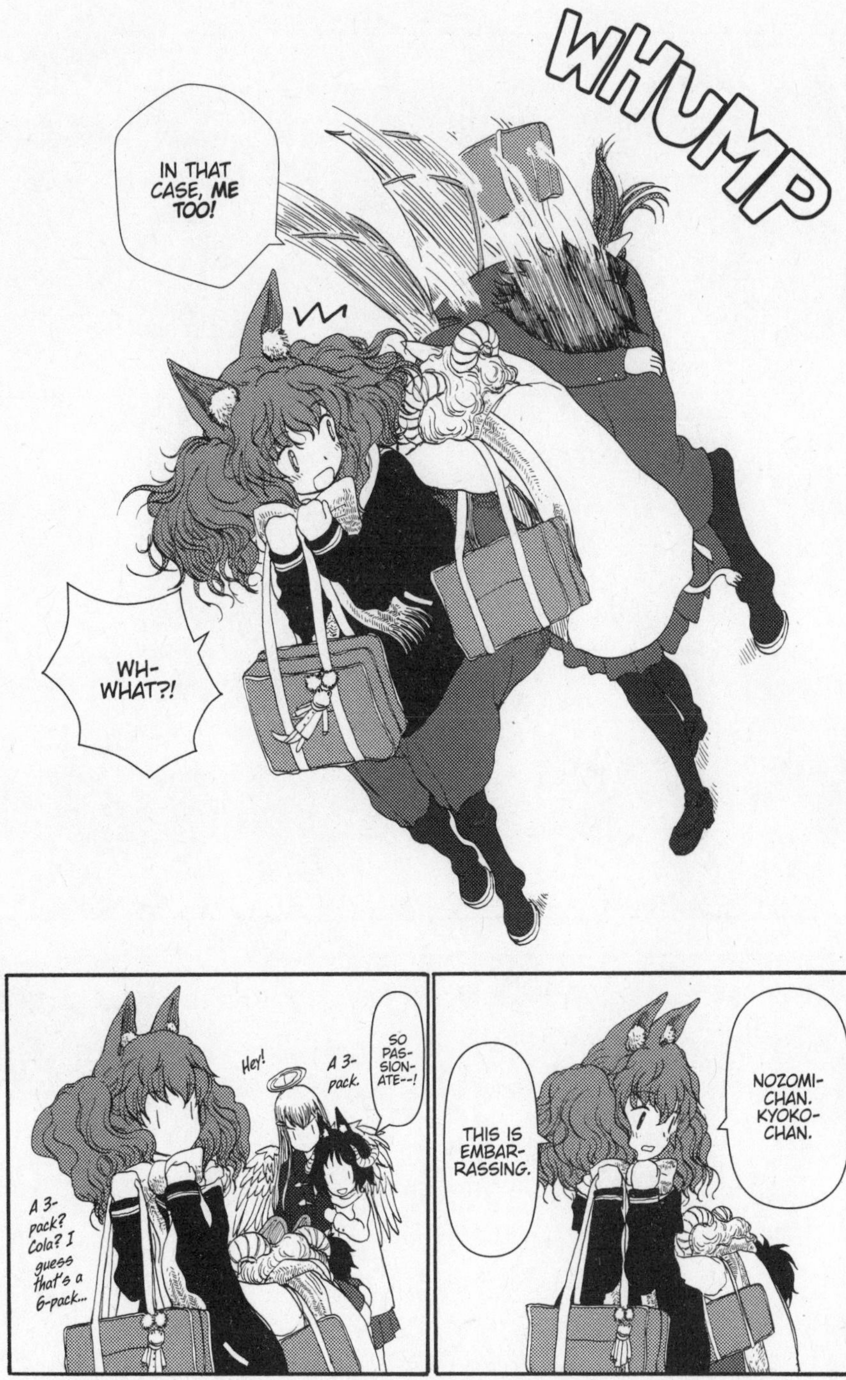
WHUMP
IN THAT CASE, ME TOO!
WH-WHAT?!
NOZOMI-CHAN. KYOKO-CHAN.
THIS IS EMBARRASSING.
SO PASSIONATE--!
A 3-pack.
Hey!
A 3-pack? Cola? I guess that's a 6-pack...

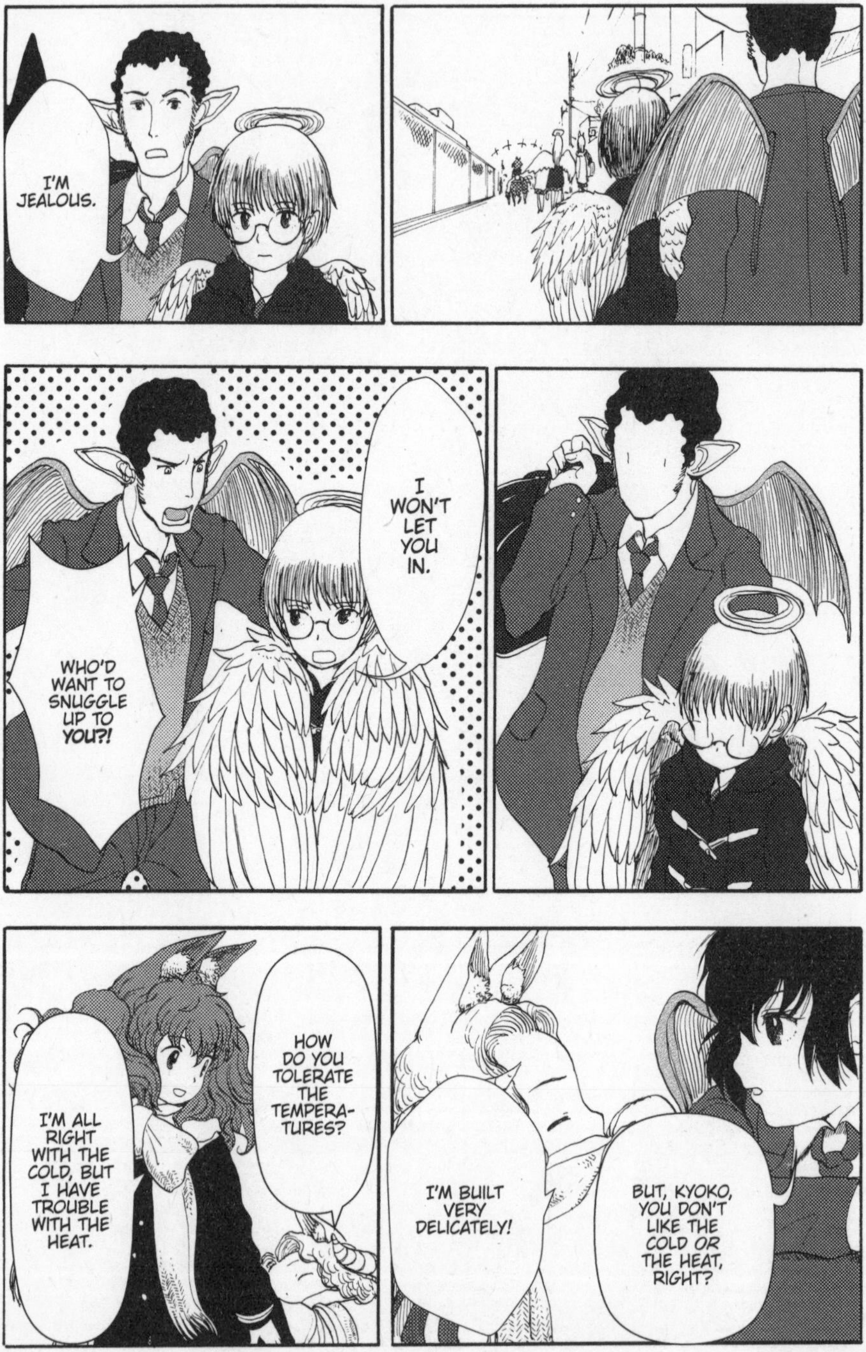
I'M JEALOUS.
I WON'T LET YOU IN.
WHO'D WANT TO SNUGGLE UP TO **YOU**?!
BUT, KYOKO, YOU DON'T LIKE THE COLD OR THE HEAT, RIGHT?
I'M BUILT VERY DELICATELY!
HOW DO YOU TOLERATE THE TEMPERA-TURES?
I'M ALL RIGHT WITH THE COLD, BUT I HAVE TROUBLE WITH THE HEAT.

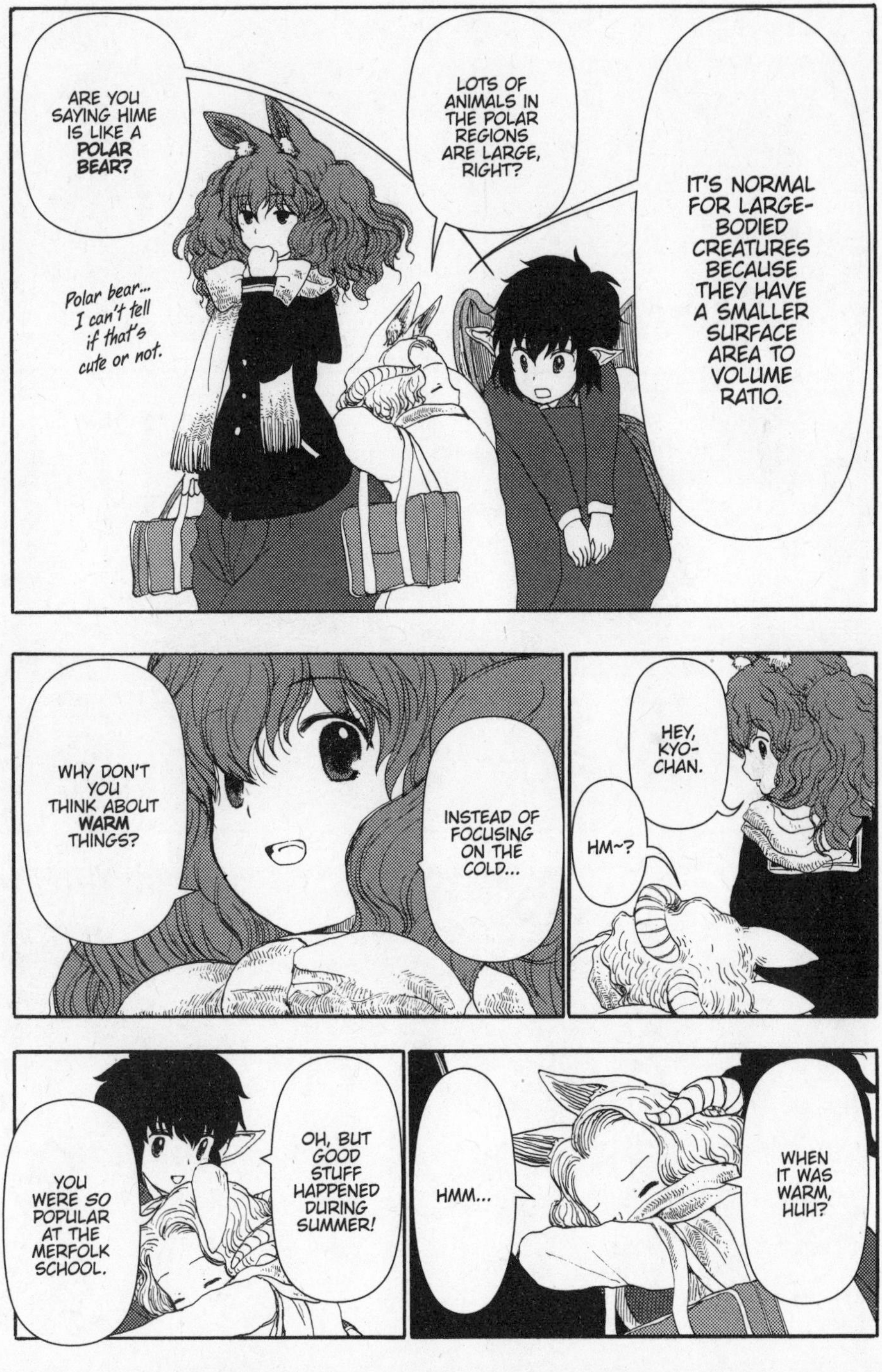
IT'S NORMAL FOR LARGE-BODIED CREATURES BECAUSE THEY HAVE A SMALLER SURFACE AREA TO VOLUME RATIO.
LOTS OF ANIMALS IN THE POLAR REGIONS ARE LARGE, RIGHT?
ARE YOU SAYING HIME IS LIKE A **POLAR BEAR?**
Polar bear... I can't tell if that's cute or not.
HEY, KYO-CHAN.
HM~?
INSTEAD OF FOCUSING ON THE COLD...
WHY DON'T YOU THINK ABOUT **WARM** THINGS?
WHEN IT WAS WARM, HUH?
HMM...
OH, BUT GOOD STUFF HAPPENED DURING SUMMER!
YOU WERE SO POPULAR AT THE MERFOLK SCHOOL.

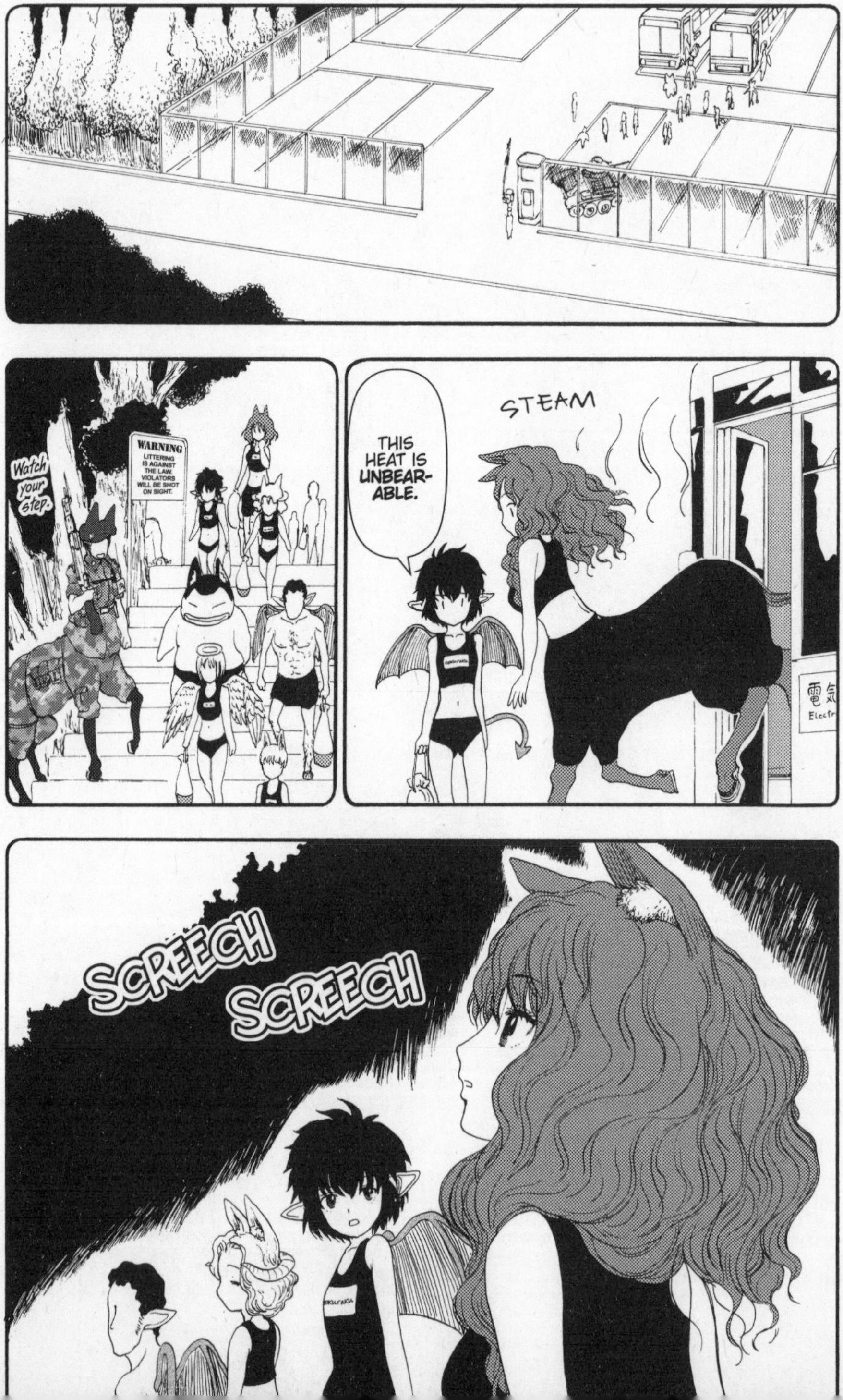
STEAM
THIS HEAT IS UNBEARABLE.
WARNING LITTERING IS AGAINST THE LAW. VIOLATORS WILL BE SHOT ON SIGHT.
Watch your step.
SCREECH SCREECH

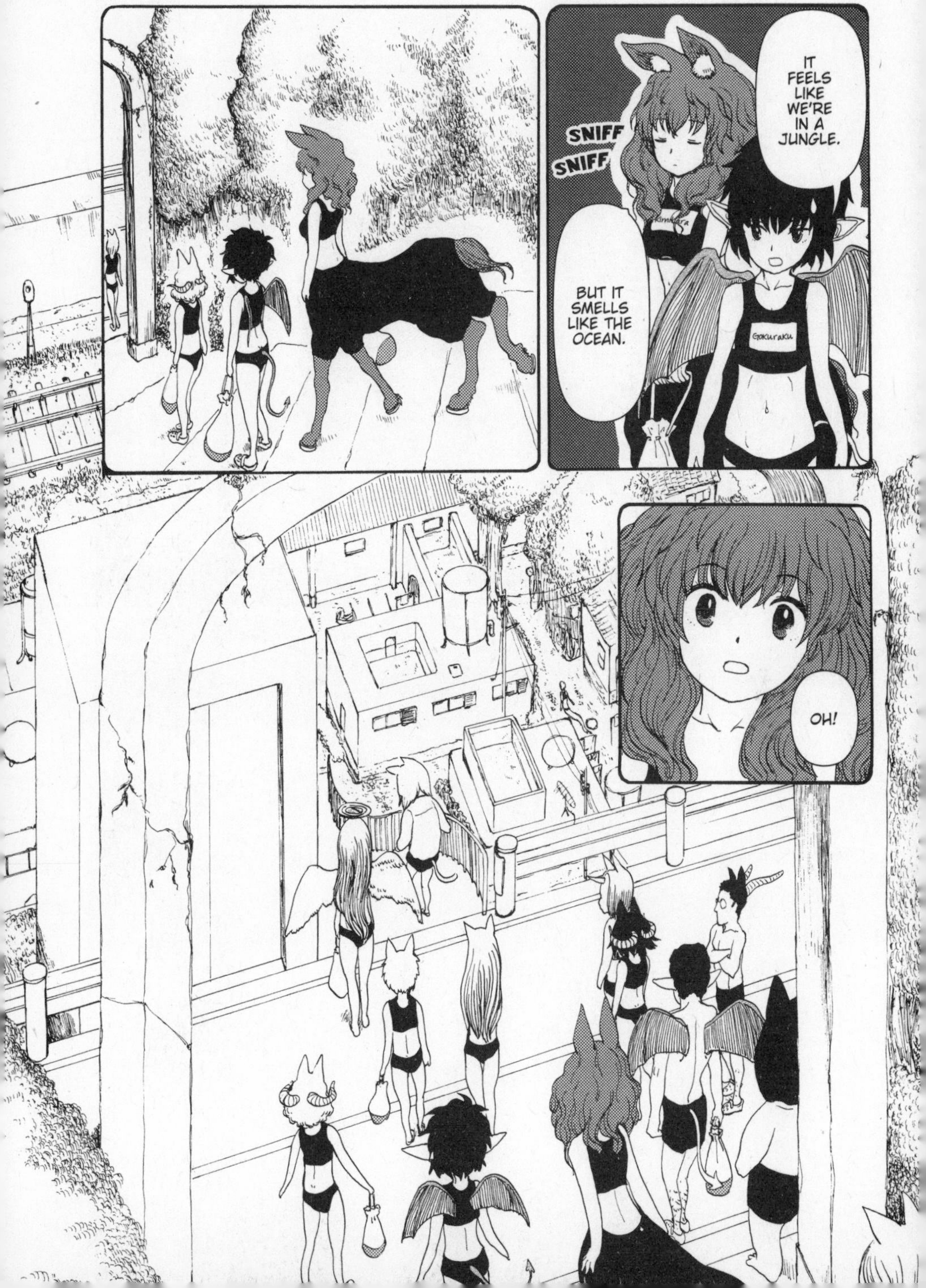
IT FEELS LIKE WE'RE IN A JUNGLE.
SNIFF SNIFF
Gokuraku
BUT IT SMELLS LIKE THE OCEAN.
OH!

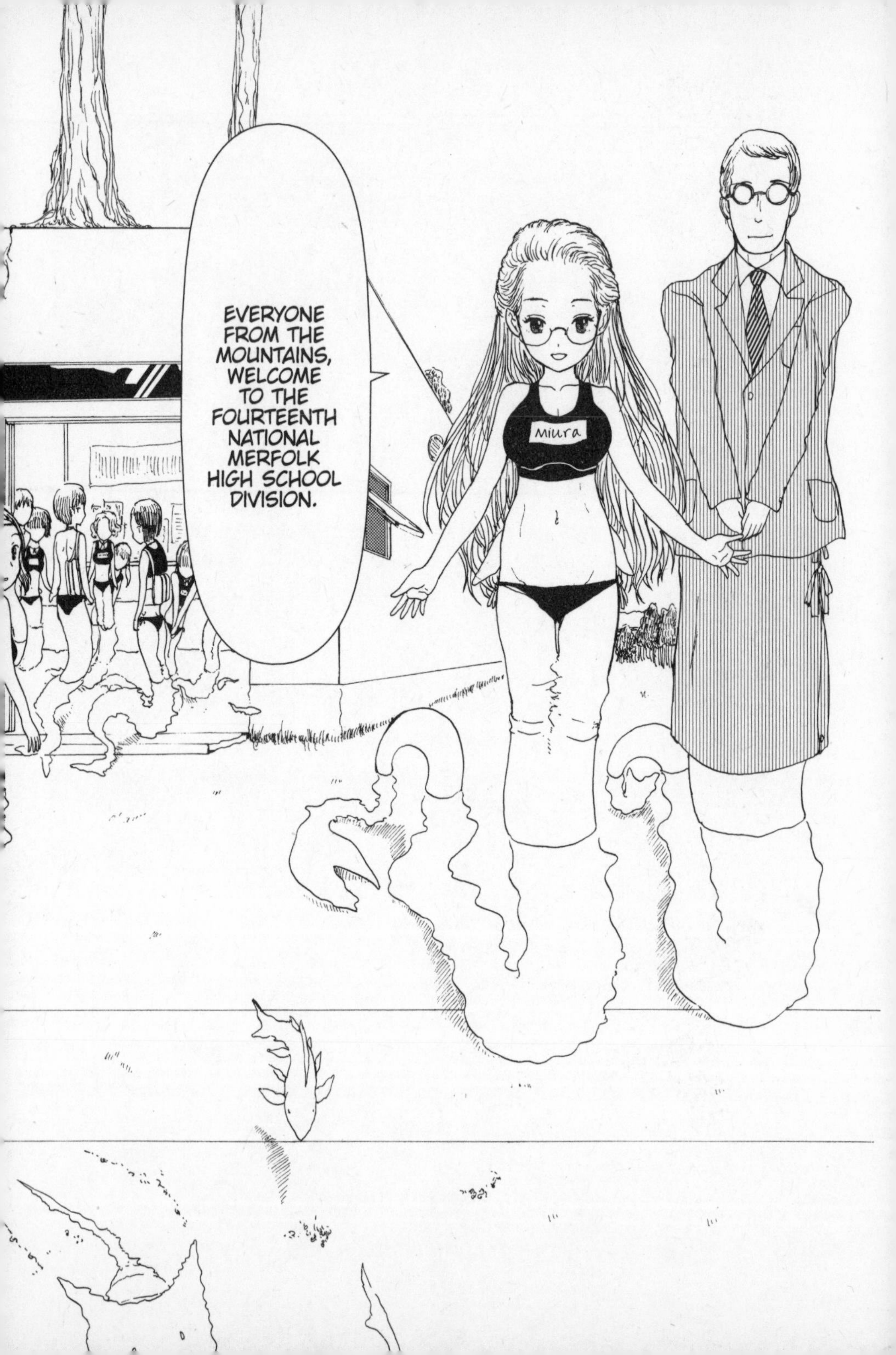
EVERYONE FROM THE MOUNTAINS, WELCOME TO THE FOURTEENTH NATIONAL MERFOLK HIGH SCHOOL DIVISION.
Miura

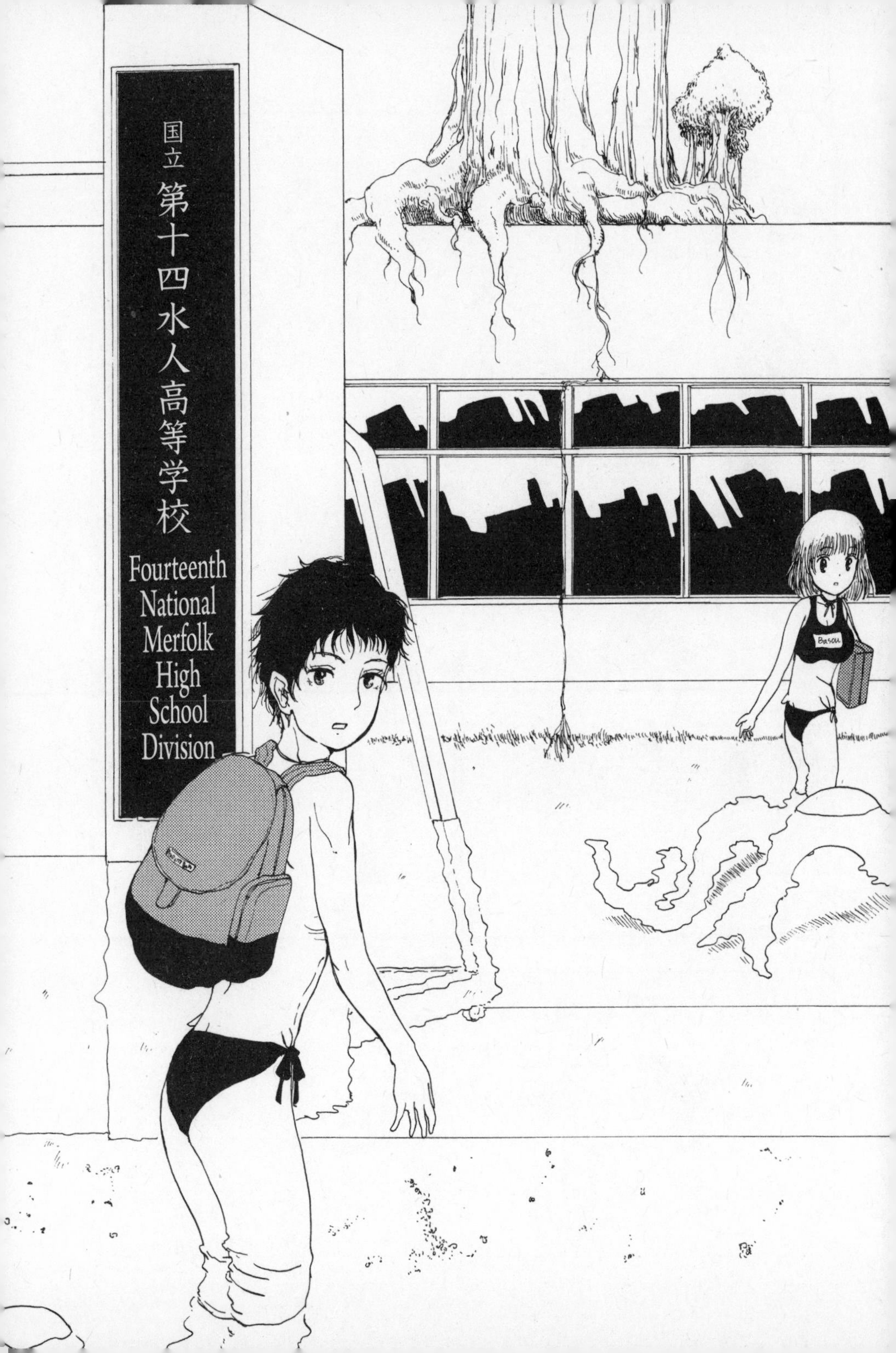
国立
第十四水人高等学校
Fourteenth National Merfolk High School Division
Basou

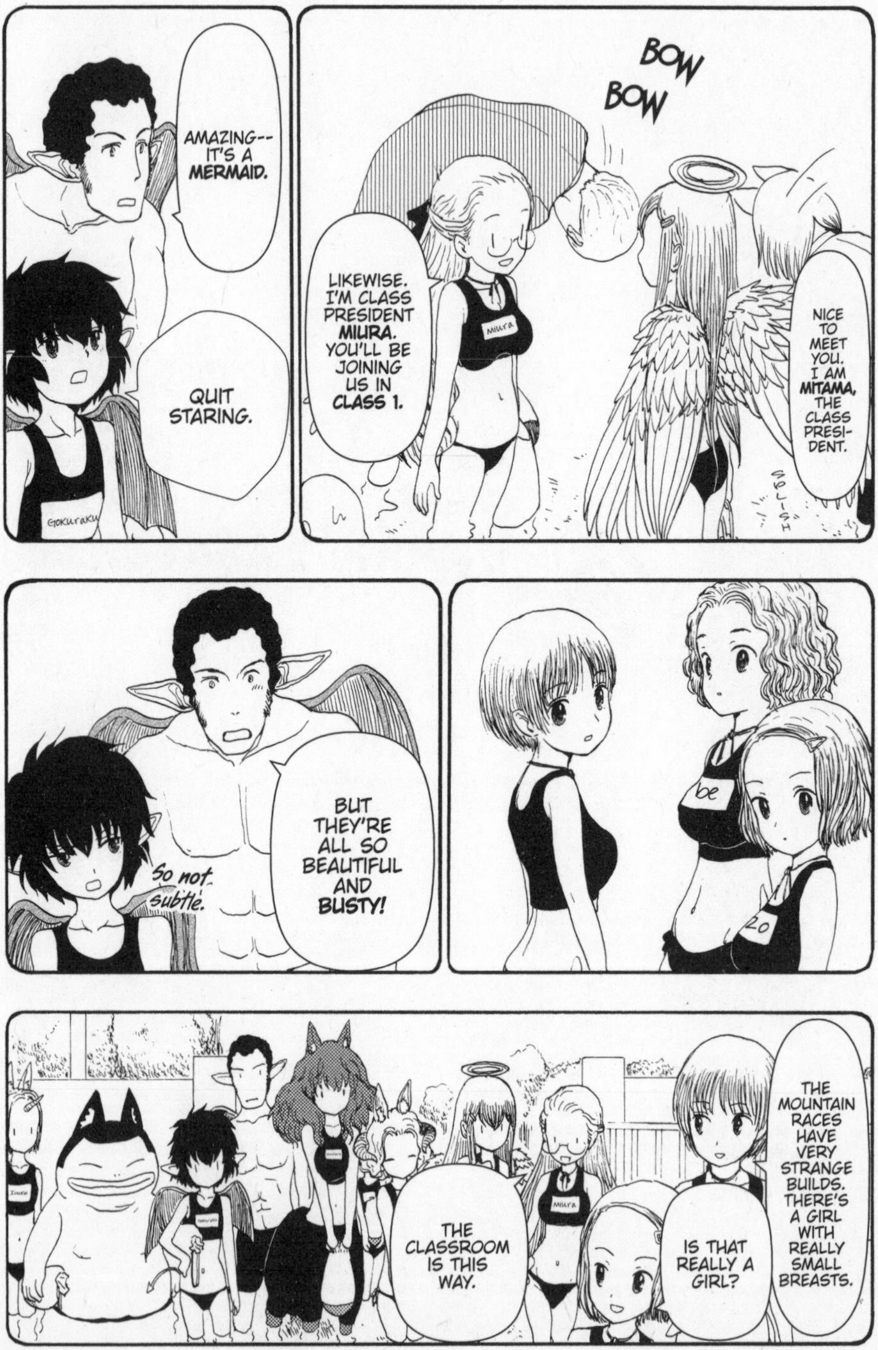
BOW BOW
NICE TO MEET YOU. I AM MITAMA, THE CLASS PRESIDENT.
SPLISH
LIKEWISE. I'M CLASS PRESIDENT MIURA. YOU'LL BE JOINING US IN CLASS 1.
AMAZING-- IT'S A MERMAID.
QUIT STARING.
BUT THEY'RE ALL SO BEAUTIFUL AND BUSTY!
So not subtle.
THE MOUNTAIN RACES HAVE VERY STRANGE BUILDS. THERE'S A GIRL WITH REALLY SMALL BREASTS.
IS THAT REALLY A GIRL?
THE CLASSROOM IS THIS WAY.

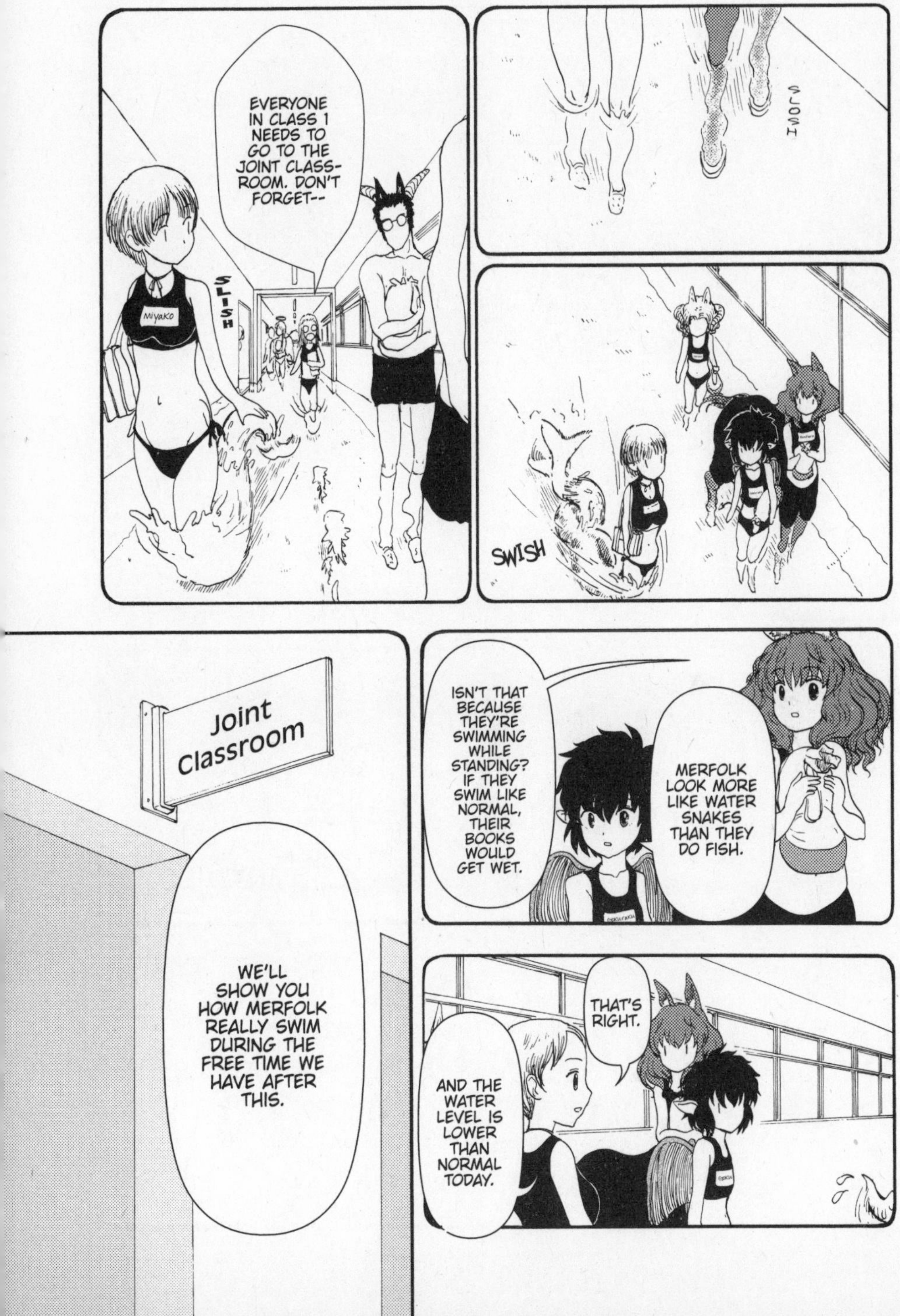
SLOSH
SWISH
EVERYONE IN CLASS 1 NEEDS TO GO TO THE JOINT CLASS-ROOM. DON'T FORGET--
SLISH
MIYAKO
MERFOLK LOOK MORE LIKE WATER SNAKES THAN THEY DO FISH.
ISN'T THAT BECAUSE THEY'RE SWIMMING WHILE STANDING? IF THEY SWIM LIKE NORMAL, THEIR BOOKS WOULD GET WET.
THAT'S RIGHT.
AND THE WATER LEVEL IS LOWER THAN NORMAL TODAY.
Joint Classroom
WE'LL SHOW YOU HOW MERFOLK REALLY SWIM DURING THE FREE TIME WE HAVE AFTER THIS.

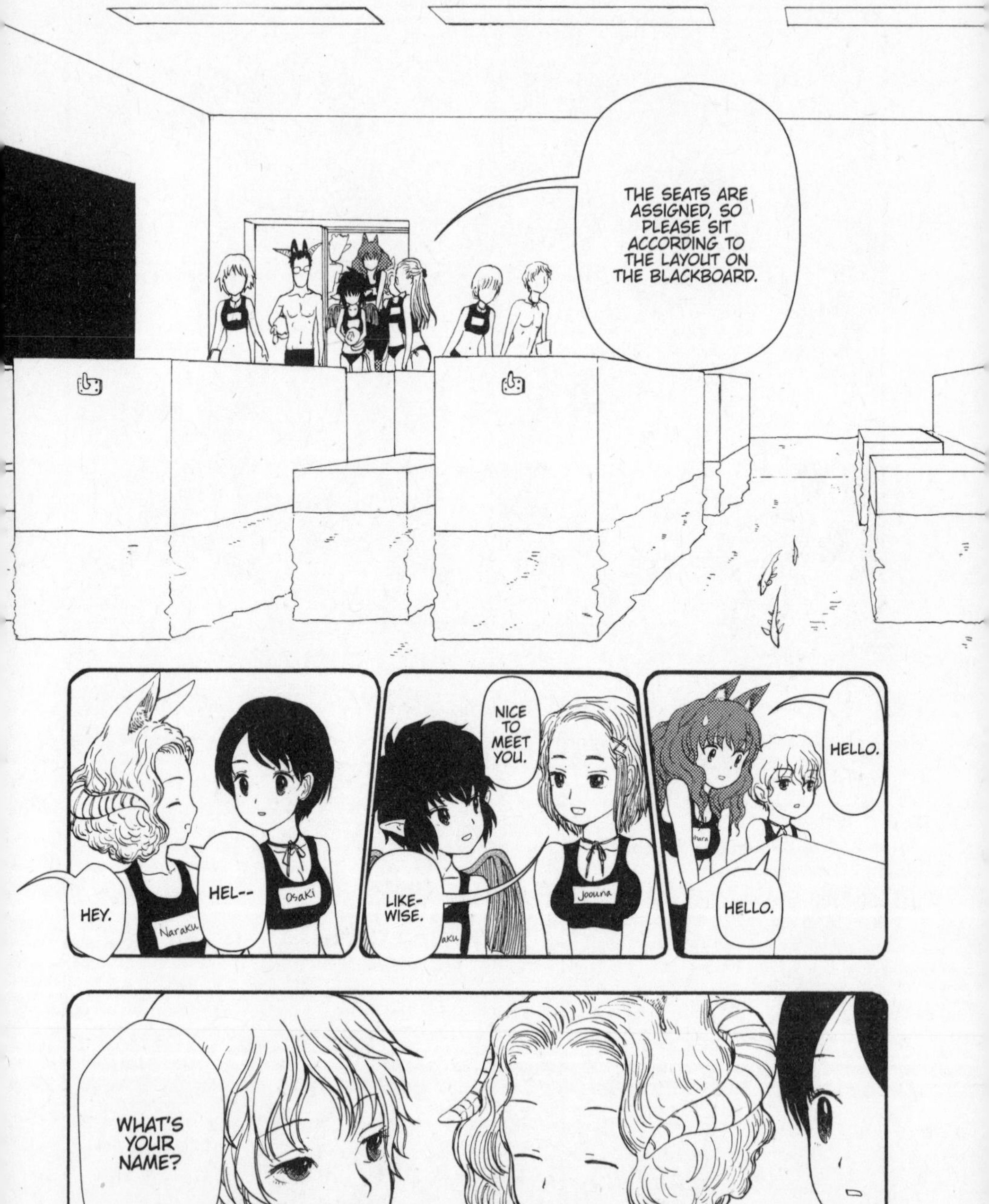
THE SEATS ARE ASSIGNED, SO PLEASE SIT ACCORDING TO THE LAYOUT ON THE BLACKBOARD.
HELLO.
HELLO.
Joouna
NICE TO MEET YOU.
LIKE-WISE.
Osaki
HEL--
Naraku
HEY.
WHAT'S YOUR NAME?

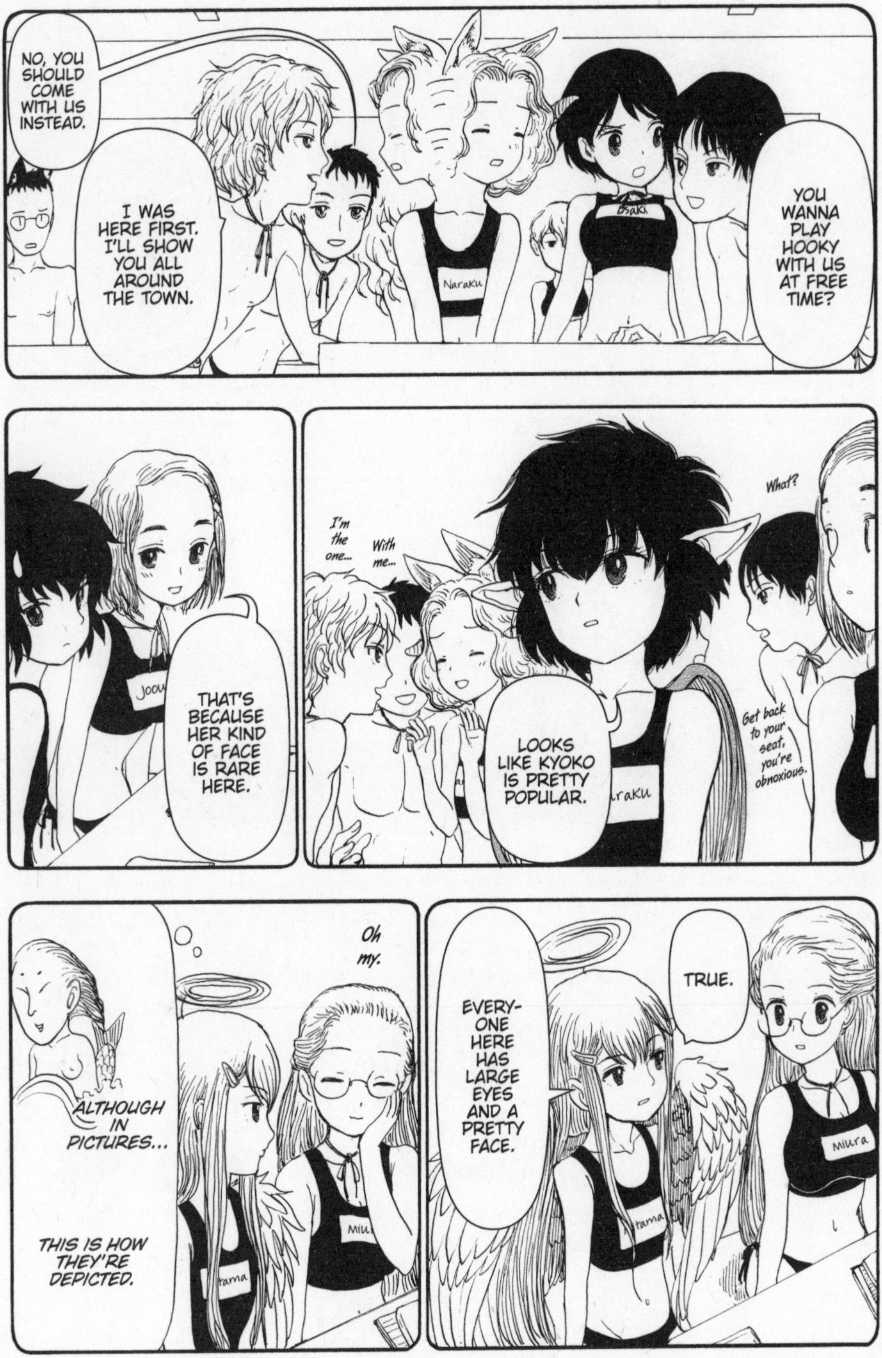
YOU WANNA PLAY HOOKY WITH US AT FREE TIME?
NO, YOU SHOULD COME WITH US INSTEAD.
I WAS HERE FIRST. I'LL SHOW YOU ALL AROUND THE TOWN.
What?
I'm the one...
With me...
Get back to your seat, you're obnoxious.
LOOKS LIKE KYOKO IS PRETTY POPULAR.
THAT'S BECAUSE HER KIND OF FACE IS RARE HERE.
TRUE.
EVERY-ONE HERE HAS LARGE EYES AND A PRETTY FACE.
Oh my.
ALTHOUGH IN PICTURES...
THIS IS HOW THEY'RE DEPICTED.

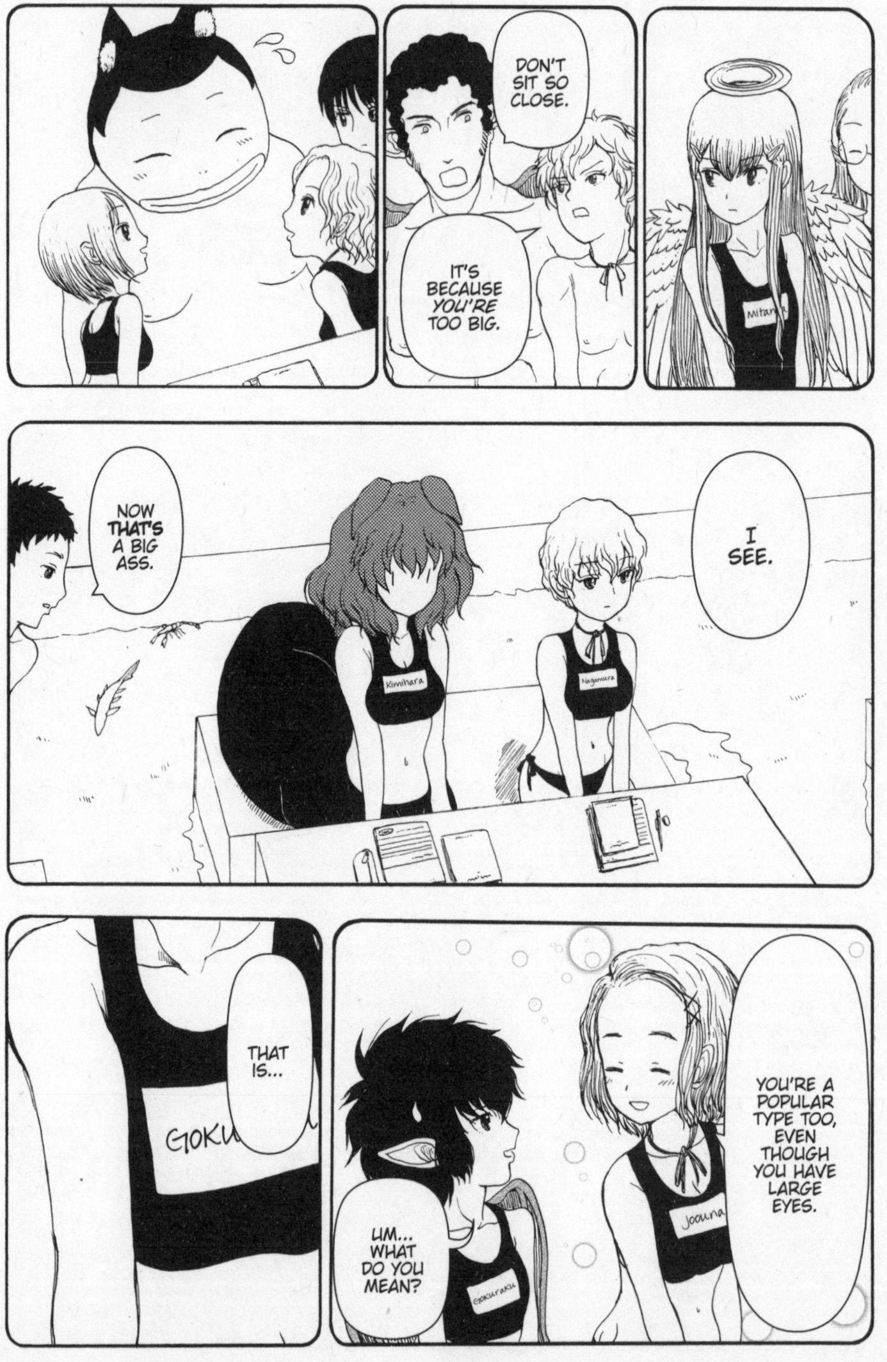
DON'T SIT SO CLOSE.
IT'S BECAUSE YOU'RE TOO BIG.
I SEE.
NOW THAT'S A BIG ASS.
YOU'RE A POPULAR TYPE TOO, EVEN THOUGH YOU HAVE LARGE EYES.
UM... WHAT DO YOU MEAN?
THAT IS...

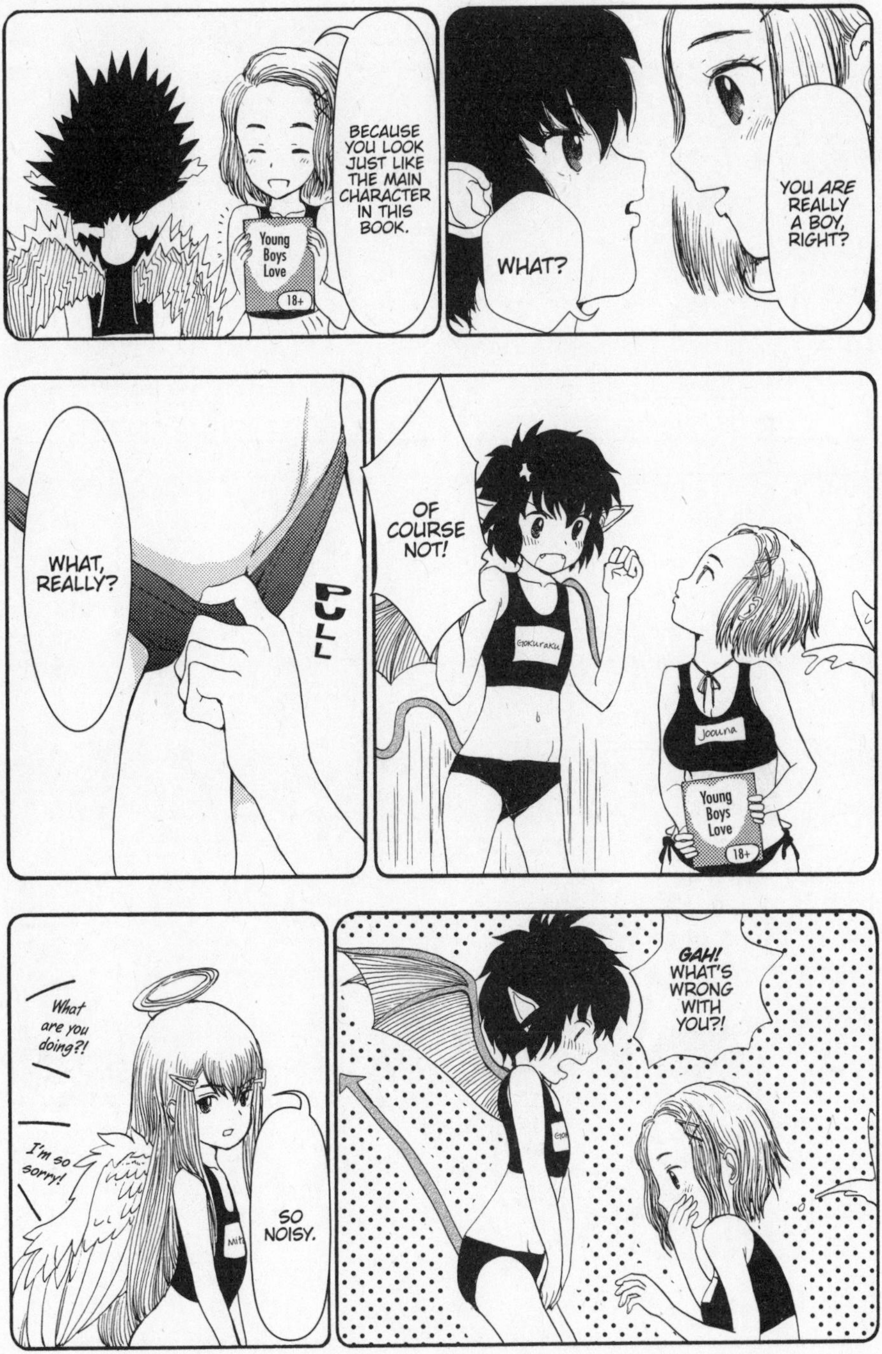
YOU ARE REALLY A BOY, RIGHT?
WHAT?
BECAUSE YOU LOOK JUST LIKE THE MAIN CHARACTER IN THIS BOOK.
Young Boys Love
18+
OF COURSE NOT!
Gokuraku
Joouna
Young Boys Love
18+
PULL
WHAT, REALLY?
GAH! WHAT'S WRONG WITH YOU?!
What are you doing?!
I'm so sorry!
SO NOISY.

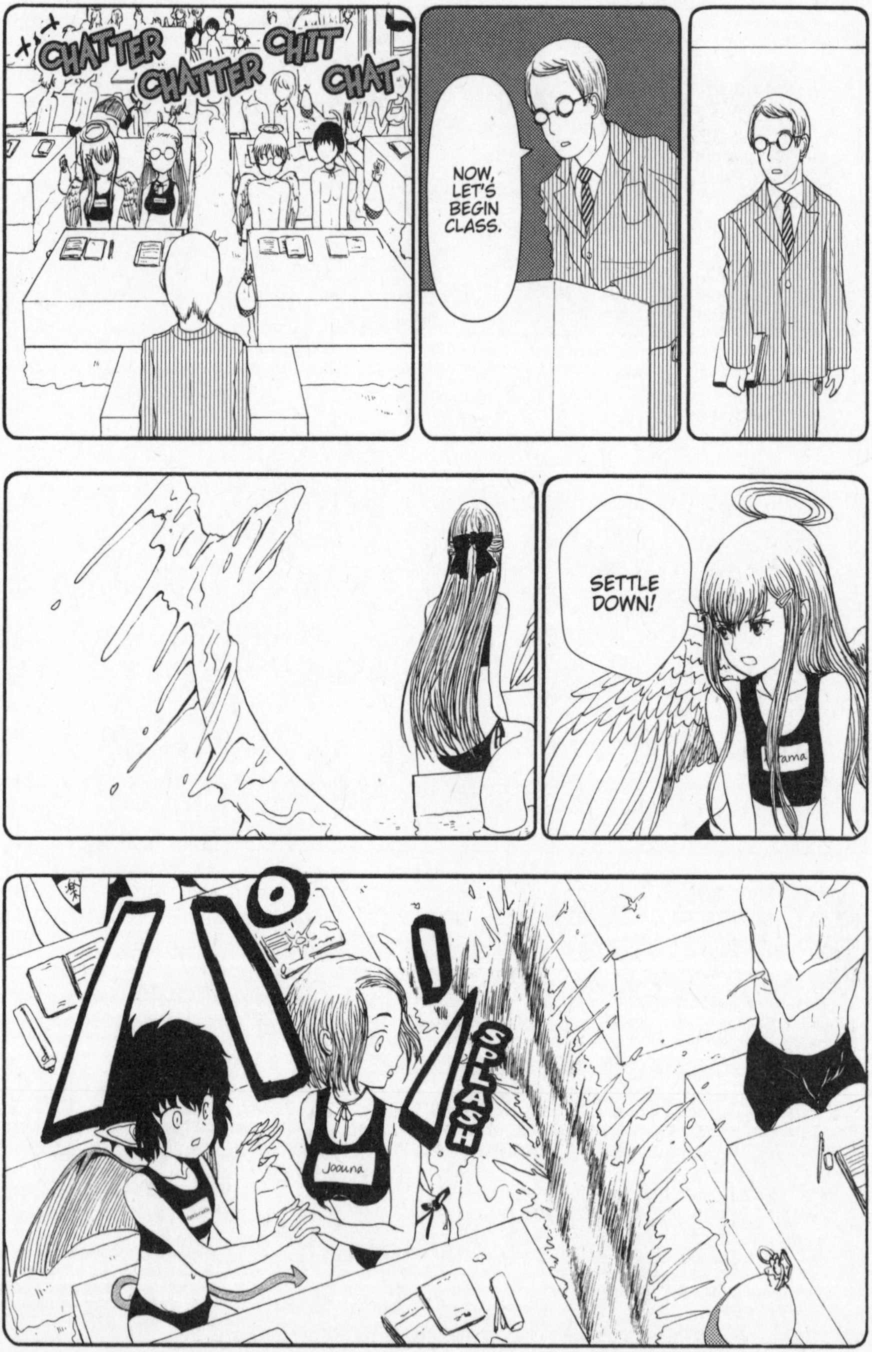
NOW, LET'S BEGIN CLASS.
CHATTER CHATTER CHIT CHAT
SETTLE DOWN!
SPLASH

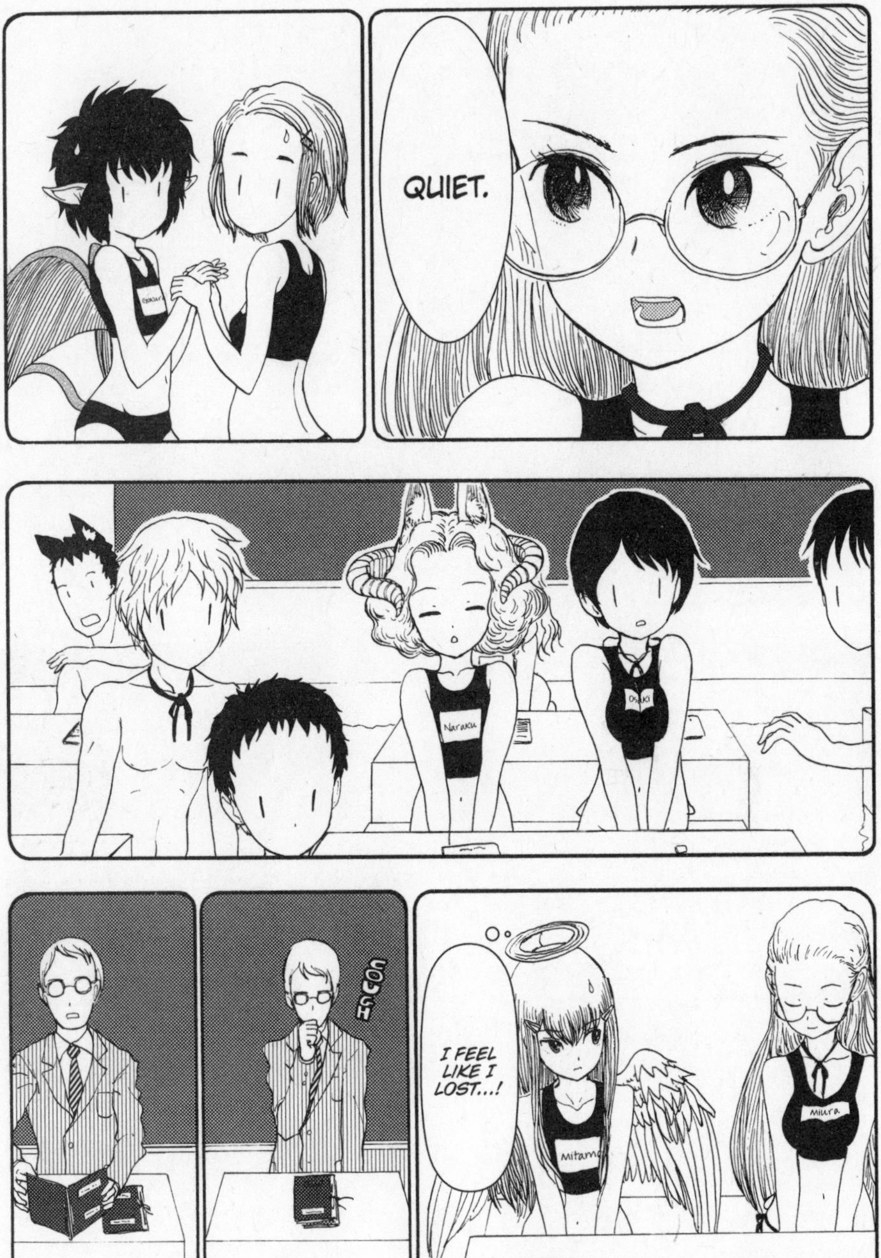
QUIET.
Osaki
Naraku
I FEEL LIKE I LOST...!
Miura
Mitama
COUGH

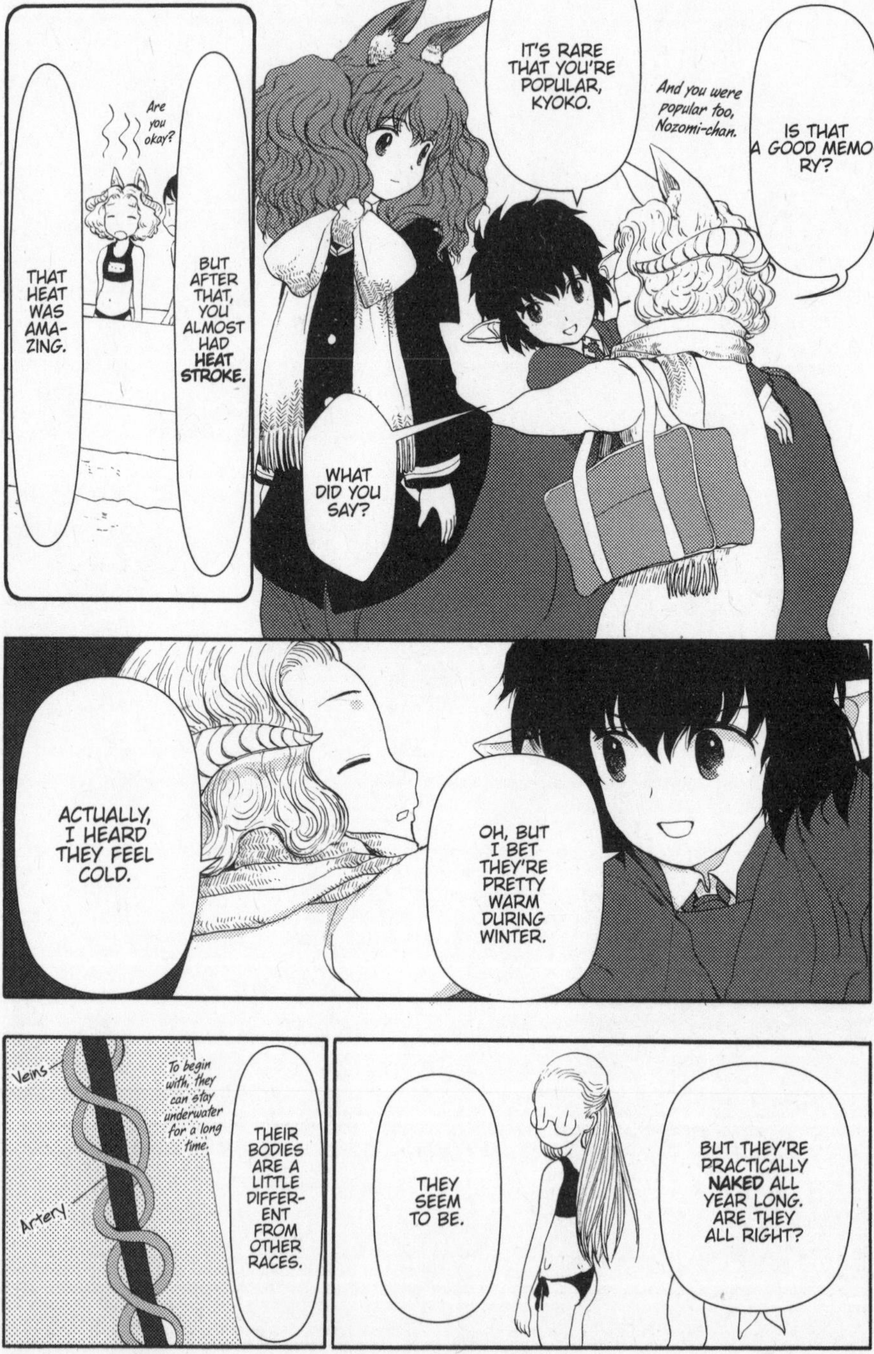
IS THAT A GOOD MEMORY?
And you were popular too, Nozomi-chan.
IT'S RARE THAT YOU'RE POPULAR, KYOKO.
WHAT DID YOU SAY?
BUT AFTER THAT, YOU ALMOST HAD **HEAT STROKE.**
Are you okay?
THAT HEAT WAS AMAZING.
OH, BUT I BET THEY'RE PRETTY WARM DURING WINTER.
ACTUALLY, I HEARD THEY FEEL COLD.
BUT THEY'RE PRACTICALLY **NAKED** ALL YEAR LONG. ARE THEY ALL RIGHT?
THEY SEEM TO BE.
THEIR BODIES ARE A LITTLE DIFFERENT FROM OTHER RACES.
To begin with, they can stay underwater for a long time.
Veins
Artery

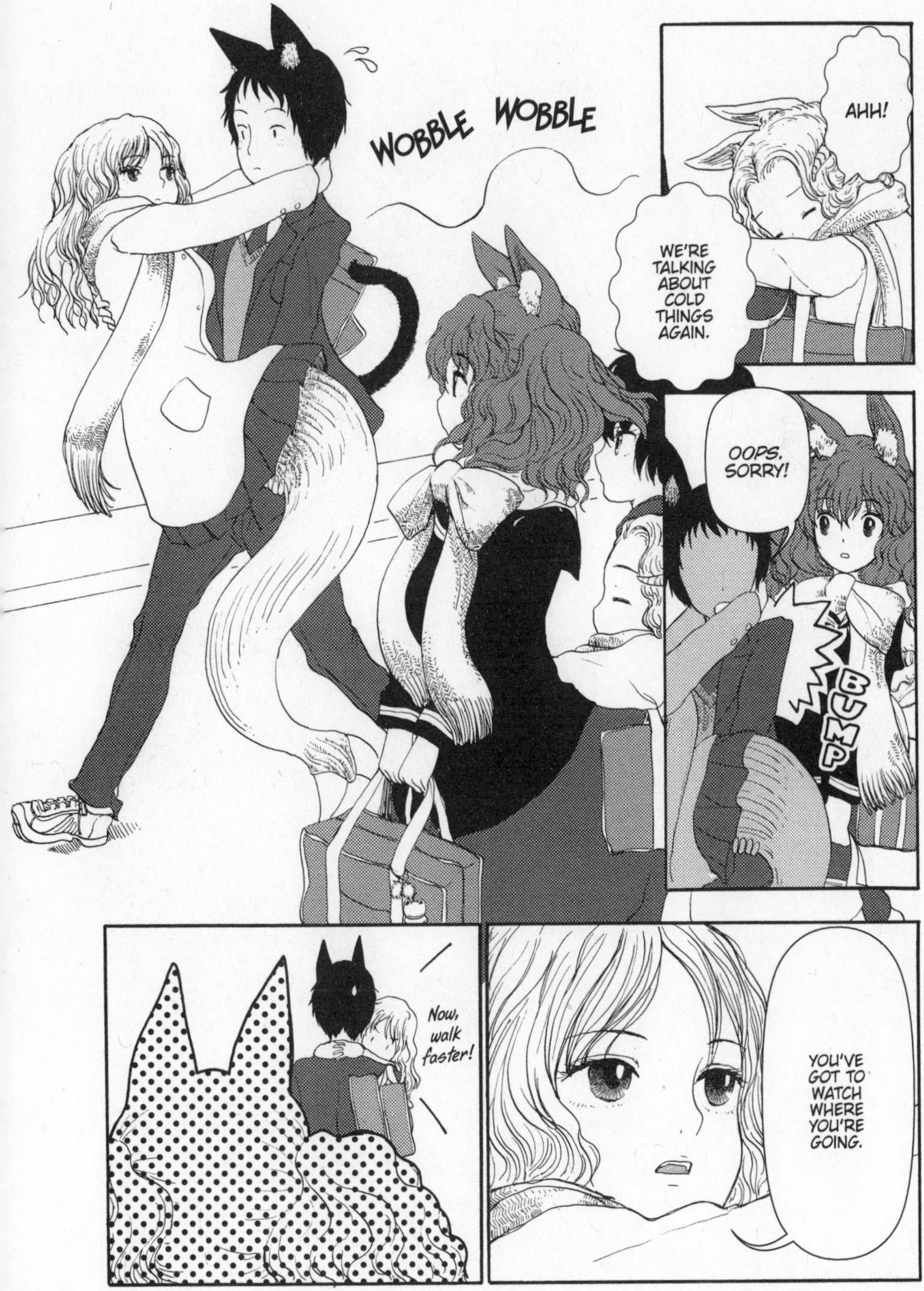
AHH!
WE'RE TALKING ABOUT COLD THINGS AGAIN.
OOPS, SORRY!
BUMP
WOBBLE WOBBLE
YOU'VE GOT TO WATCH WHERE YOU'RE GOING.
Now, walk faster!

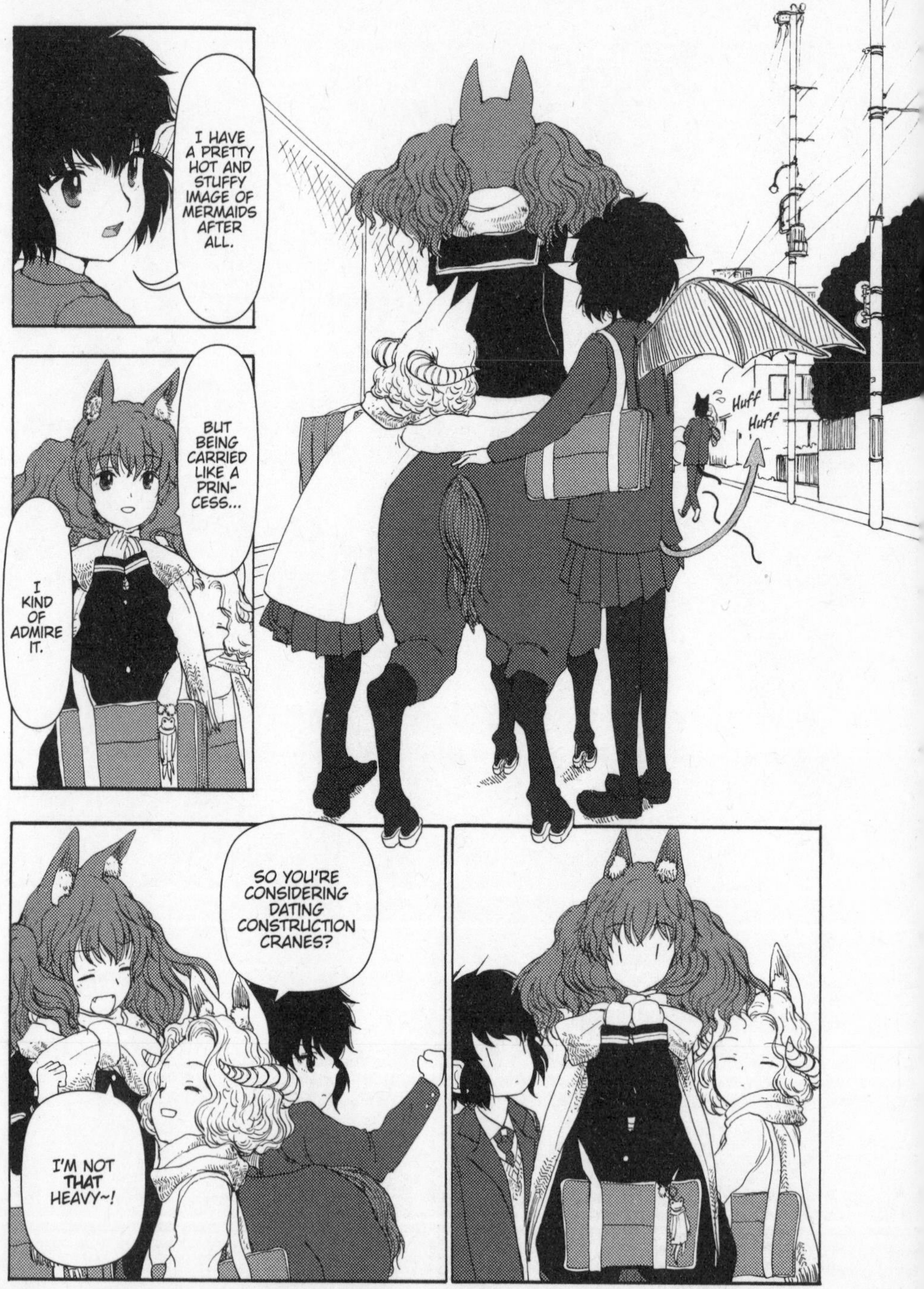
Huff
Huff
I HAVE A PRETTY HOT AND STUFFY IMAGE OF MERMAIDS AFTER ALL.
BUT BEING CARRIED LIKE A PRINCESS...
I KIND OF ADMIRE IT.
SO YOU'RE CONSIDERING DATING CONSTRUCTION CRANES?
I'M NOT THAT HEAVY~!

A Centaur's Life

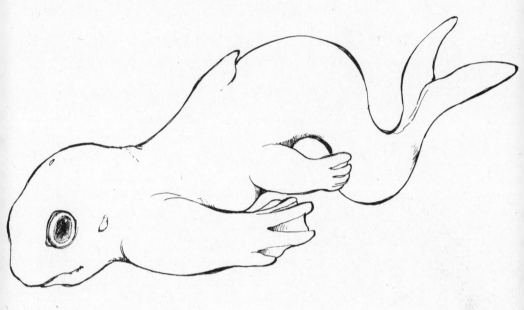

KETAPITEX

ORDER *PRIMATES*, FAMILY *HOMINIDAE*, GENUS *KETAPITEX*. EXTINCT.
ONE OF THE RACES OF HUMANITY THAT RETURNED TO THE SEA.

MUCH LIKE THE MERFOLK, KETAPITEX COULD LIVE THEIR ENTIRE LIVES
UNDERWATER. ALTHOUGH OTHERWISE SIMILAR TO TOOTHED WHALES
(ORDER *CETACEA*, SUBORDER *ODONTOCETI*), THEY COULD NOT USE
ECHOLOCATION TO SURVEY THEIR SURROUNDINGS AND HAD TO RELY ON
SIGHT. IT IS BELIEVED THAT THIS DISADVANTAGE LED TO THEIR EXTINCTION.

THE MERFOLK RACE, ON THE OTHER HAND, RETAINED THE HOMINID UPPER
BODY AND WERE ABLE TO FILL A NICHE WITH NO COMPETITION FROM OTHER
SEA CREATURES, ALLOWING THEM TO SURVIVE TO THE PRESENT DAY.

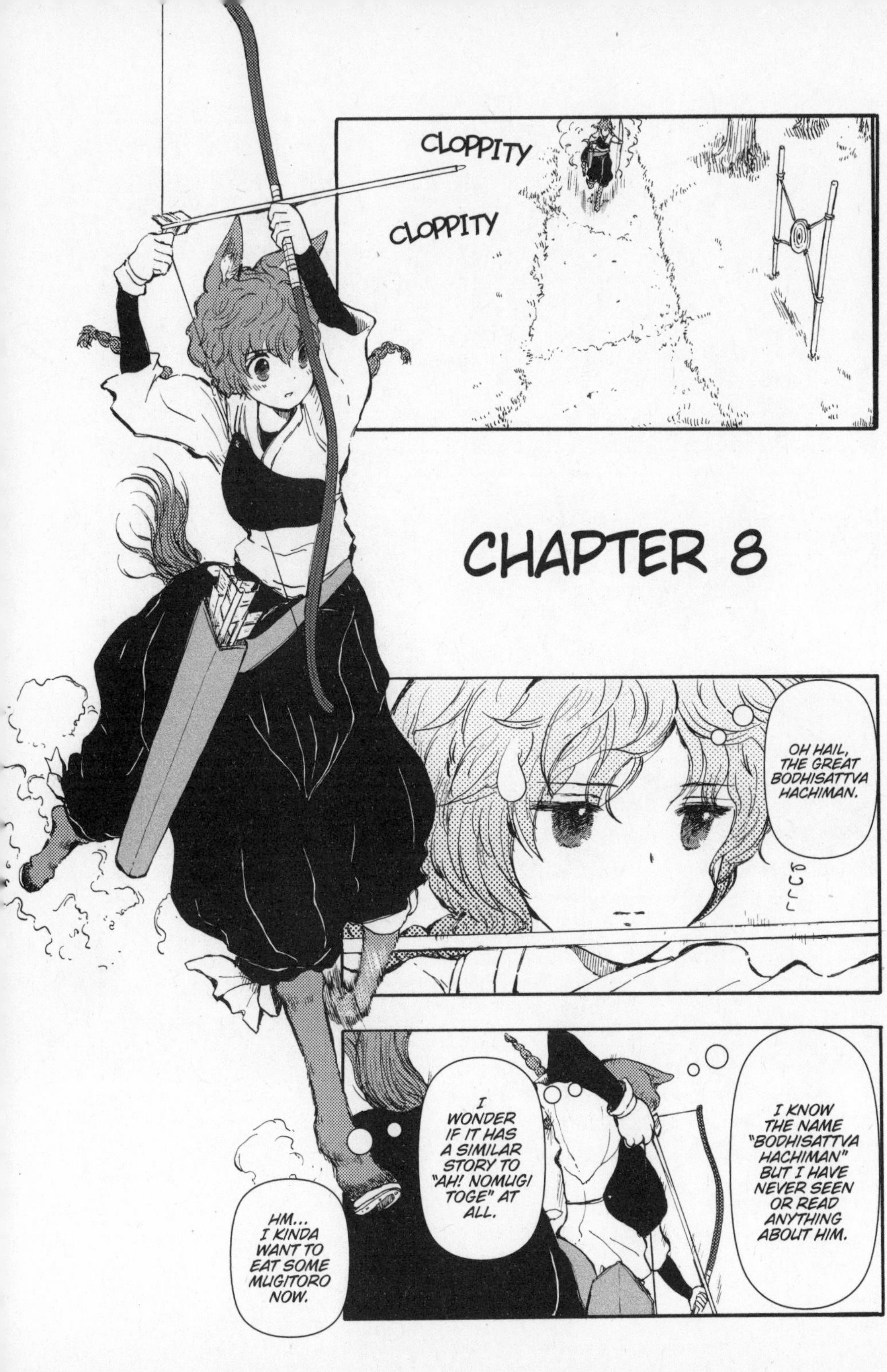
CLOPPITY
CLOPPITY
CHAPTER 8
OH HAIL, THE GREAT BODHISATTVA HACHIMAN.
I KNOW THE NAME "BODHISATTVA HACHIMAN" BUT I HAVE NEVER SEEN OR READ ANYTHING ABOUT HIM.
I WONDER IF IT HAS A SIMILAR STORY TO "AH! NOMUGI TOGE" AT ALL.
HM... I KINDA WANT TO EAT SOME MUGITORO NOW.

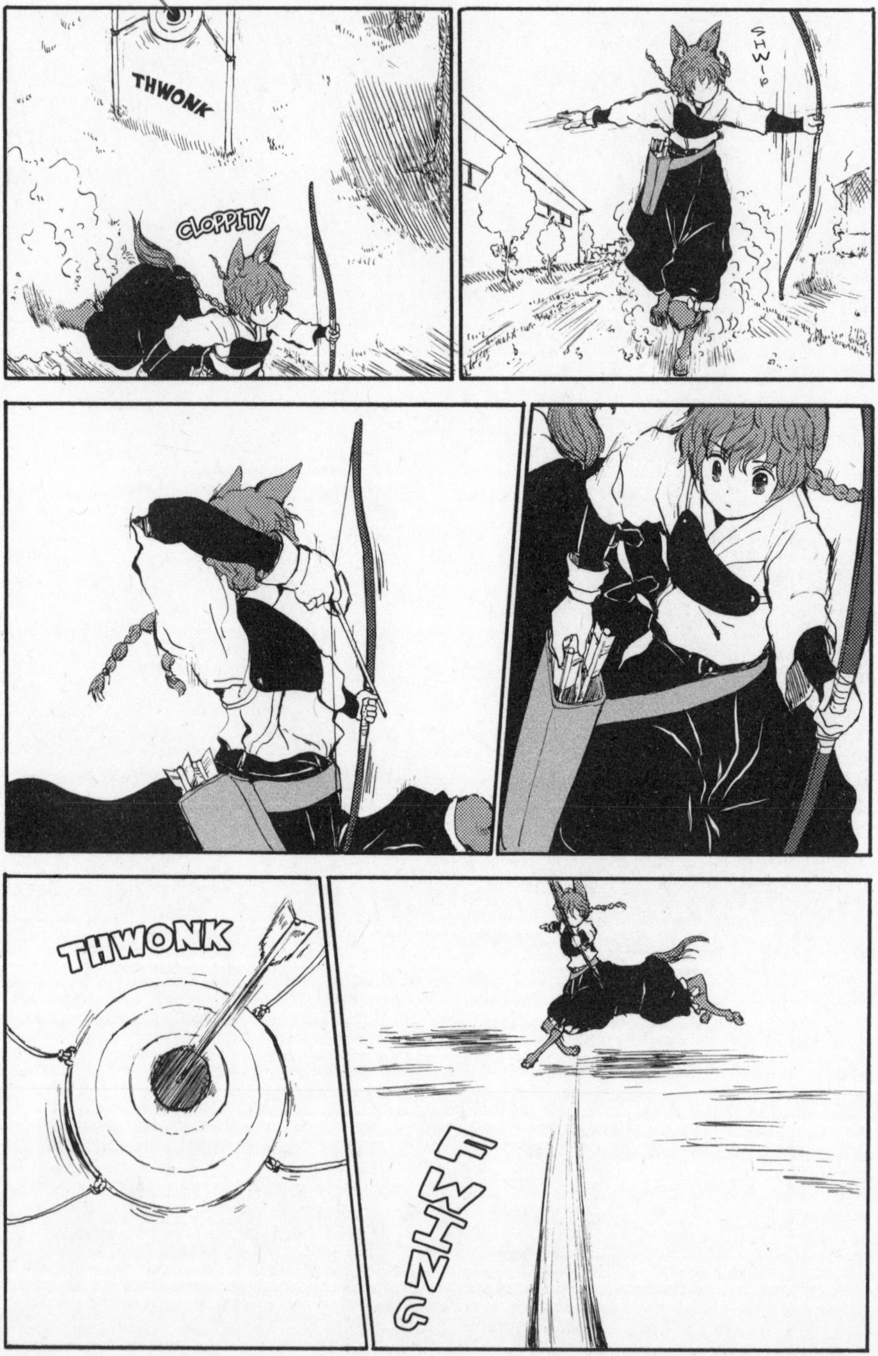
SHWIP
THWONK
CLOPPITY
FWING
THWONK

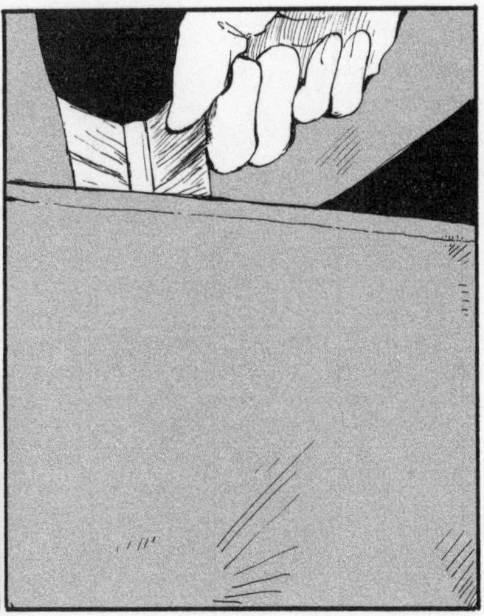

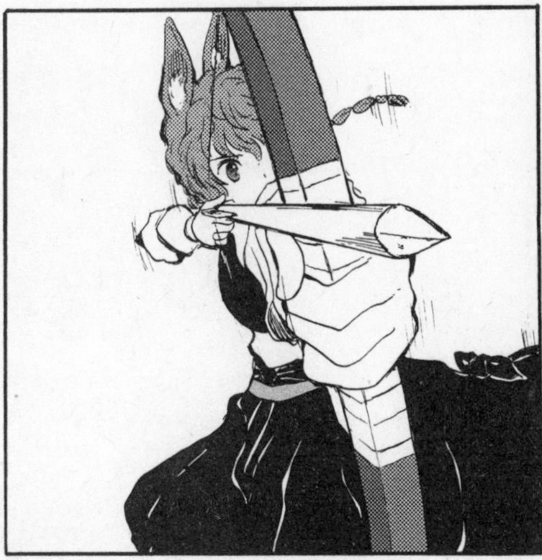

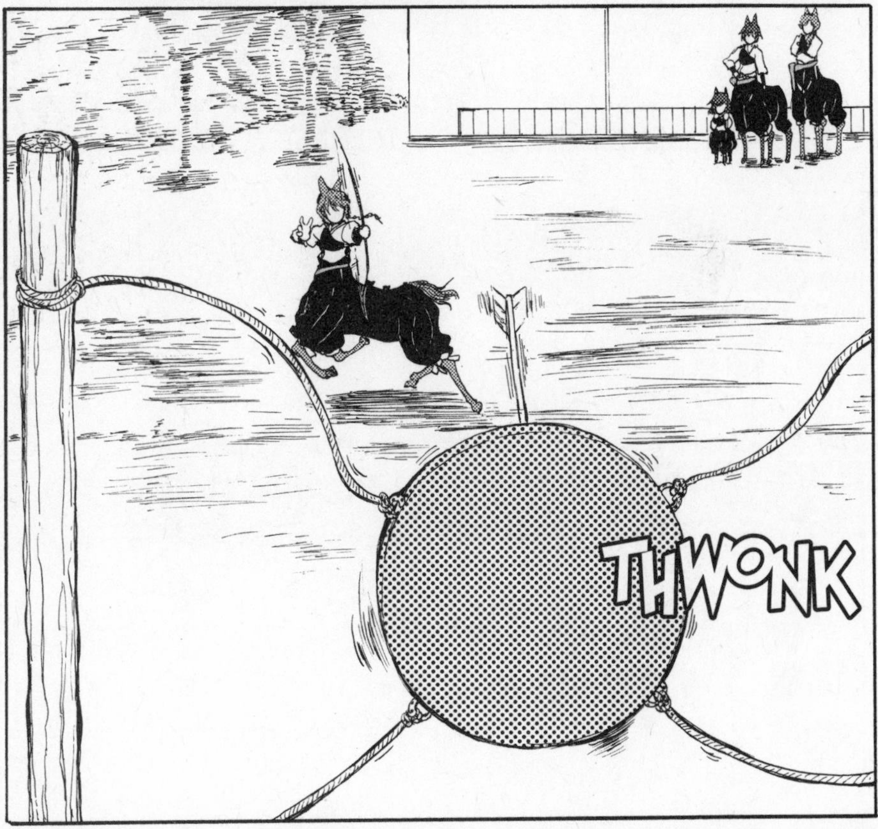
THWONK

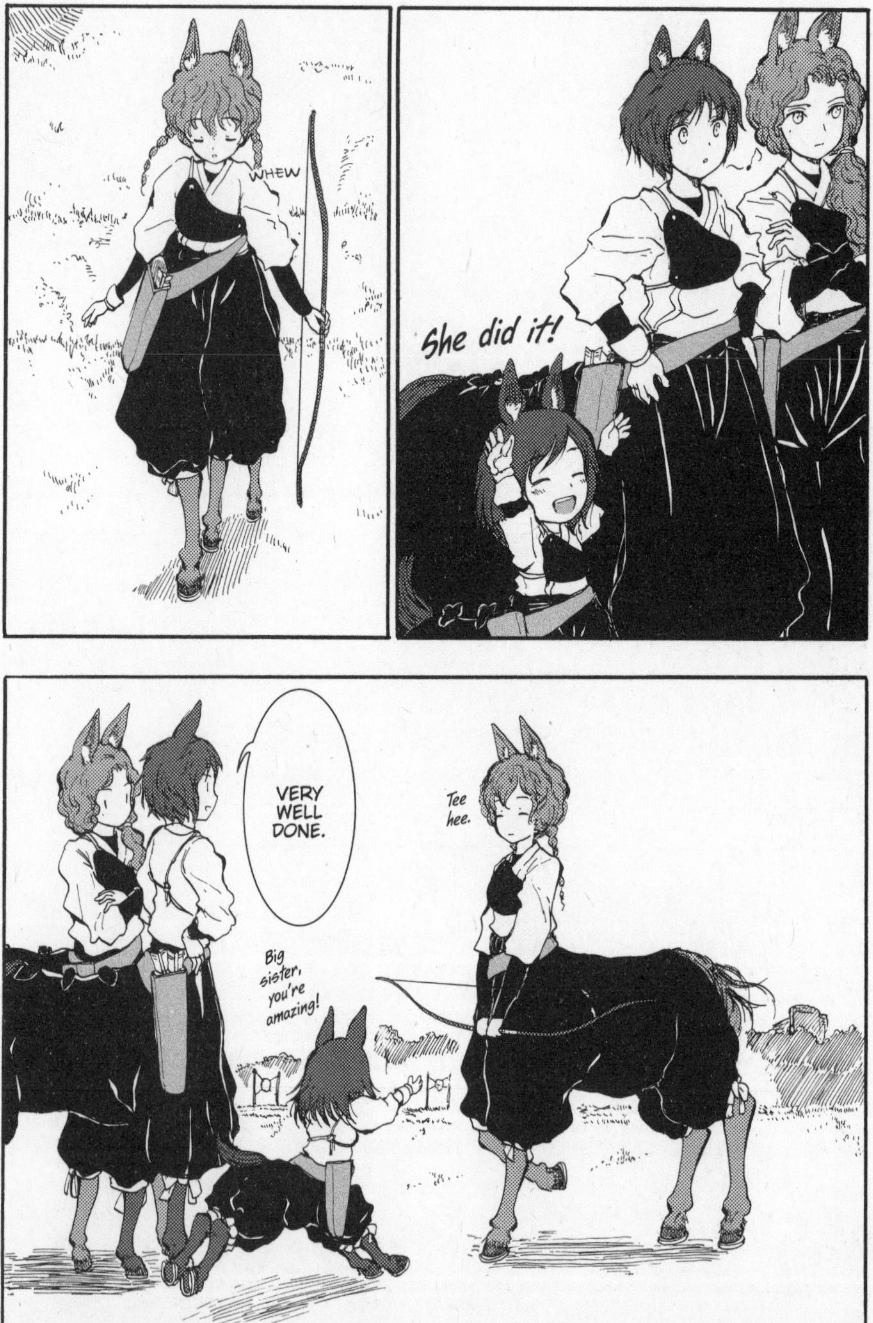
She did it!
WHEW
Tee hee.
VERY WELL DONE.
Big sister, you're amazing!

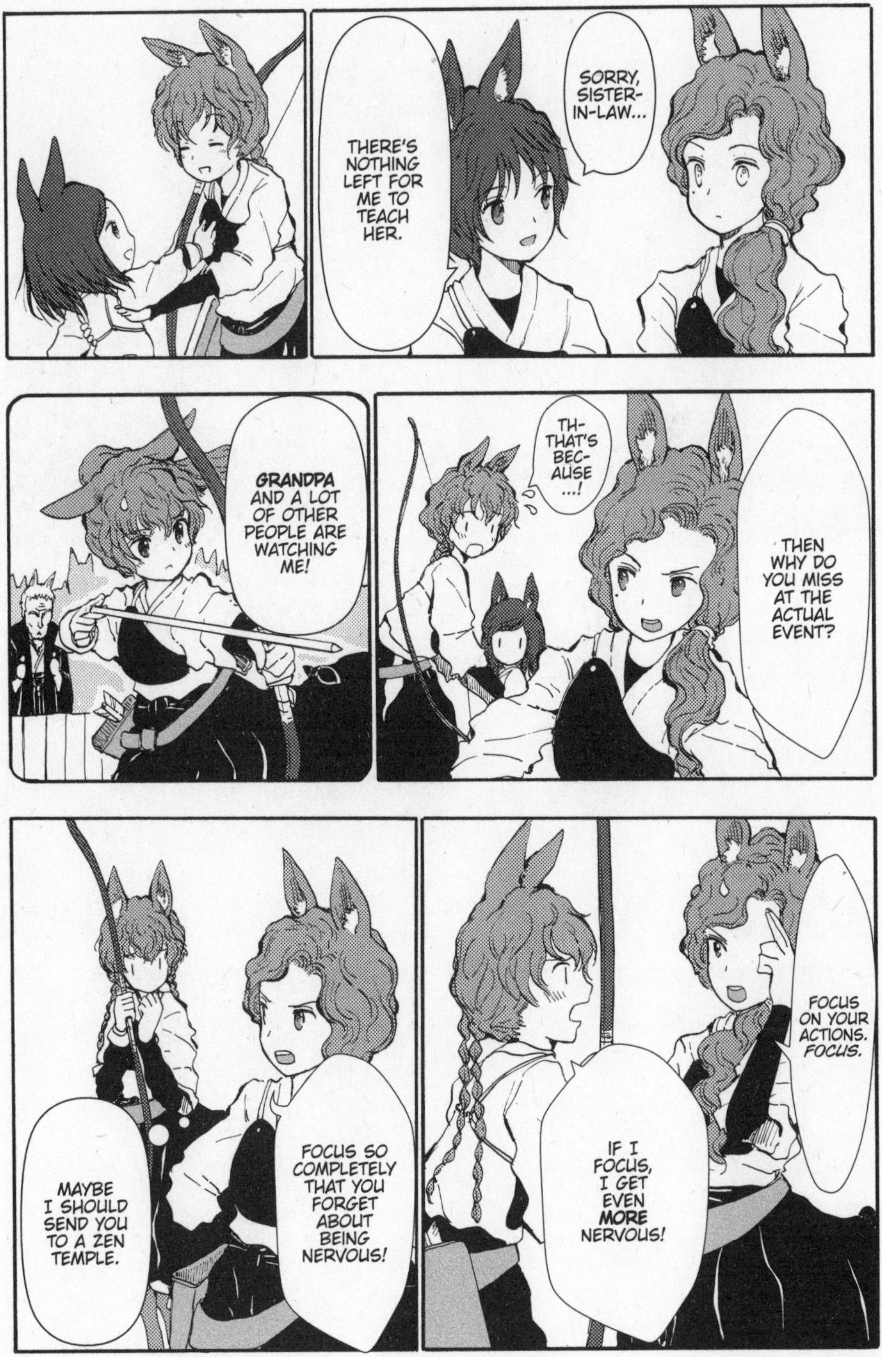
SORRY, SISTER-IN-LAW...
THERE'S NOTHING LEFT FOR ME TO TEACH HER.
THEN WHY DO YOU MISS AT THE ACTUAL EVENT?
TH-THAT'S BECAUSE ...!
GRANDPA AND A LOT OF OTHER PEOPLE ARE WATCHING ME!
FOCUS ON YOUR ACTIONS. FOCUS.
IF I FOCUS, I GET EVEN **MORE** NERVOUS!
FOCUS SO COMPLETELY THAT YOU FORGET ABOUT BEING NERVOUS!
MAYBE I SHOULD SEND YOU TO A ZEN TEMPLE.

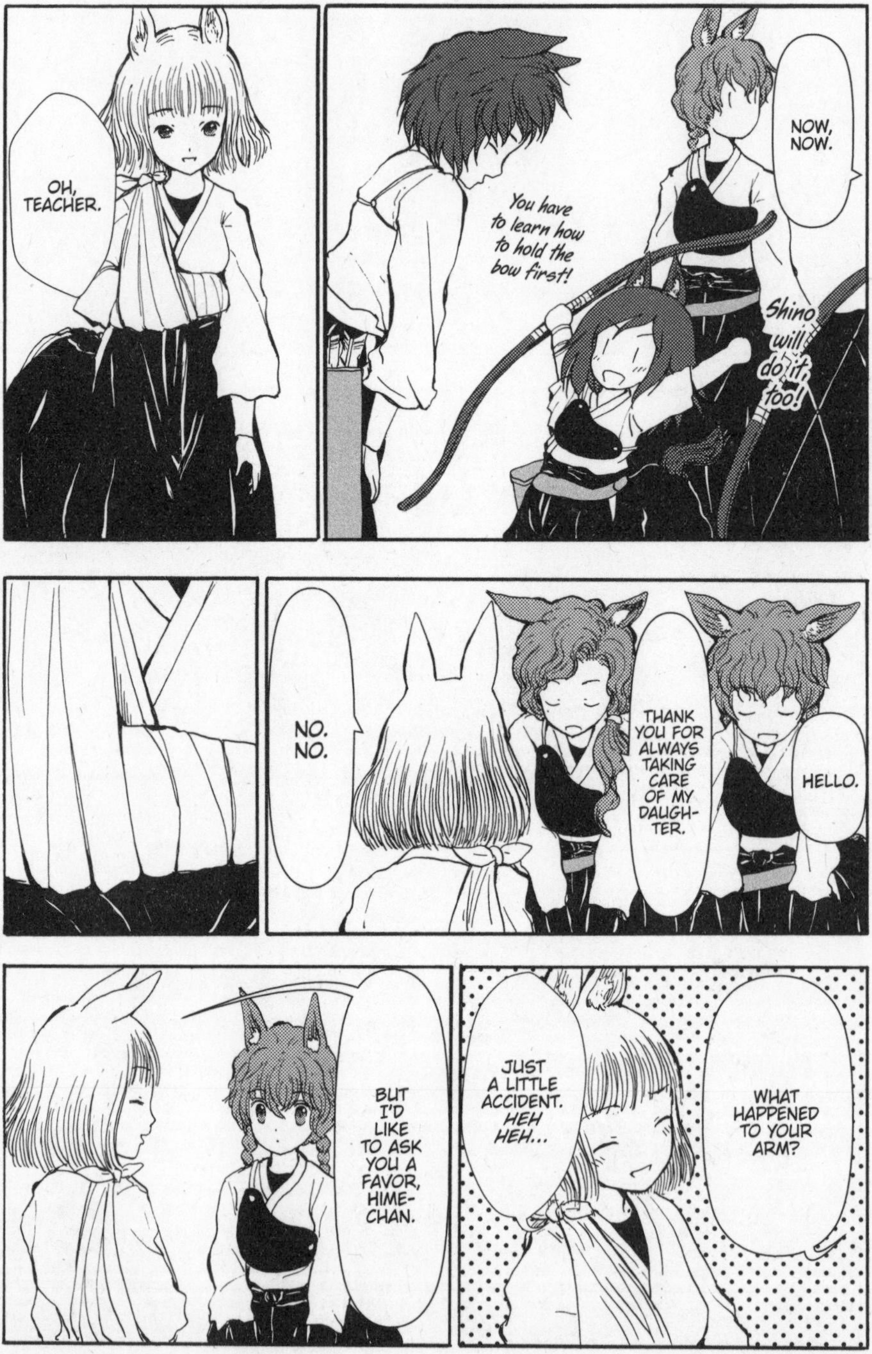
NOW, NOW.
You have to learn how to hold the bow first!
Shino will do it, too!
OH, TEACHER.
HELLO.
THANK YOU FOR ALWAYS TAKING CARE OF MY DAUGHTER.
NO. NO.
WHAT HAPPENED TO YOUR ARM?
JUST A LITTLE ACCIDENT. HEH HEH...
BUT I'D LIKE TO ASK YOU A FAVOR, HIME-CHAN.

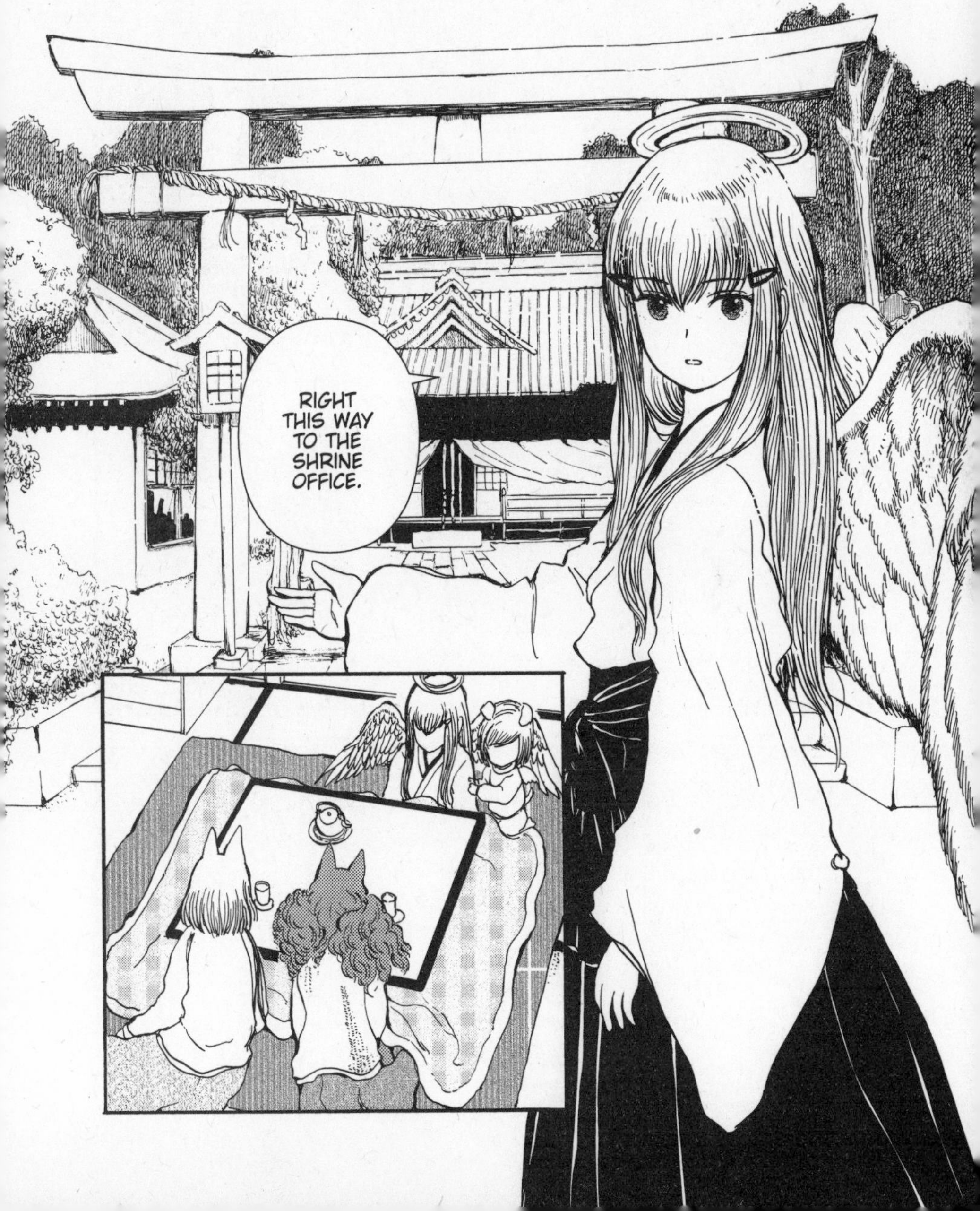
RIGHT THIS WAY TO THE SHRINE OFFICE.

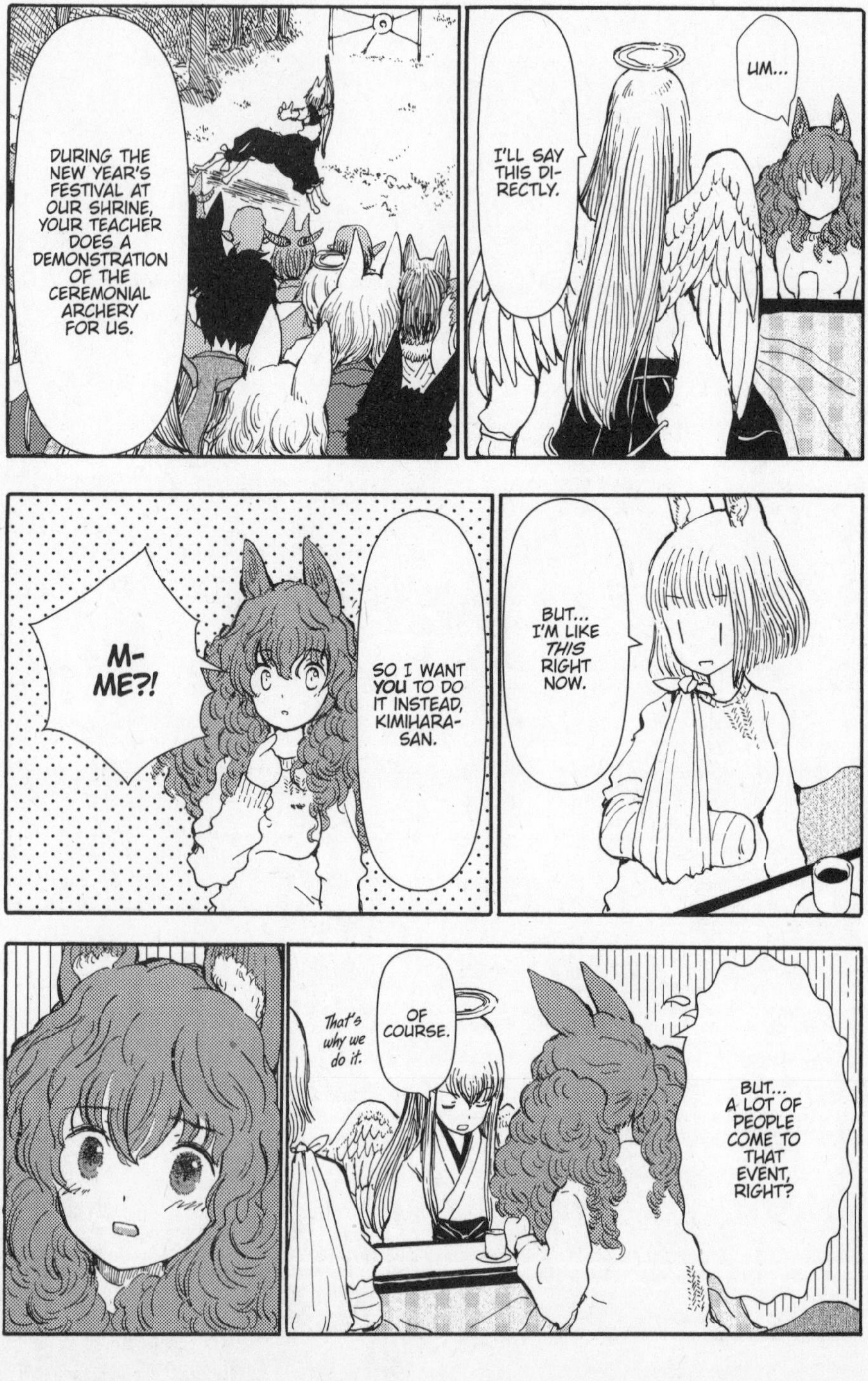
UM...
I'LL SAY THIS DIRECTLY.
DURING THE NEW YEAR'S FESTIVAL AT OUR SHRINE, YOUR TEACHER DOES A DEMONSTRATION OF THE CEREMONIAL ARCHERY FOR US.
BUT... I'M LIKE *THIS* RIGHT NOW.
SO I WANT **YOU** TO DO IT INSTEAD, KIMIHARA-SAN.
M-ME?!
BUT... A LOT OF PEOPLE COME TO THAT EVENT, RIGHT?
OF COURSE.
That's why we do it.

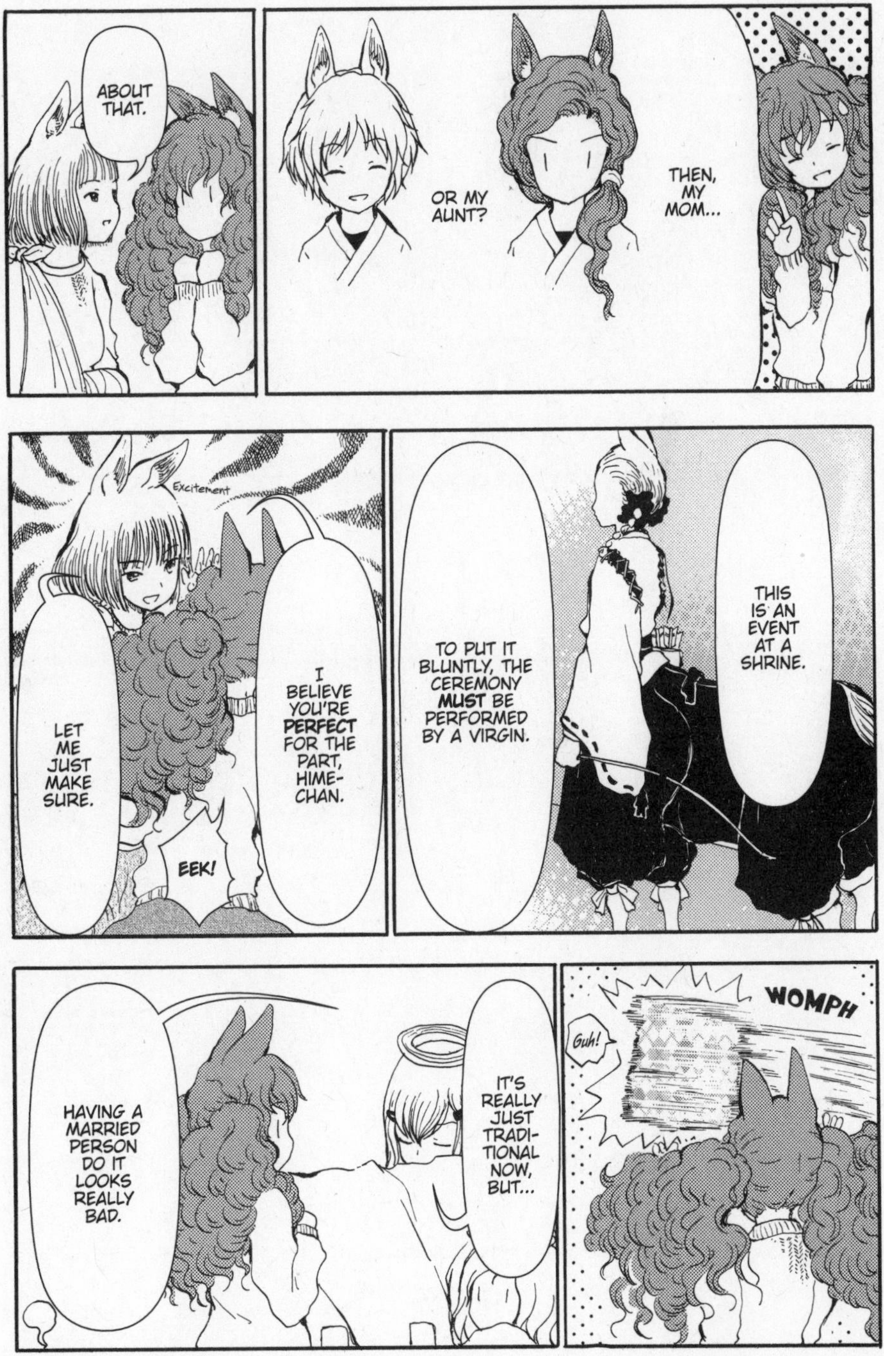
THEN, MY MOM...
OR MY AUNT?
ABOUT THAT.
THIS IS AN EVENT AT A SHRINE.
TO PUT IT BLUNTLY, THE CEREMONY **MUST** BE PERFORMED BY A VIRGIN.
Excitement
I BELIEVE YOU'RE **PERFECT** FOR THE PART, HIME-CHAN.
LET ME JUST MAKE SURE.
EEK!
WOMPH
Guh!
IT'S REALLY JUST TRADITIONAL NOW, BUT...
HAVING A MARRIED PERSON DO IT LOOKS REALLY BAD.

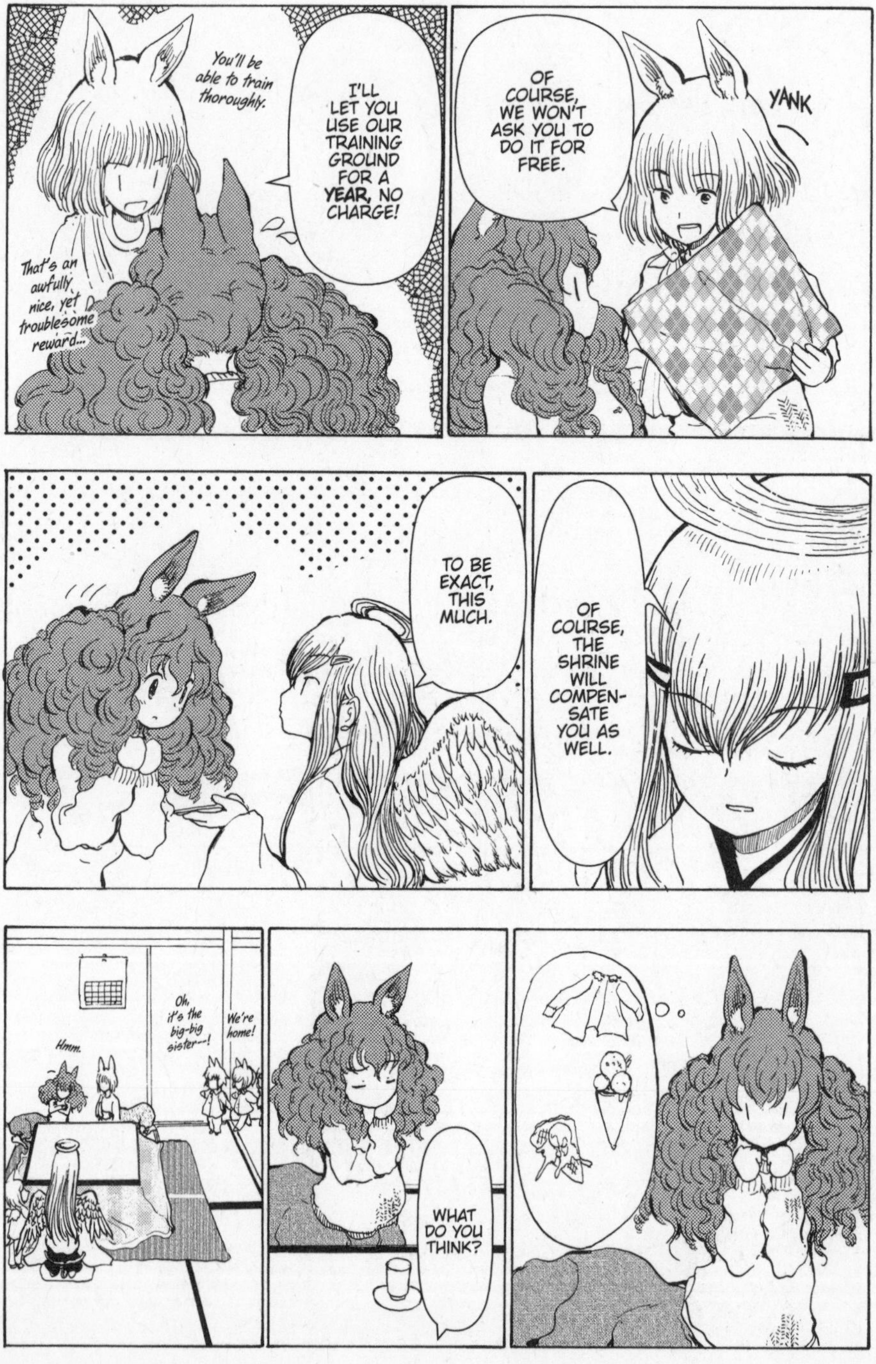
OF COURSE, WE WON'T ASK YOU TO DO IT FOR FREE.
YANK
I'LL LET YOU USE OUR TRAINING GROUND FOR A **YEAR,** NO CHARGE!
You'll be able to train thoroughly.
That's an awfully nice, yet troublesome reward...
OF COURSE, THE SHRINE WILL COMPENSATE YOU AS WELL.
TO BE EXACT, THIS MUCH.
WHAT DO YOU THINK?
We're home!
Oh, it's the big-big sister--!
Hmm.

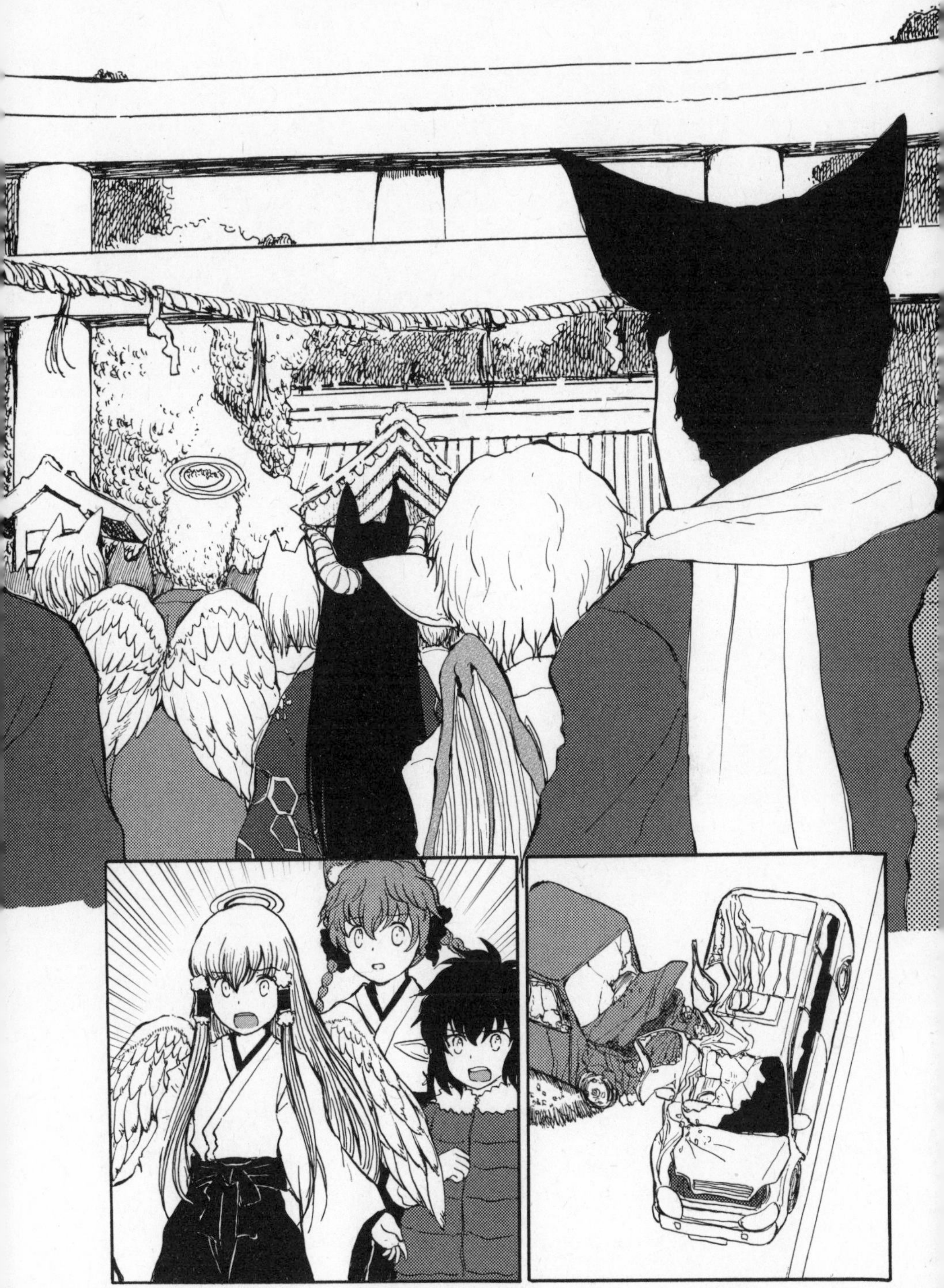

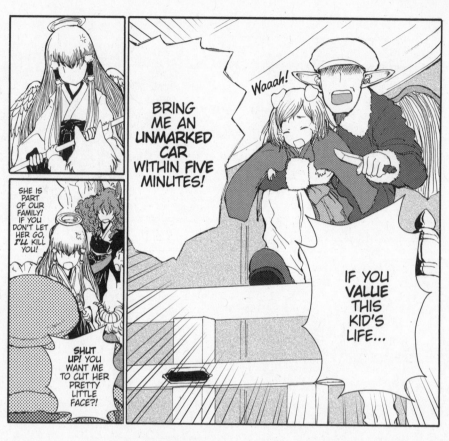

BRING ME AN UNMARKED CAR WITHIN FIVE MINUTES!

Waaah!

IF YOU VALUE THIS KID'S LIFE...

SHE IS PART OF OUR FAMILY! IF YOU DON'T LET HER GO, *I'LL* KILL YOU!

SHUT UP! YOU WANT ME TO CUT HER PRETTY LITTLE FACE?!

PLEASE DON'T THREATEN HIM, YOU WILL ONLY ESCALATE THE SITUATION.

WE CALL THE POLICE FOR HELP AND ALL THEY SEND IS YOU?

WAIT A SECOND...

I'M AFRAID SO.

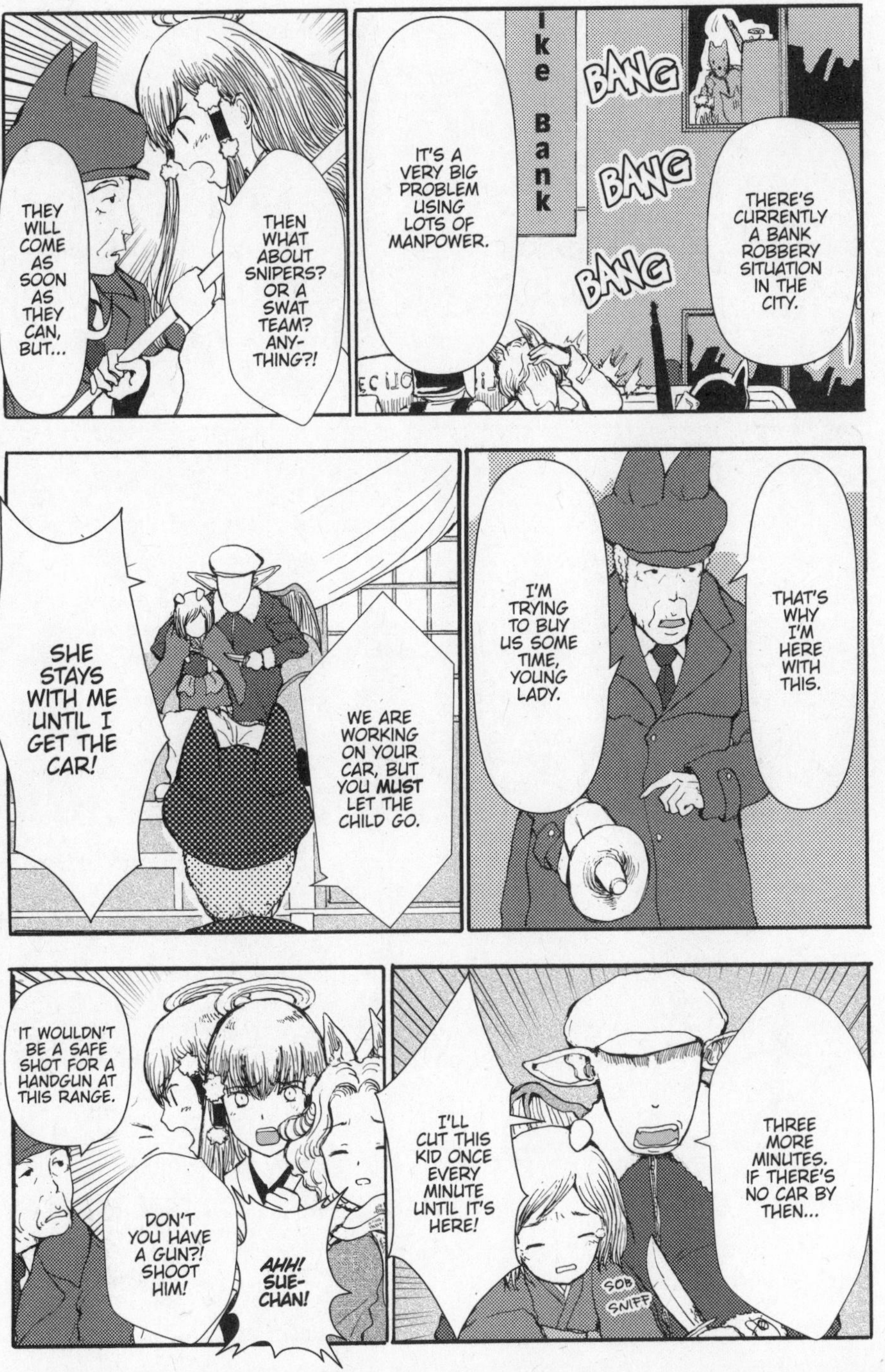
ike Bank
BANG
BANG
BANG
THERE'S CURRENTLY A BANK ROBBERY SITUATION IN THE CITY.
IT'S A VERY BIG PROBLEM USING LOTS OF MANPOWER.
THEN WHAT ABOUT SNIPERS? OR A SWAT TEAM? ANY-THING?!
THEY WILL COME AS SOON AS THEY CAN, BUT...
THAT'S WHY I'M HERE WITH THIS.
I'M TRYING TO BUY US SOME TIME, YOUNG LADY.
WE ARE WORKING ON YOUR CAR, BUT YOU **MUST** LET THE CHILD GO.
SHE STAYS WITH ME UNTIL I GET THE CAR!
THREE MORE MINUTES. IF THERE'S NO CAR BY THEN...
I'LL CUT THIS KID ONCE EVERY MINUTE UNTIL IT'S HERE!
SOB
SNIFF
AHH! SUE-CHAN!
DON'T YOU HAVE A GUN?! SHOOT HIM!
IT WOULDN'T BE A SAFE SHOT FOR A HANDGUN AT THIS RANGE.

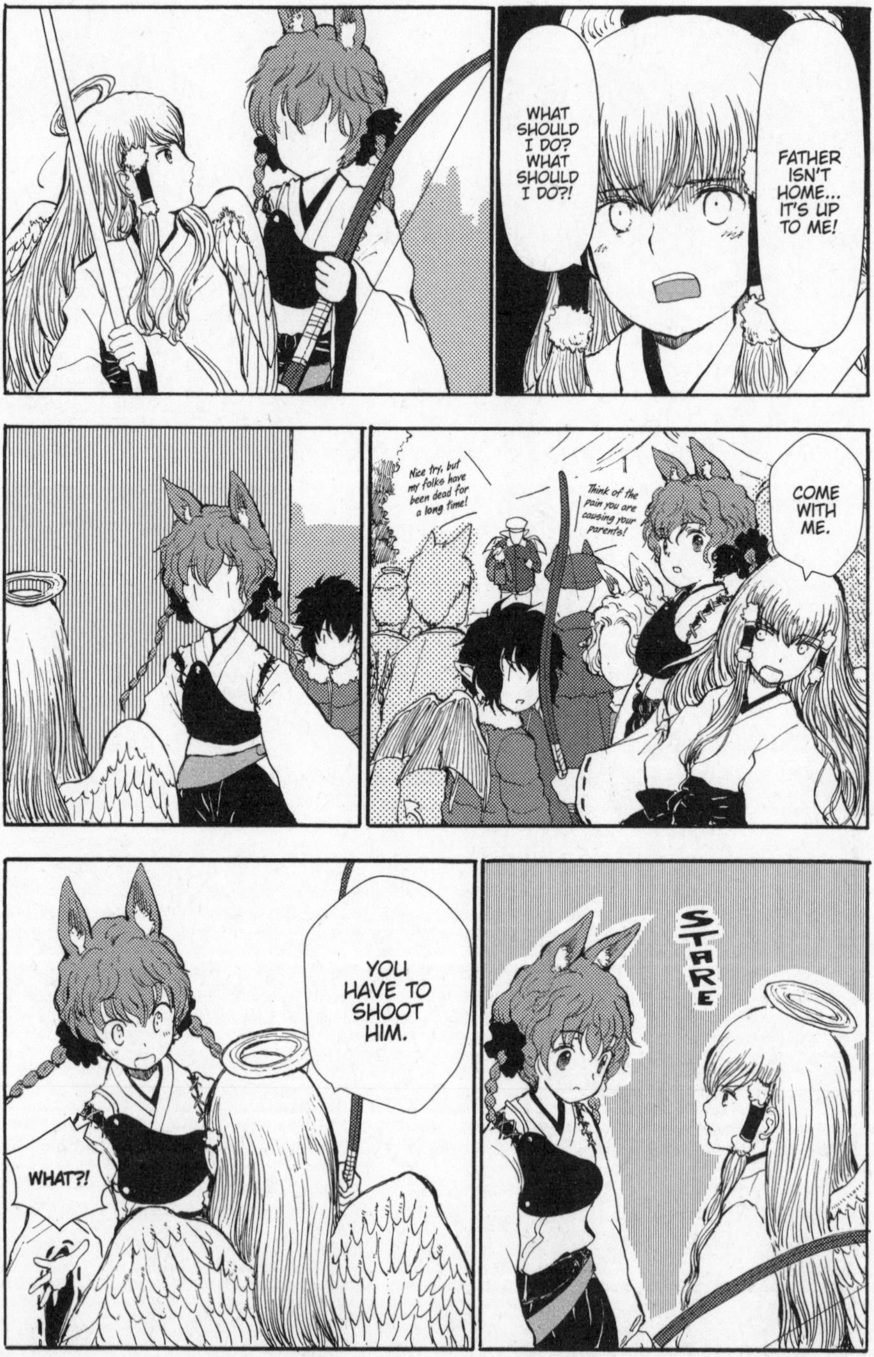
FATHER ISN'T HOME... IT'S UP TO ME!
WHAT SHOULD I DO? WHAT SHOULD I DO?!
COME WITH ME.
Think of the pain you are causing your parents!
Nice try, but my folks have been dead for a long time!
STARE
YOU HAVE TO SHOOT HIM.
WHAT?!

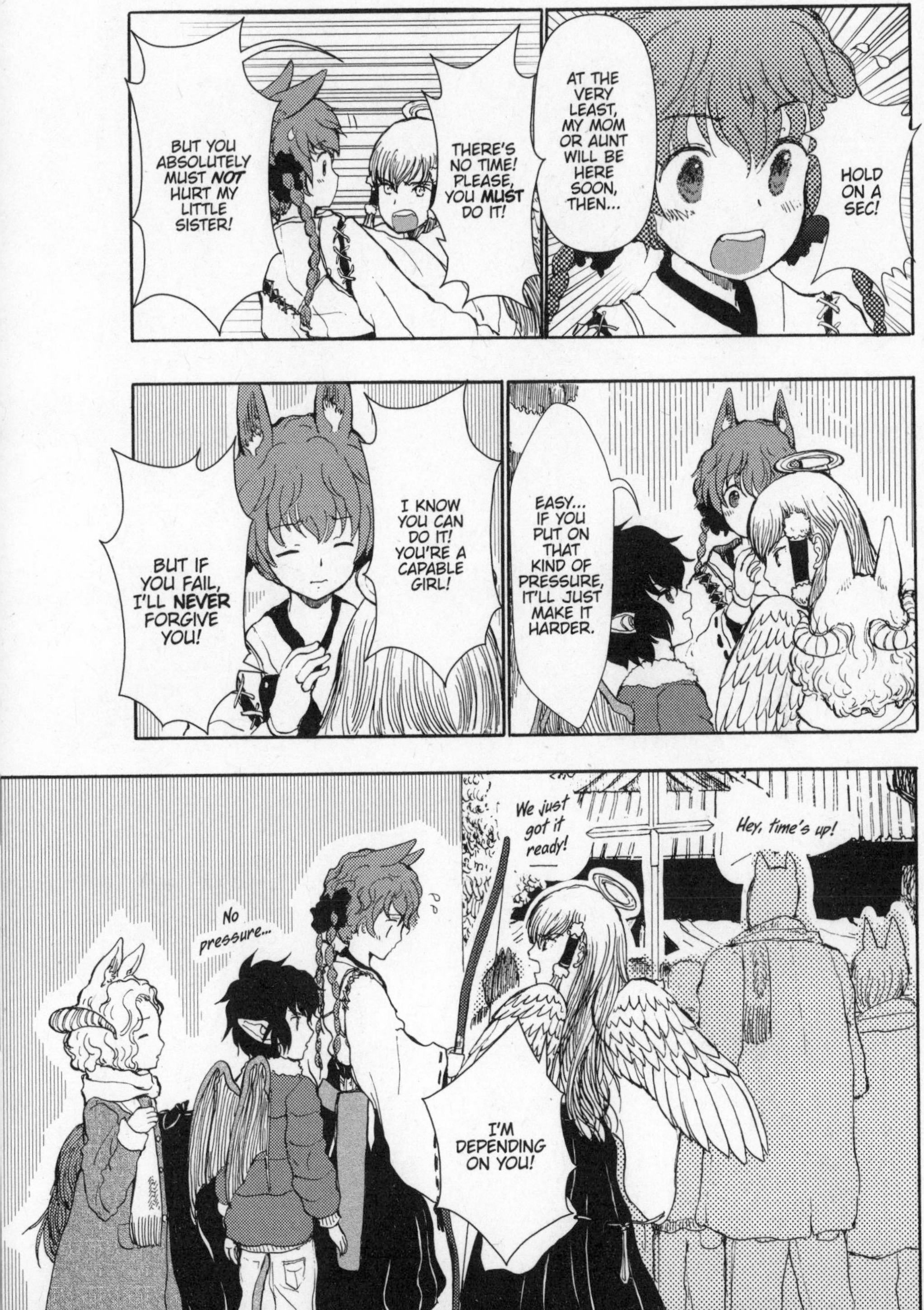
HOLD ON A SEC!
AT THE VERY LEAST, MY MOM OR AUNT WILL BE HERE SOON, THEN...
THERE'S NO TIME! PLEASE, YOU **MUST** DO IT!
BUT YOU ABSOLUTELY MUST ***NOT*** HURT MY LITTLE SISTER!
EASY... IF YOU PUT ON THAT KIND OF PRESSURE, IT'LL JUST MAKE IT HARDER.
I KNOW YOU CAN DO IT! YOU'RE A CAPABLE GIRL!
BUT IF YOU FAIL, I'LL **NEVER** FORGIVE YOU!
Hey, time's up!
We just got it ready!
I'M DEPENDING ON YOU!
No pressure...

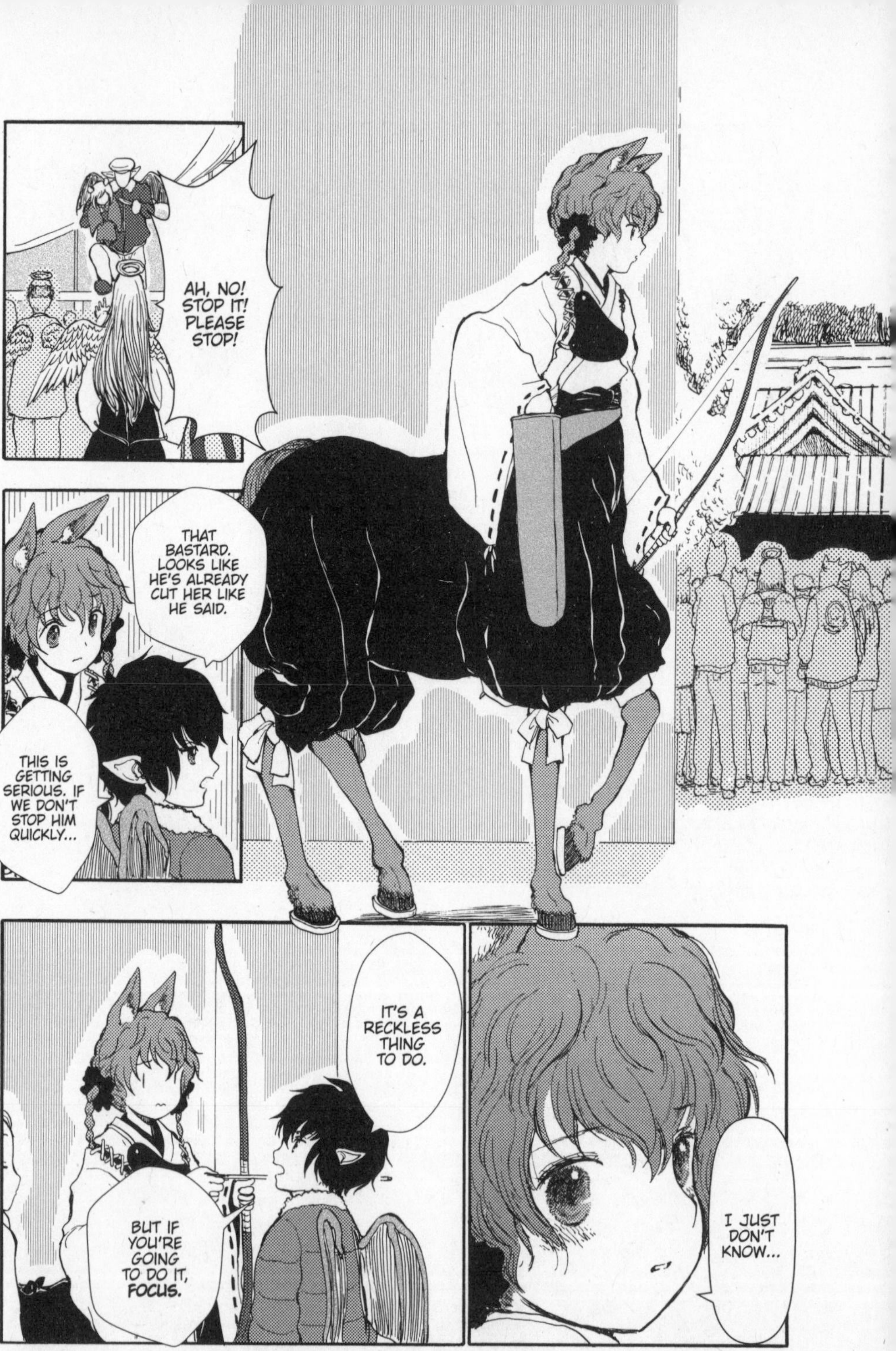
AH, NO! STOP IT! PLEASE STOP!
THAT BASTARD. LOOKS LIKE HE'S ALREADY CUT HER LIKE HE SAID.
THIS IS GETTING SERIOUS. IF WE DON'T STOP HIM QUICKLY...
I JUST DON'T KNOW...
IT'S A RECKLESS THING TO DO.
BUT IF YOU'RE GOING TO DO IT, FOCUS.

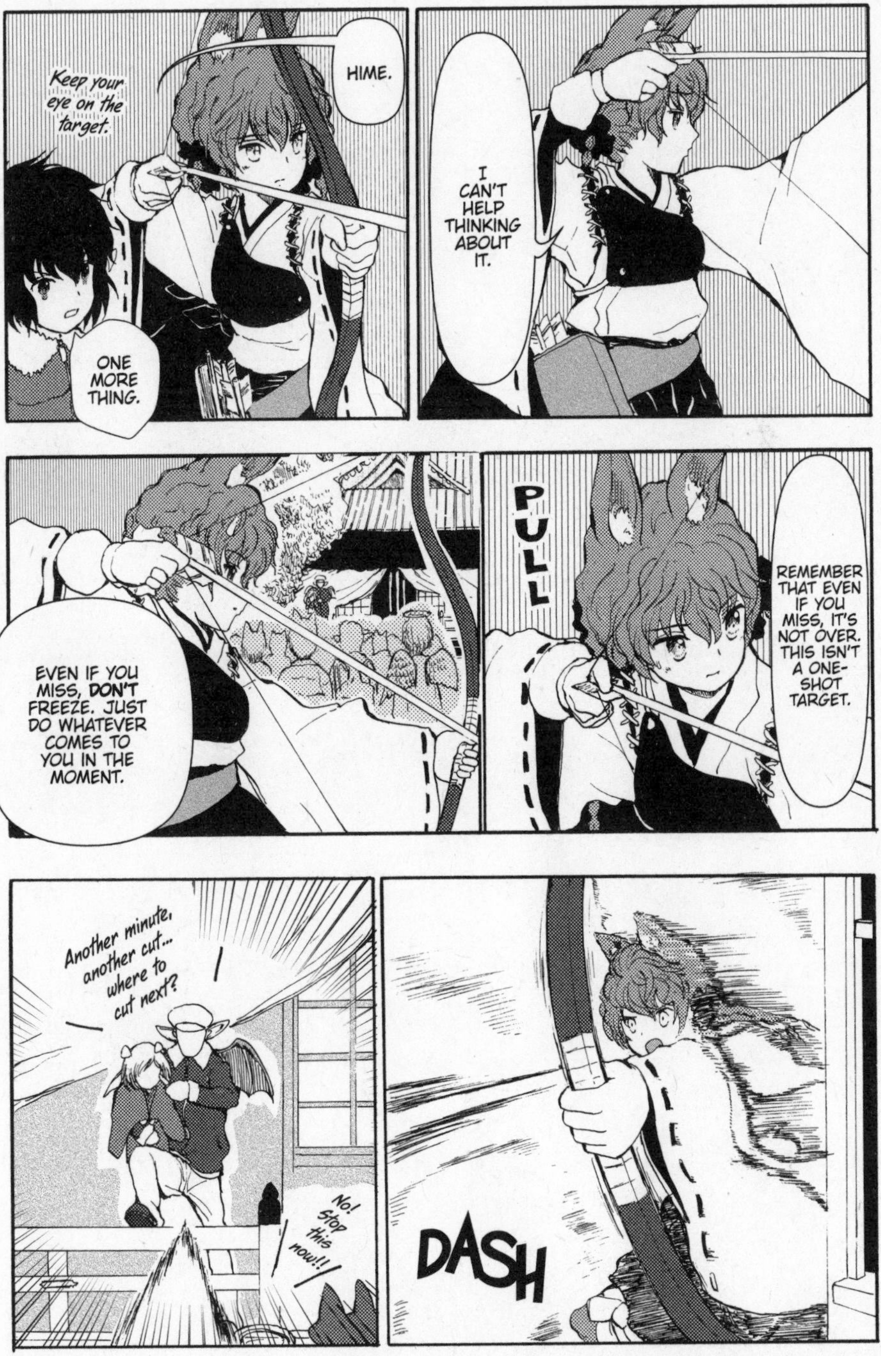
I CAN'T HELP THINKING ABOUT IT.
HIME.
Keep your eye on the target.
ONE MORE THING.
REMEMBER THAT EVEN IF YOU MISS, IT'S NOT OVER. THIS ISN'T A ONE-SHOT TARGET.
PULL
EVEN IF YOU MISS, **DON'T** FREEZE. JUST DO WHATEVER COMES TO YOU IN THE MOMENT.
DASH
Another minute, another cut... where to cut next?
No! Stop this now!!

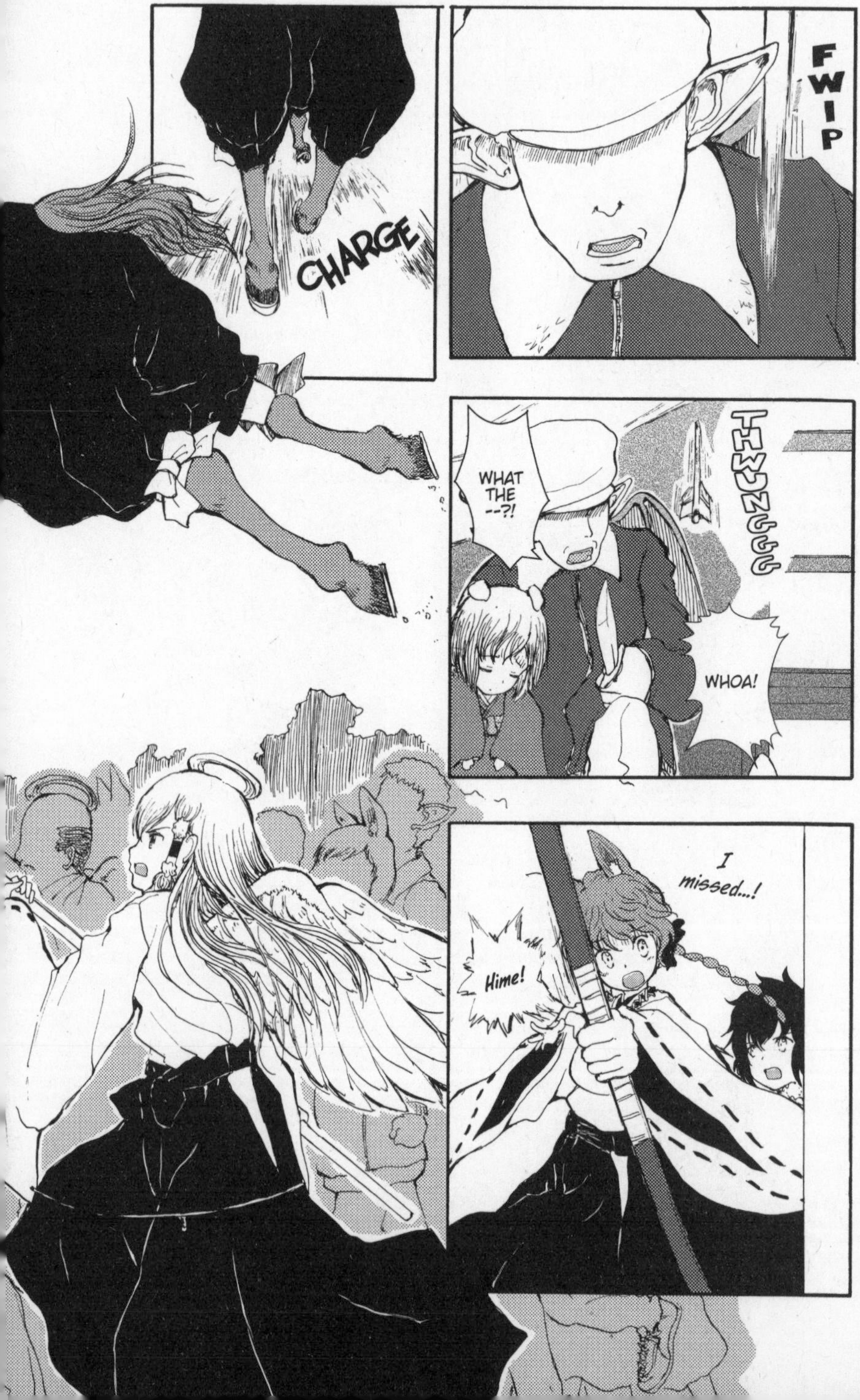
FWIP
CHARGE
THWUNGGG
WHAT THE --?!
WHOA!
I missed...!
Hime!

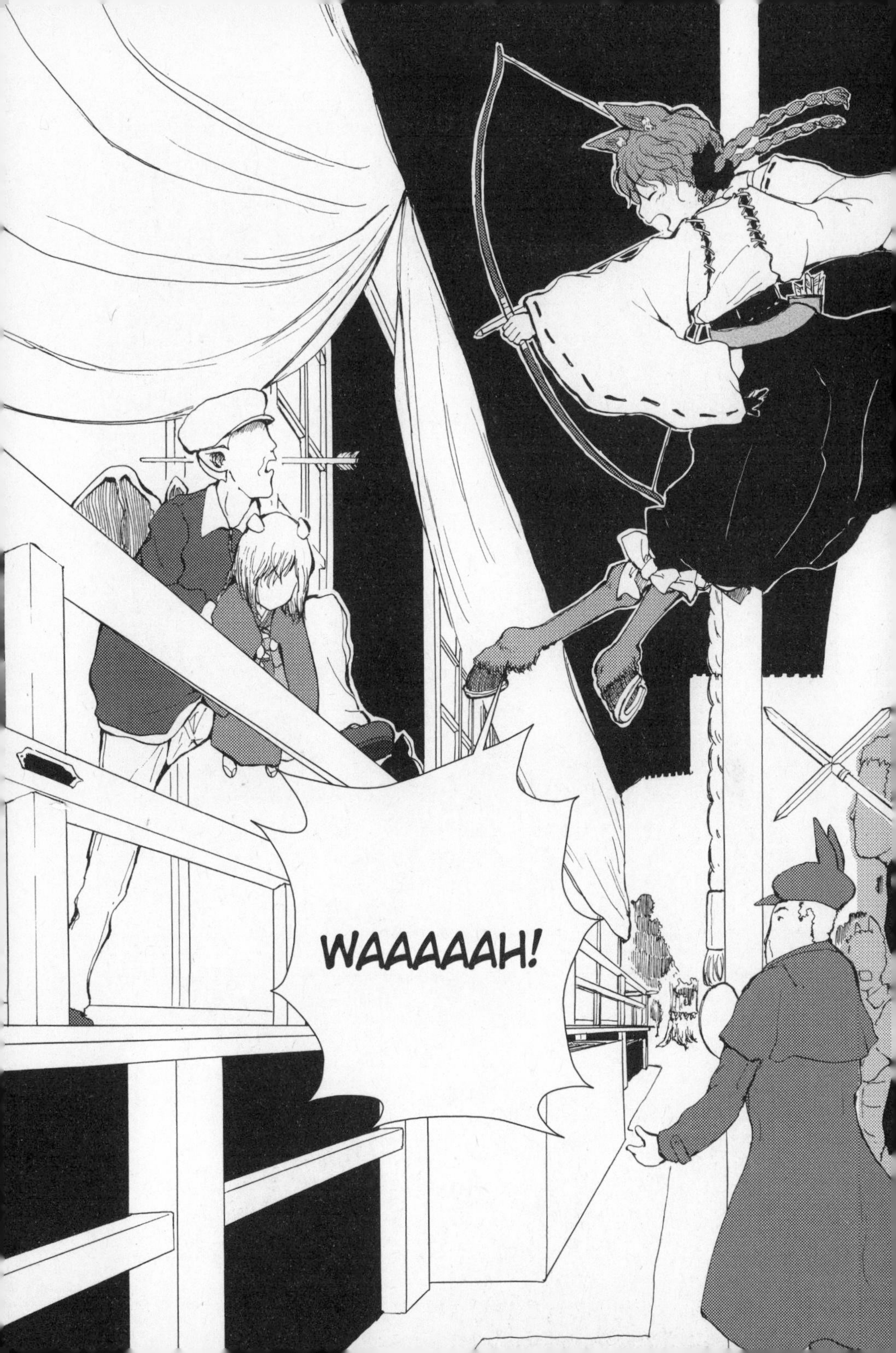
WAAAAAH!

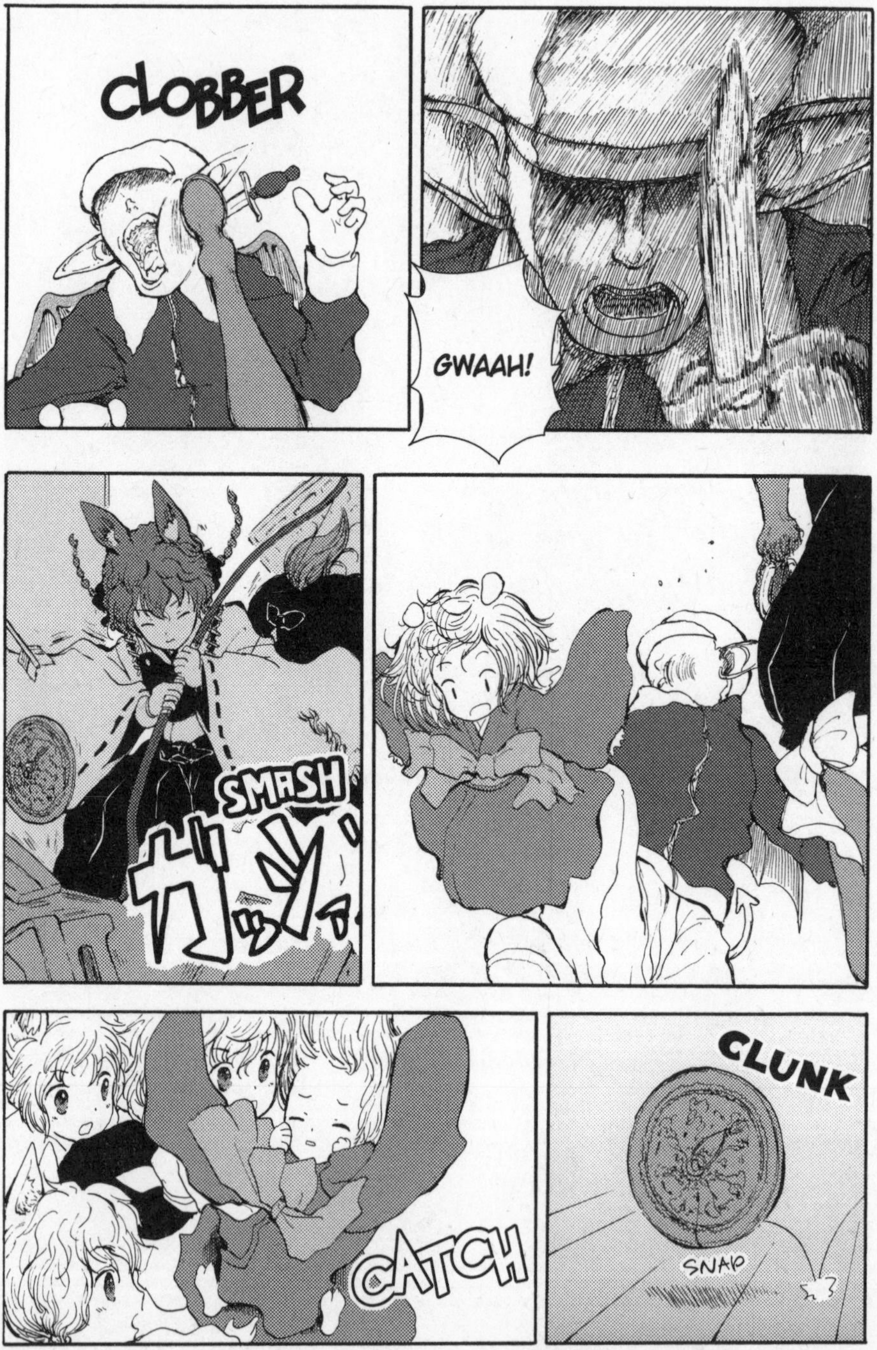
GWAAH!
CLOBBER
SMASH
CLUNK
SNAP
CATCH

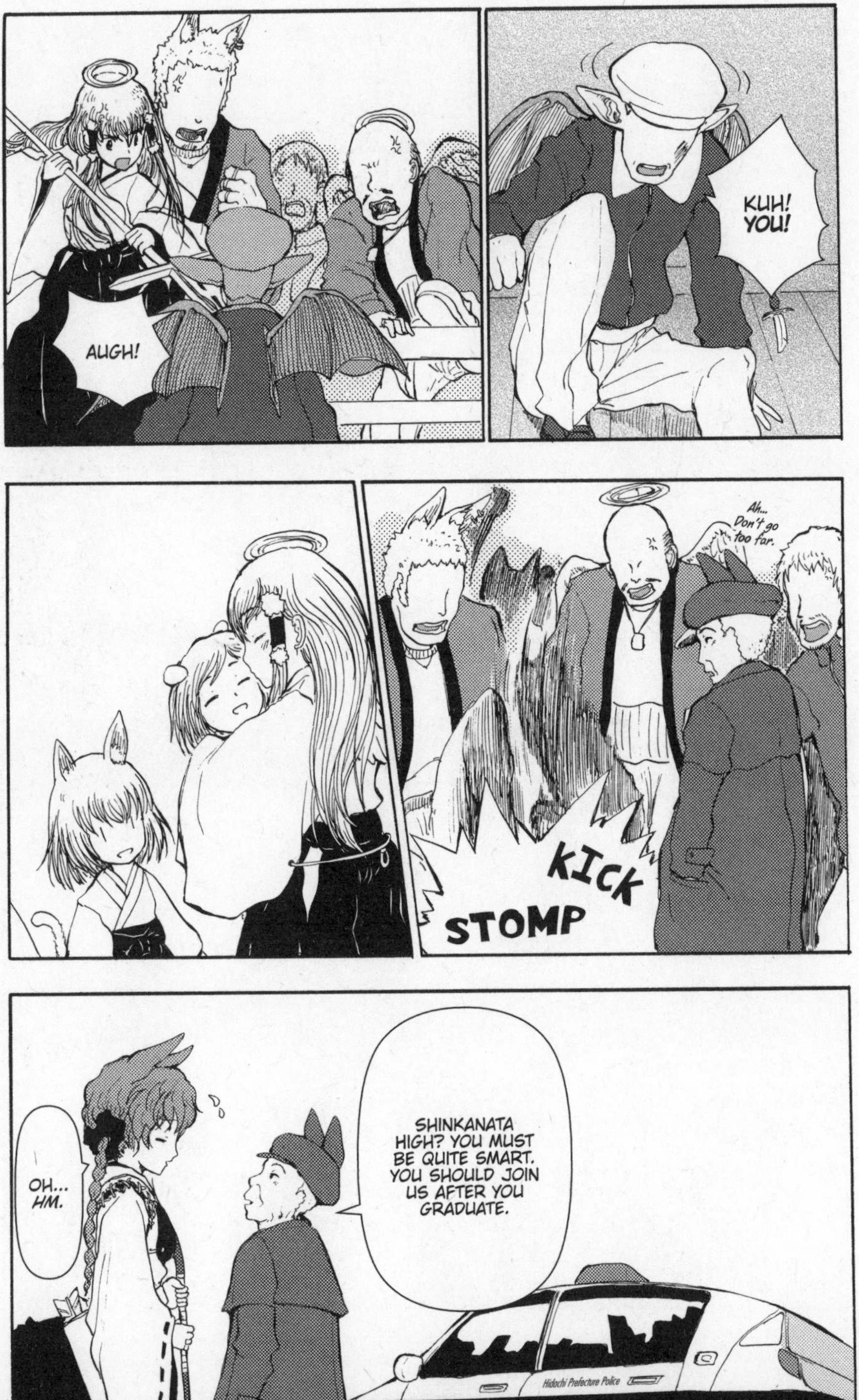
KUH! YOU!
AUGH!
Ah... Don't go too far.
KICK
STOMP
SHINKANATA HIGH? YOU MUST BE QUITE SMART. YOU SHOULD JOIN US AFTER YOU GRADUATE.
OH... HM.
Hidochi Prefecture Police

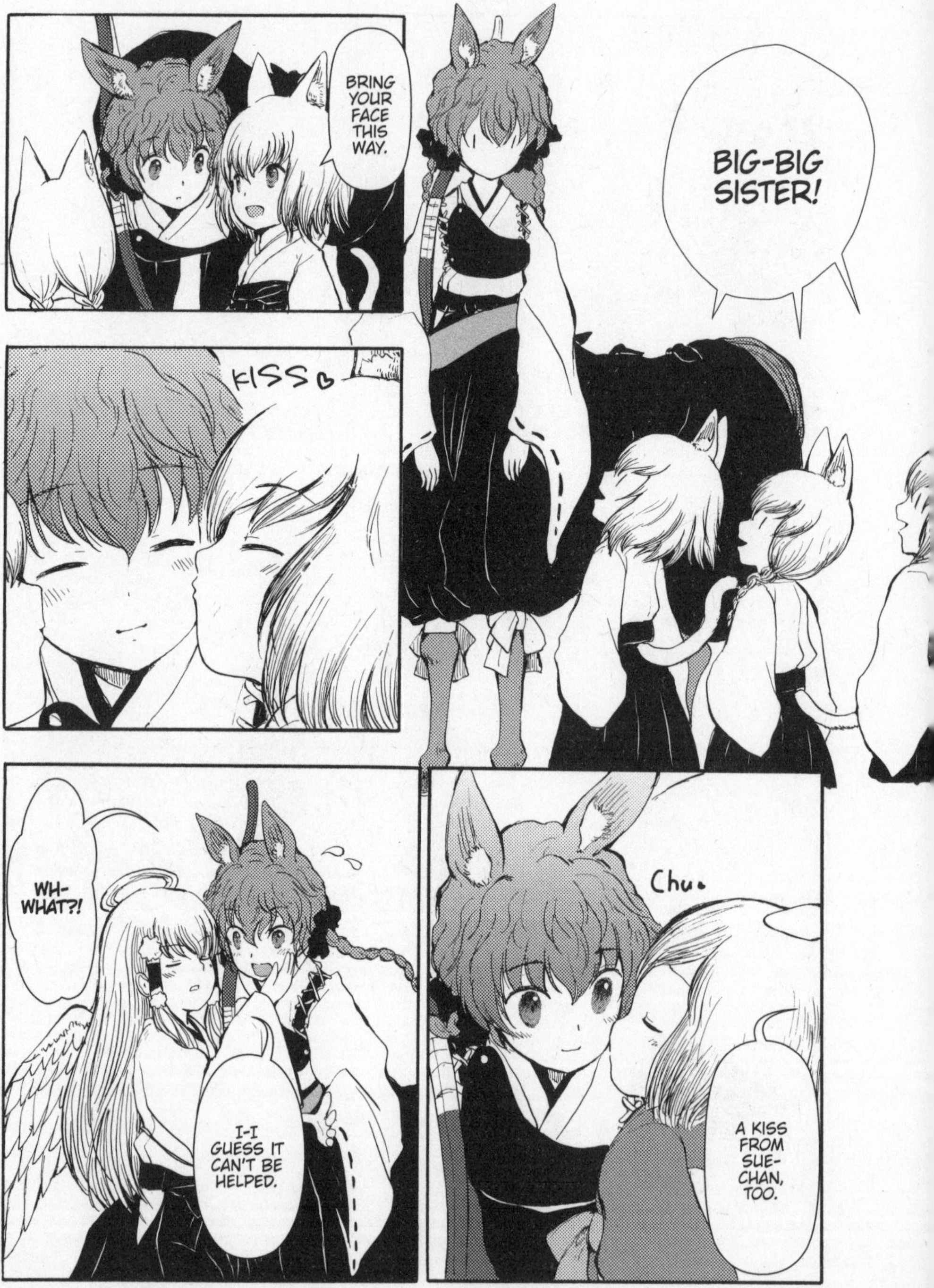
BIG-BIG SISTER!
BRING YOUR FACE THIS WAY.
KISS ♡
Chu•
A KISS FROM SUE-CHAN, TOO.
WH-WHAT?!
I-I GUESS IT CAN'T BE HELPED.

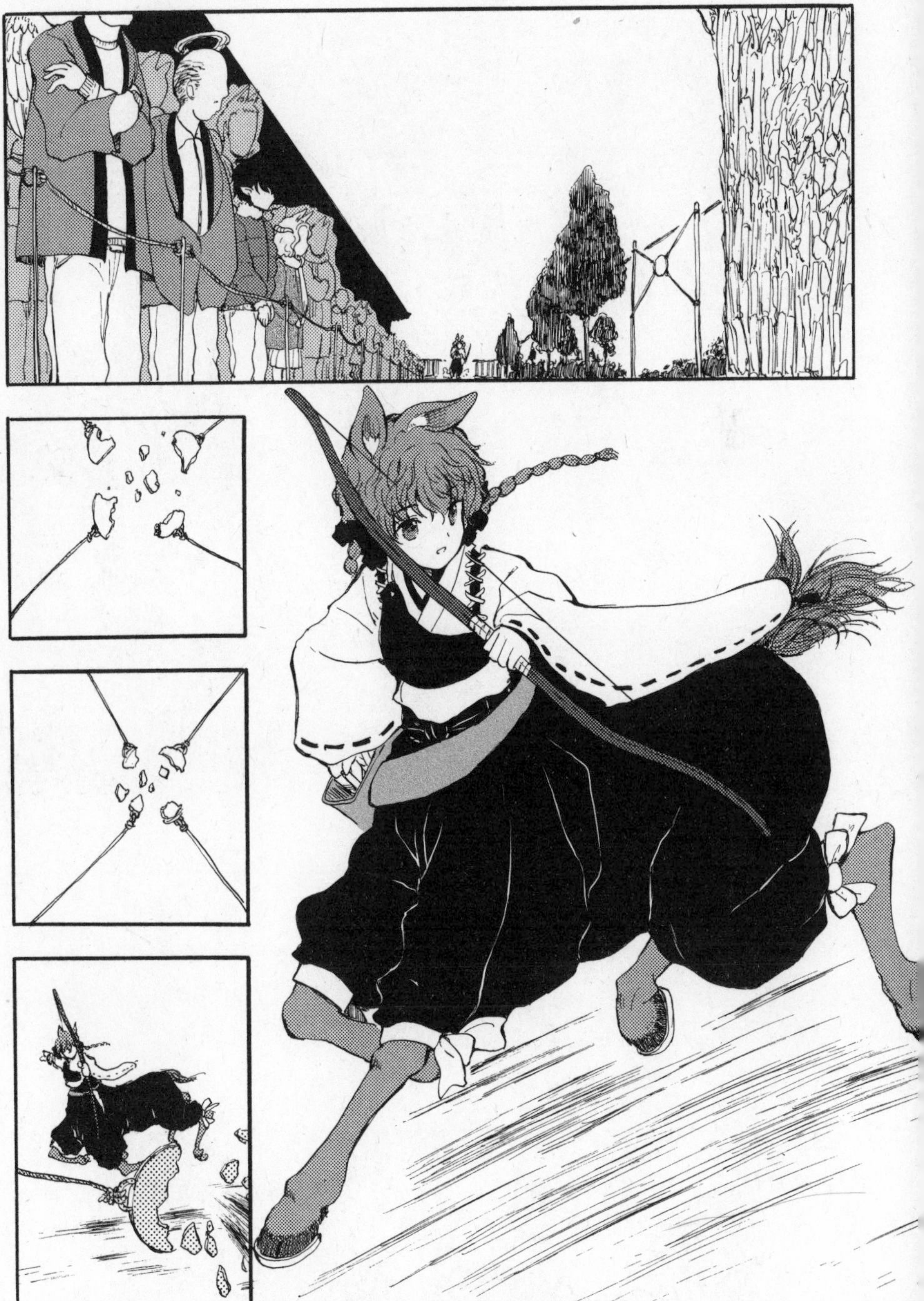

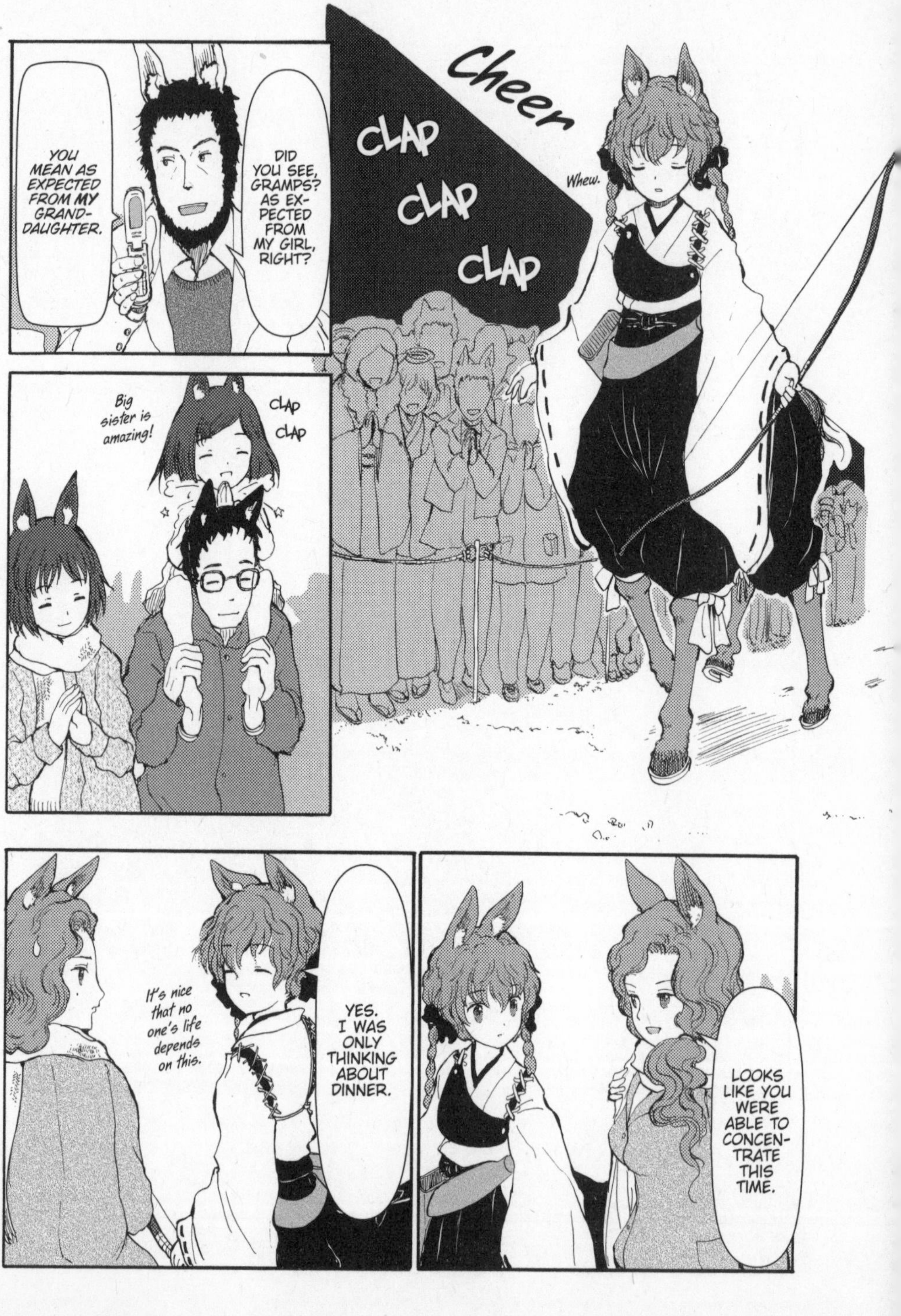
Cheer
Whew.
CLAP
CLAP
CLAP
DID YOU SEE, GRAMPS? AS EXPECTED FROM MY GIRL, RIGHT?
YOU MEAN AS EXPECTED FROM MY GRAND-DAUGHTER.
CLAP
CLAP
Big sister is amazing!
LOOKS LIKE YOU WERE ABLE TO CONCEN-TRATE THIS TIME.
YES. I WAS ONLY THINKING ABOUT DINNER.
It's nice that no one's life depends on this.

A CentaUr's Life

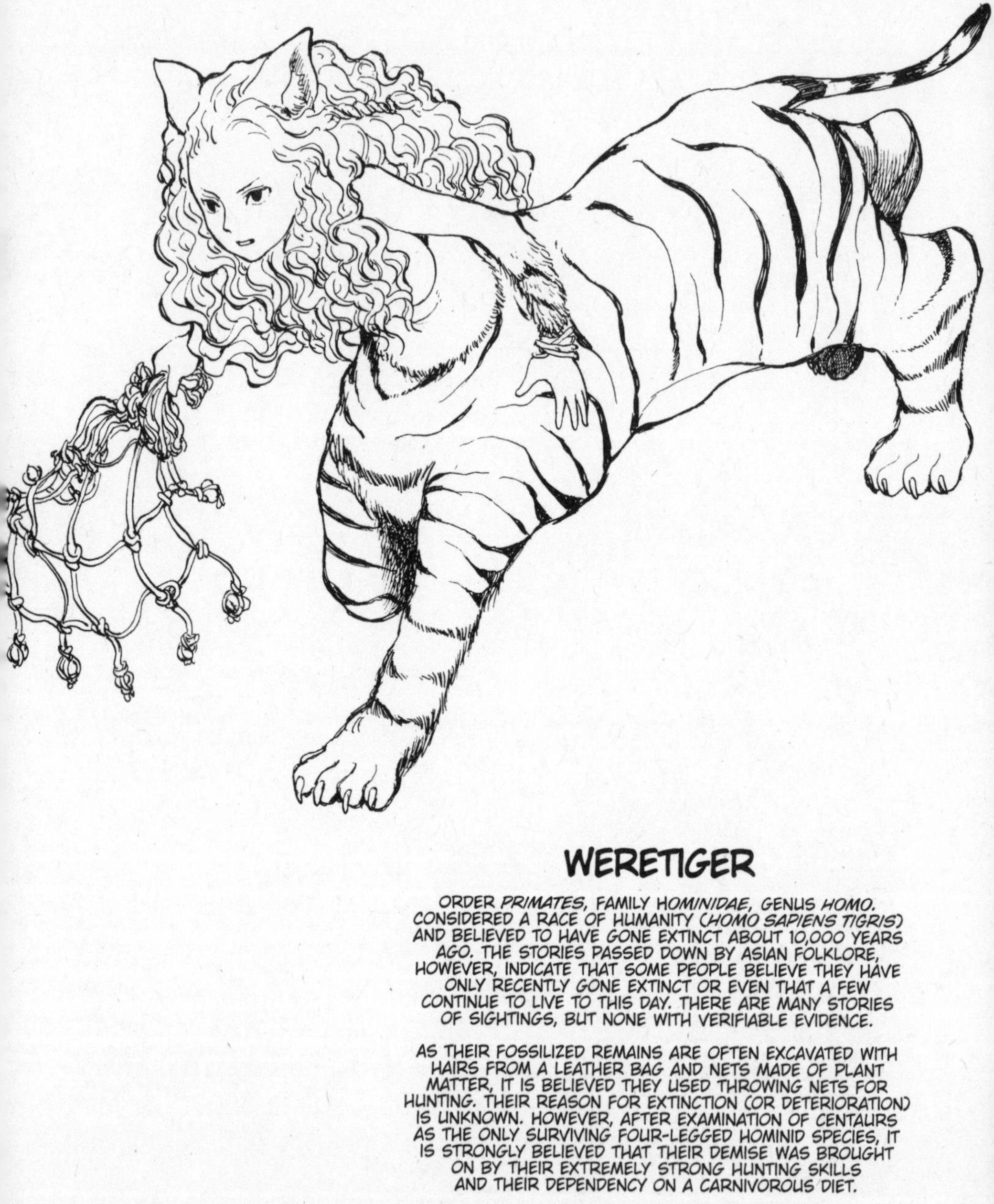

WERETIGER

ORDER *PRIMATES*, FAMILY *HOMINIDAE*, GENUS *HOMO*. CONSIDERED A RACE OF HUMANITY (*HOMO SAPIENS TIGRIS*) AND BELIEVED TO HAVE GONE EXTINCT ABOUT 10,000 YEARS AGO. THE STORIES PASSED DOWN BY ASIAN FOLKLORE, HOWEVER, INDICATE THAT SOME PEOPLE BELIEVE THEY HAVE ONLY RECENTLY GONE EXTINCT OR EVEN THAT A FEW CONTINUE TO LIVE TO THIS DAY. THERE ARE MANY STORIES OF SIGHTINGS, BUT NONE WITH VERIFIABLE EVIDENCE.

AS THEIR FOSSILIZED REMAINS ARE OFTEN EXCAVATED WITH HAIRS FROM A LEATHER BAG AND NETS MADE OF PLANT MATTER, IT IS BELIEVED THEY USED THROWING NETS FOR HUNTING. THEIR REASON FOR EXTINCTION (OR DETERIORATION) IS UNKNOWN. HOWEVER, AFTER EXAMINATION OF CENTAURS AS THE ONLY SURVIVING FOUR-LEGGED HOMINID SPECIES, IT IS STRONGLY BELIEVED THAT THEIR DEMISE WAS BROUGHT ON BY THEIR EXTREMELY STRONG HUNTING SKILLS AND THEIR DEPENDENCY ON A CARNIVOROUS DIET.

FEARS OF A HUMAN FACED DOG

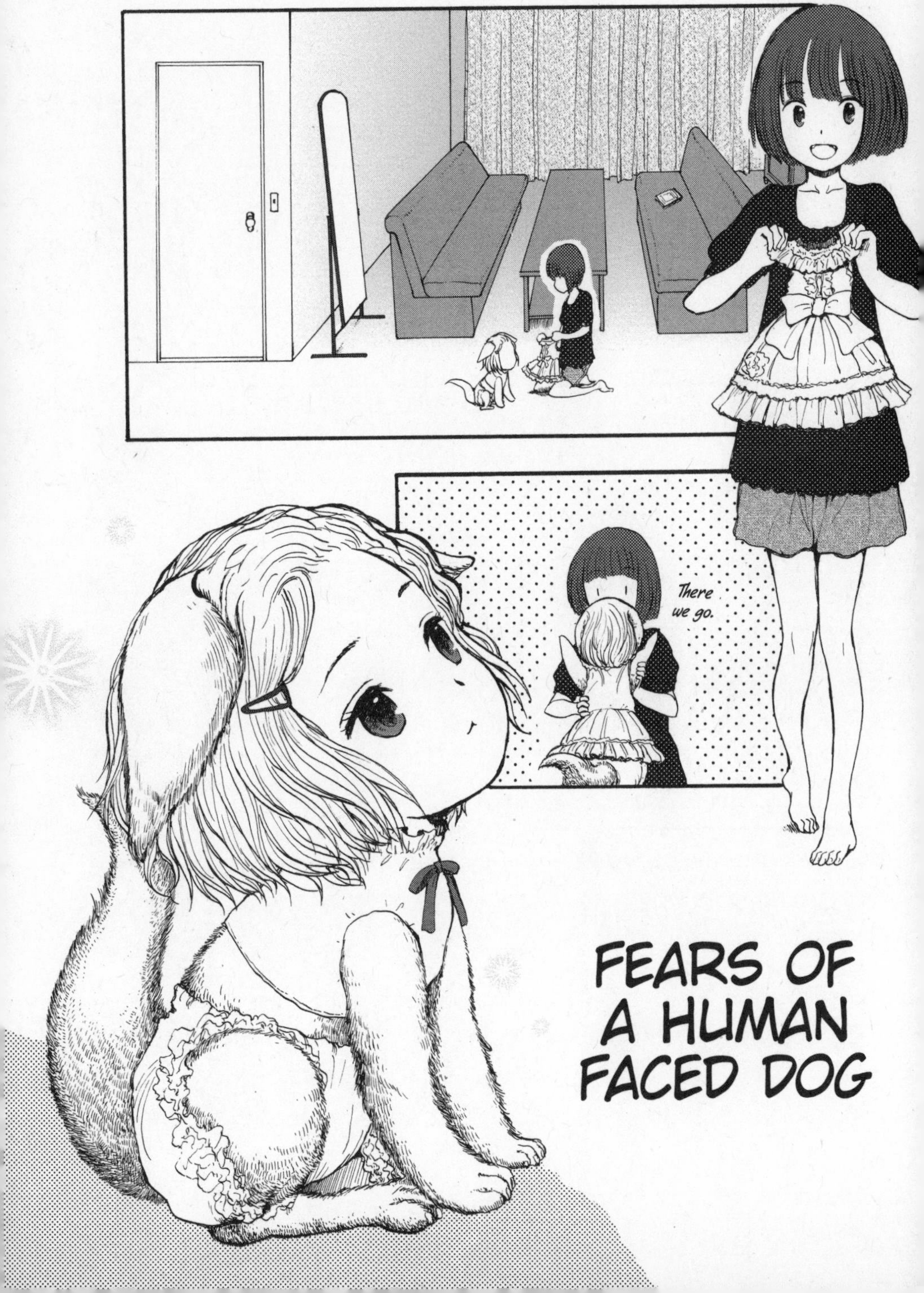
There we go.

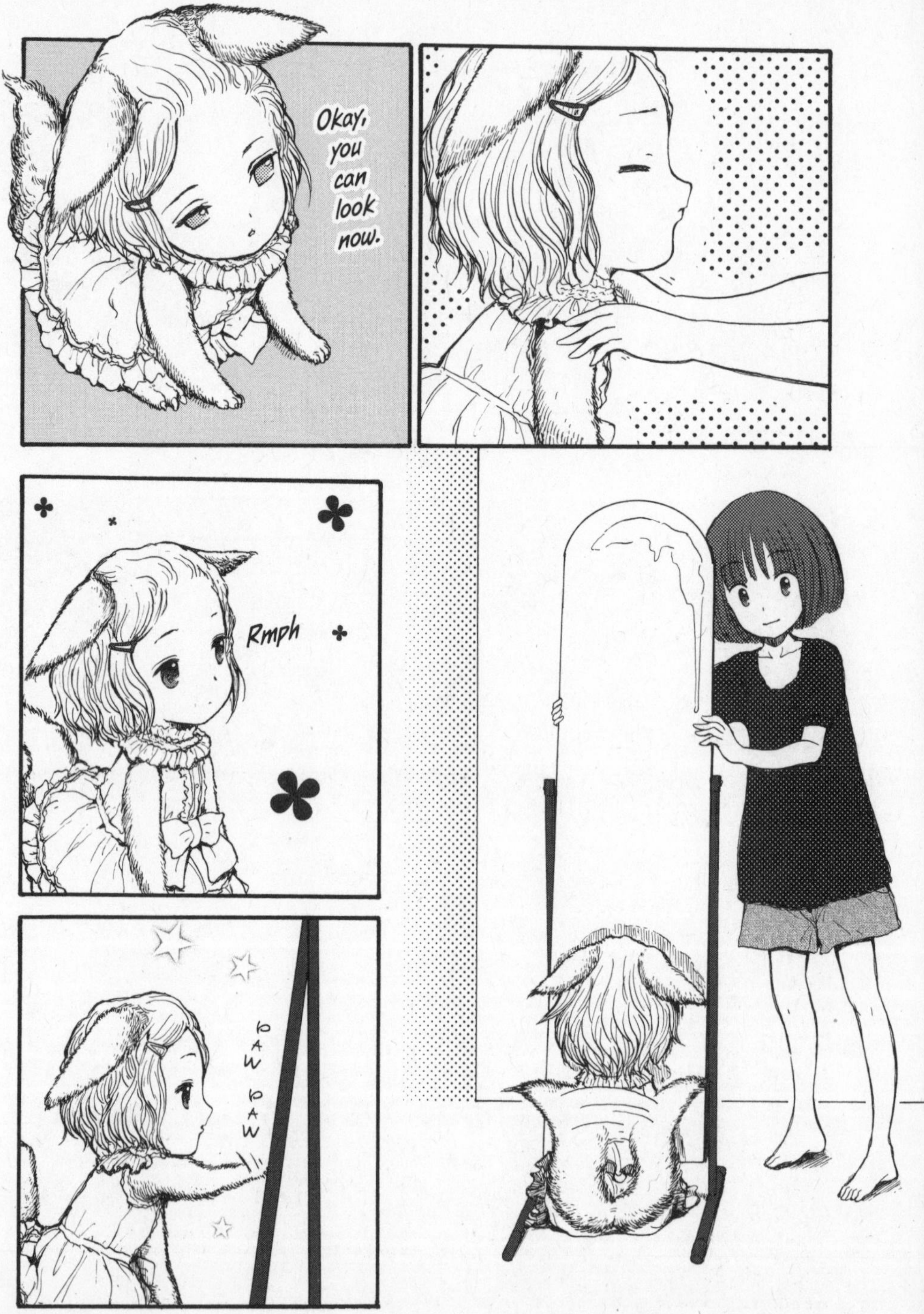
Okay, you can look now.
Rmph
PAW PAW

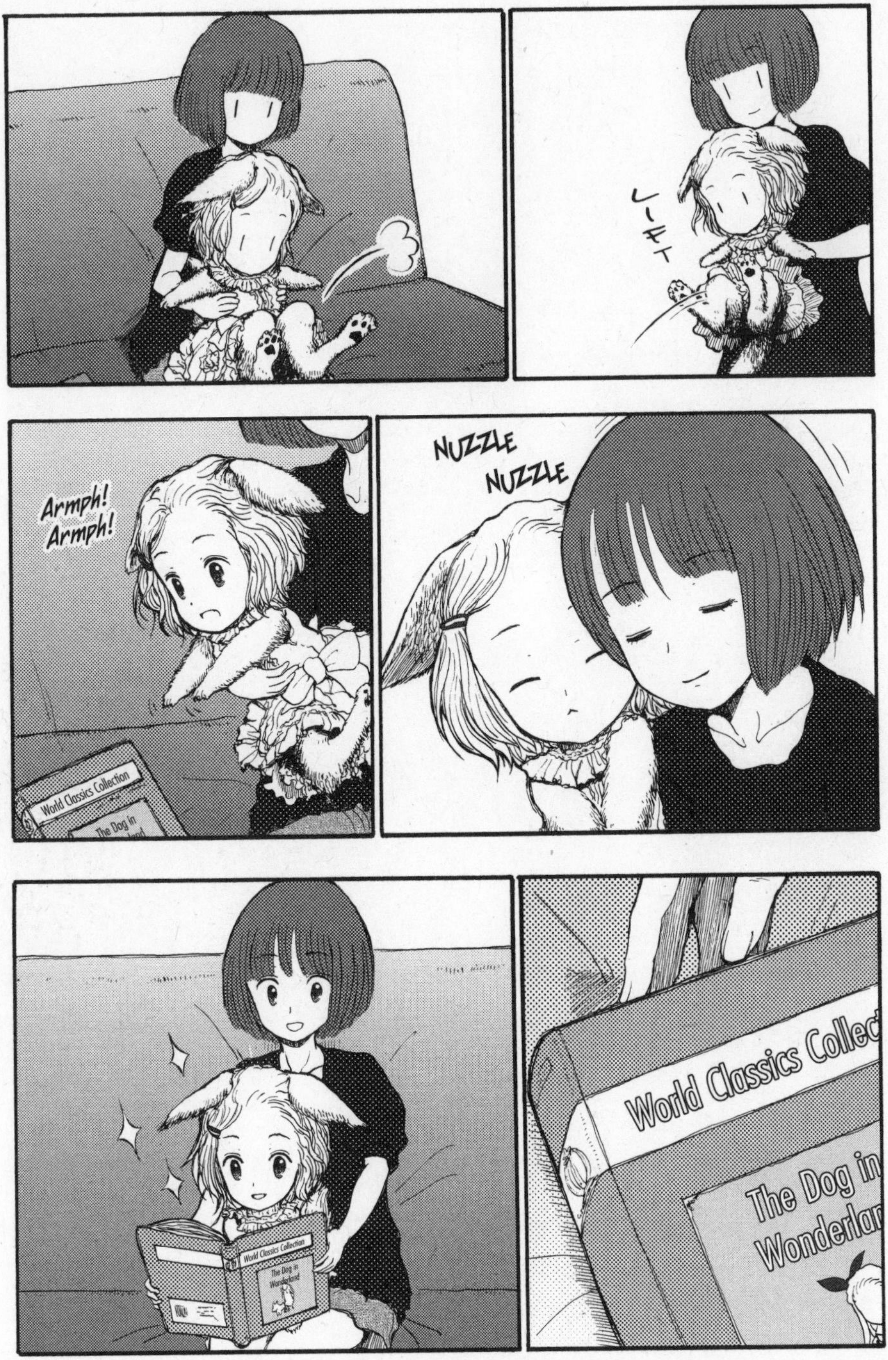
LIFT
NUZZLE NUZZLE
Armph! Armph!
World Classics Collection
World Classics Collec
The Dog in Wonderlan
World Classics Collection

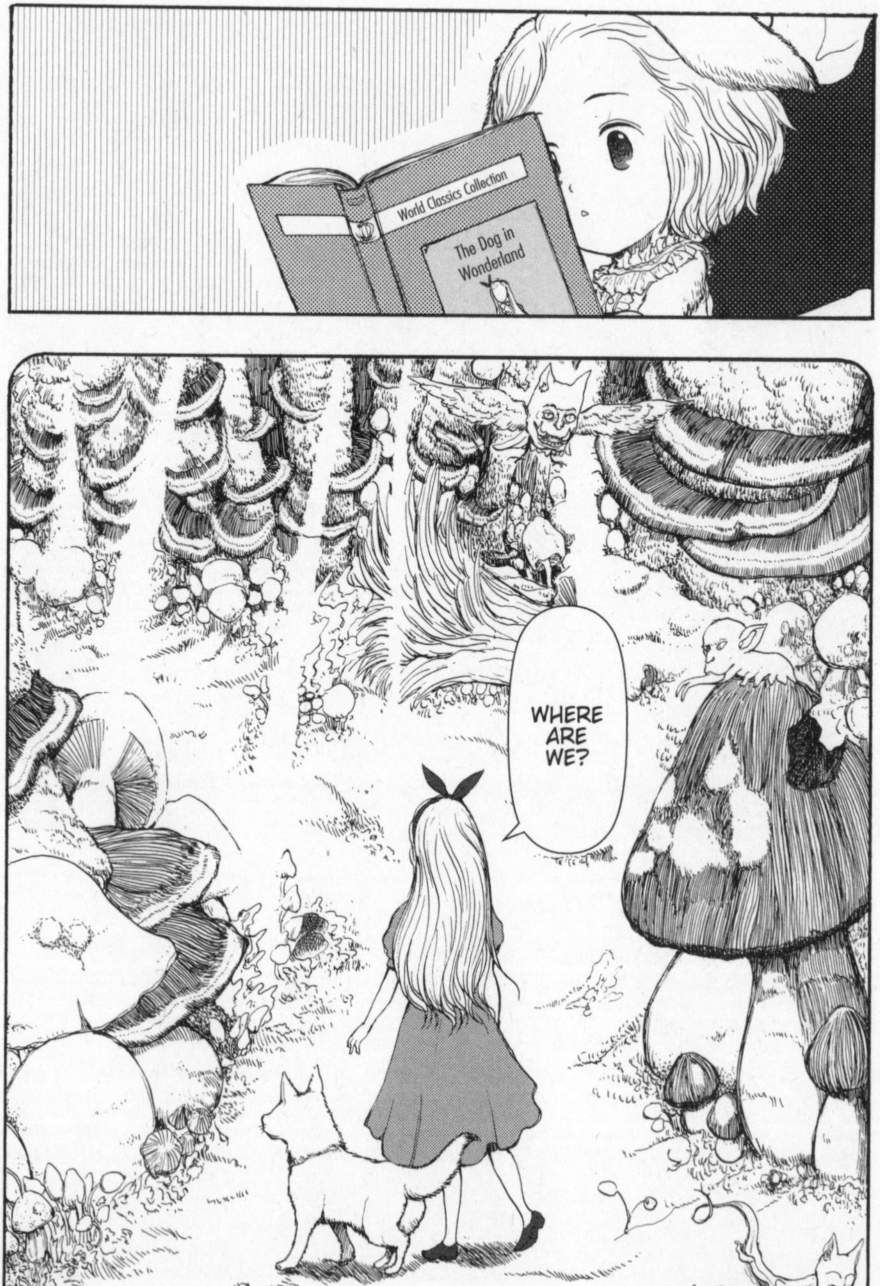
World Classics Collection
The Dog in Wonderland
WHERE ARE WE?

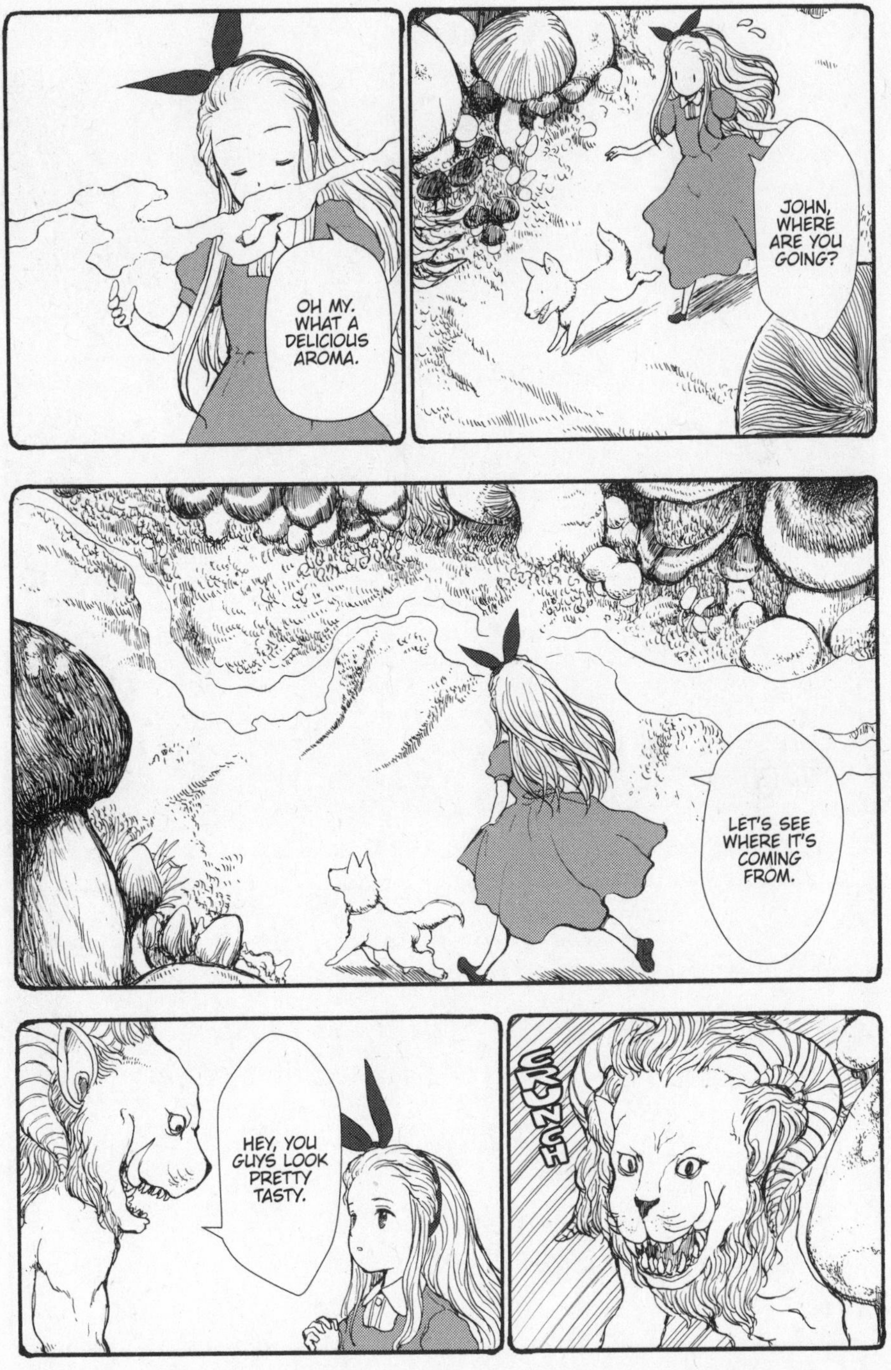

JOHN, WHERE ARE YOU GOING?
OH MY. WHAT A DELICIOUS AROMA.
LET'S SEE WHERE IT'S COMING FROM.
CRUNCH
HEY, YOU GUYS LOOK PRETTY TASTY.

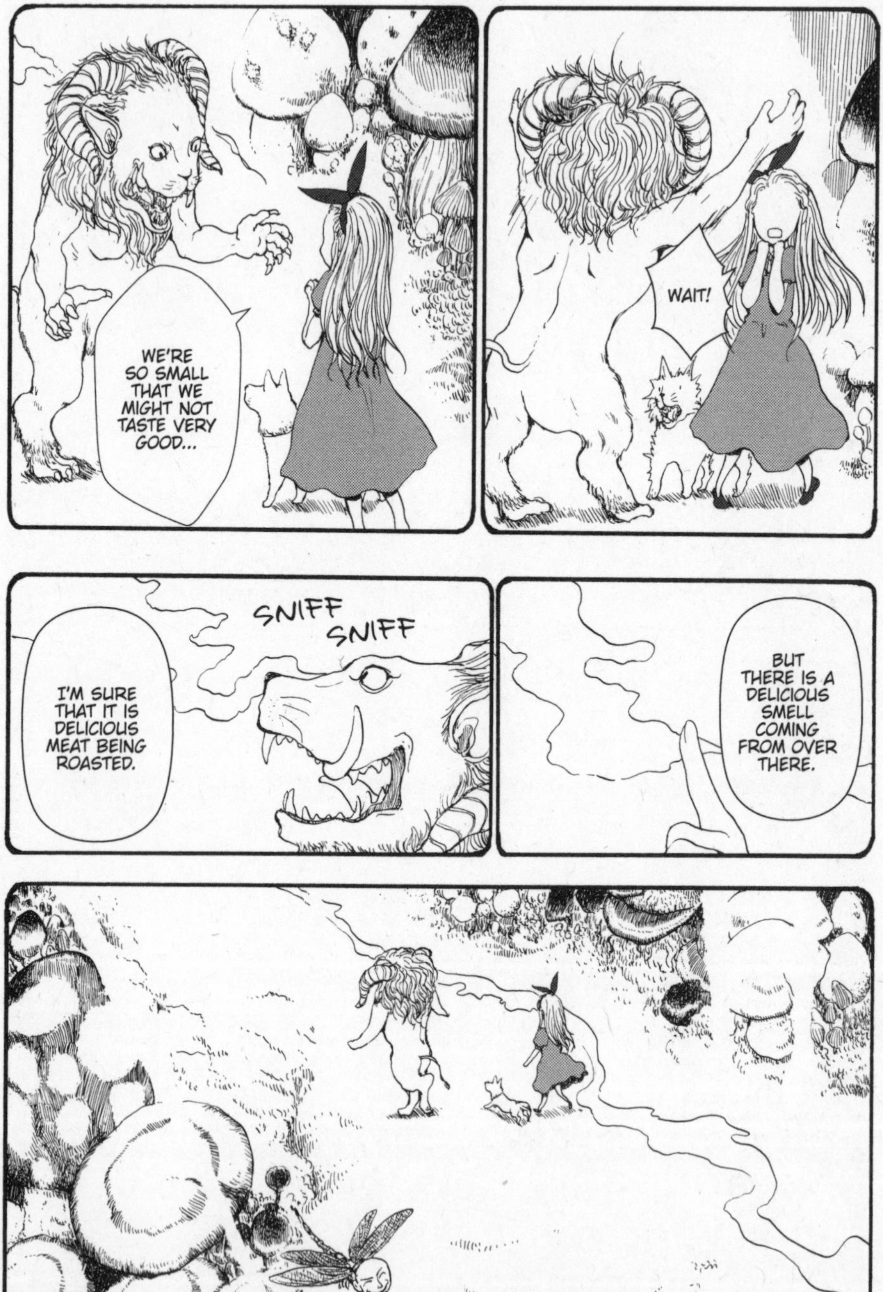
WAIT!
WE'RE SO SMALL THAT WE MIGHT NOT TASTE VERY GOOD...
BUT THERE IS A DELICIOUS SMELL COMING FROM OVER THERE.
SNIFF SNIFF
I'M SURE THAT IT IS DELICIOUS MEAT BEING ROASTED.

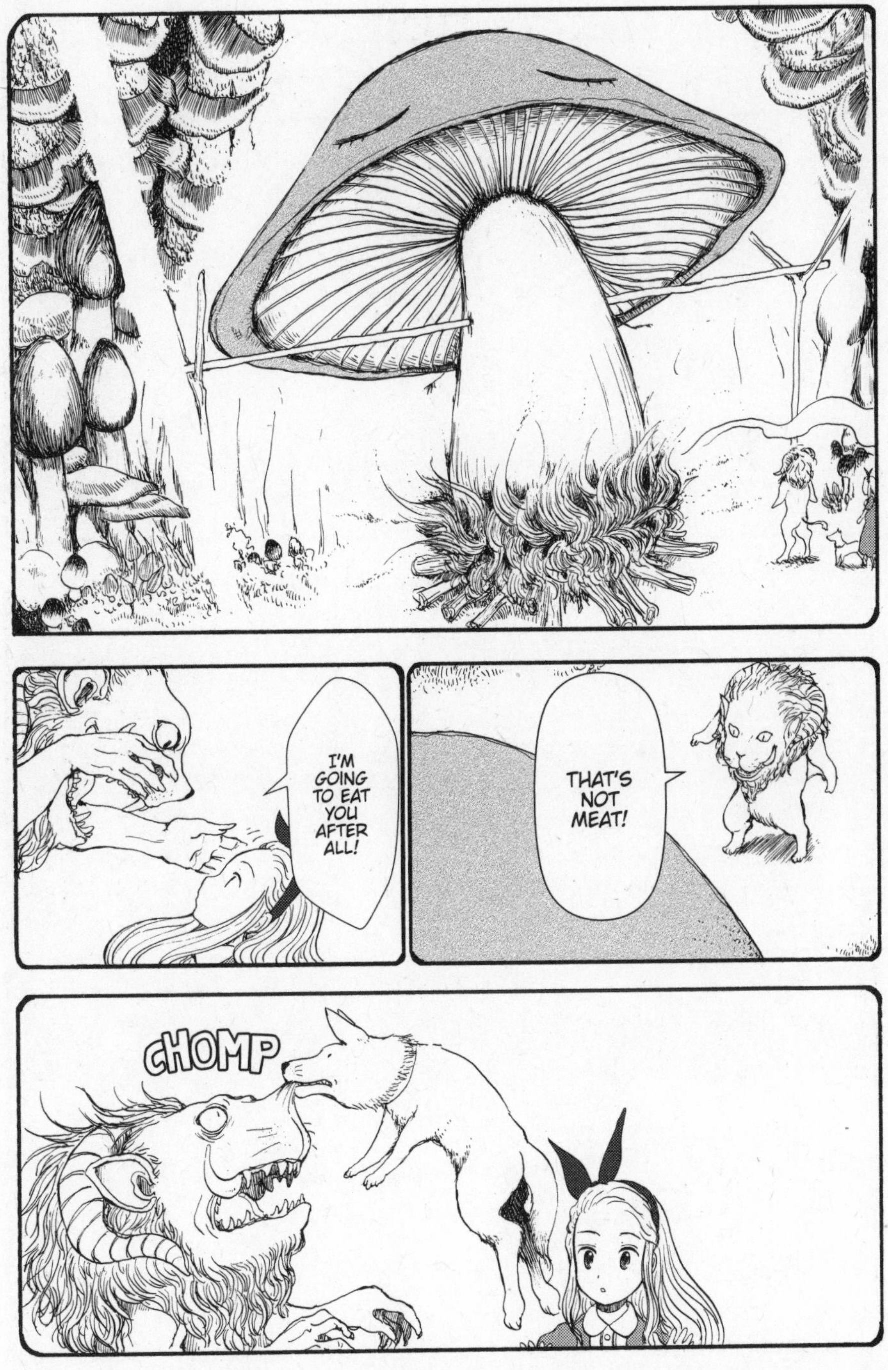
THAT'S NOT MEAT!
I'M GOING TO EAT YOU AFTER ALL!
CHOMP

S-Save me! I'm going to be eaten--!
Settle, boy.
BARK
BARK
TWIST
I WONDER IF THIS IS EDIBLE.
カッ
OPEN
KO
OM!

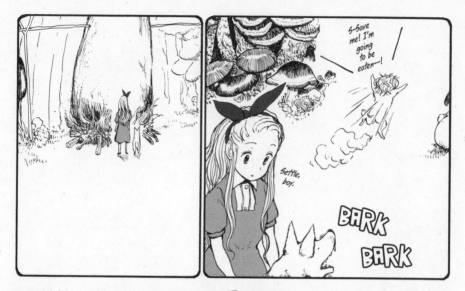

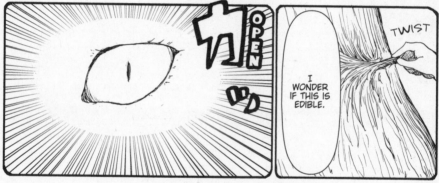

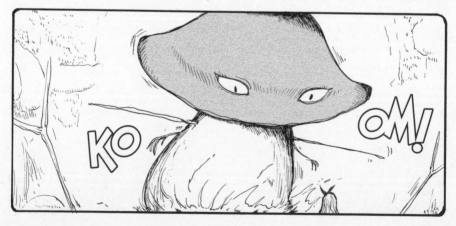

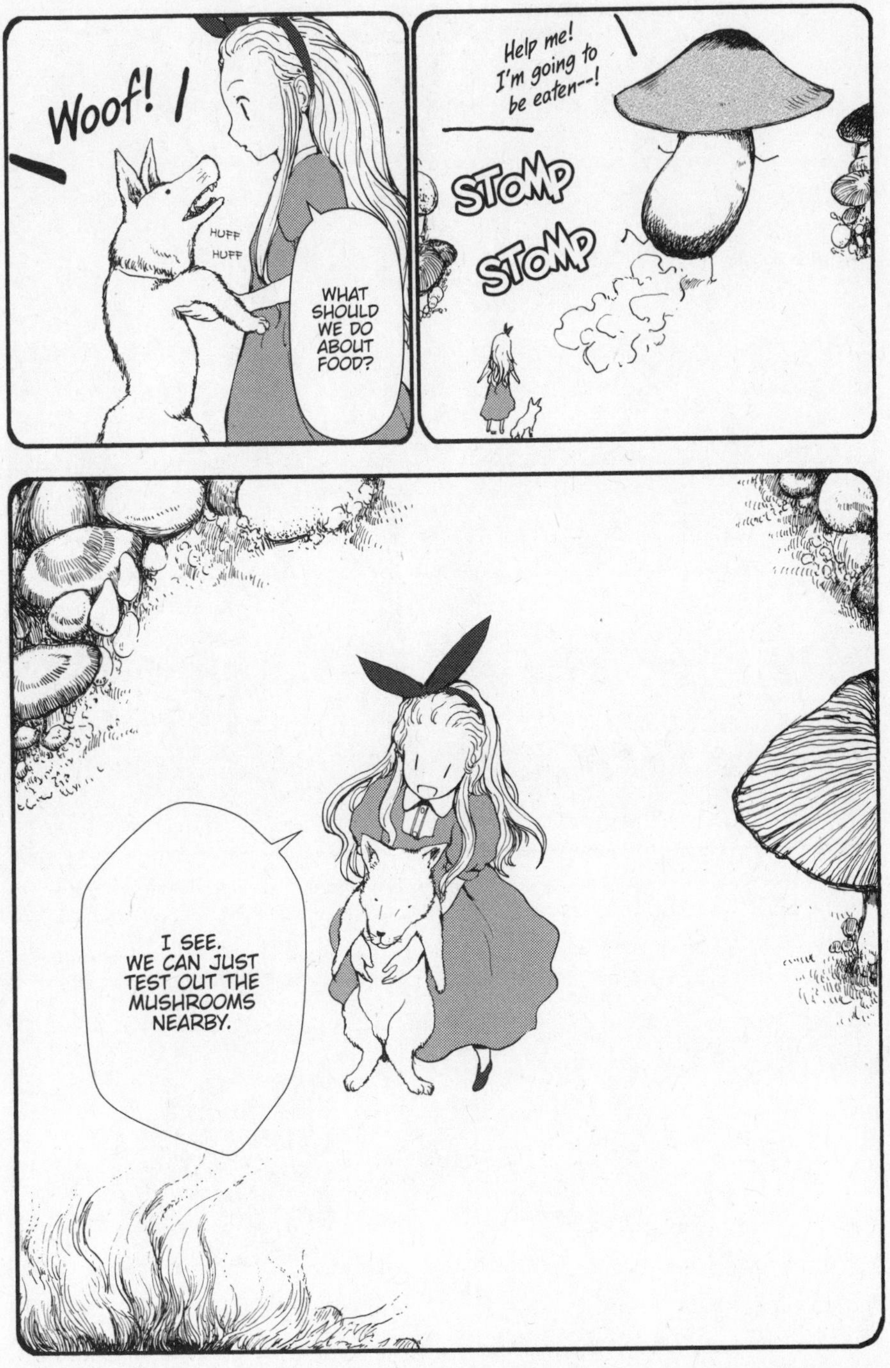
Help me! I'm going to be eaten--!
STOMP
STOMP
Woof!
HUFF HUFF
WHAT SHOULD WE DO ABOUT FOOD?
I SEE. WE CAN JUST TEST OUT THE MUSHROOMS NEARBY.

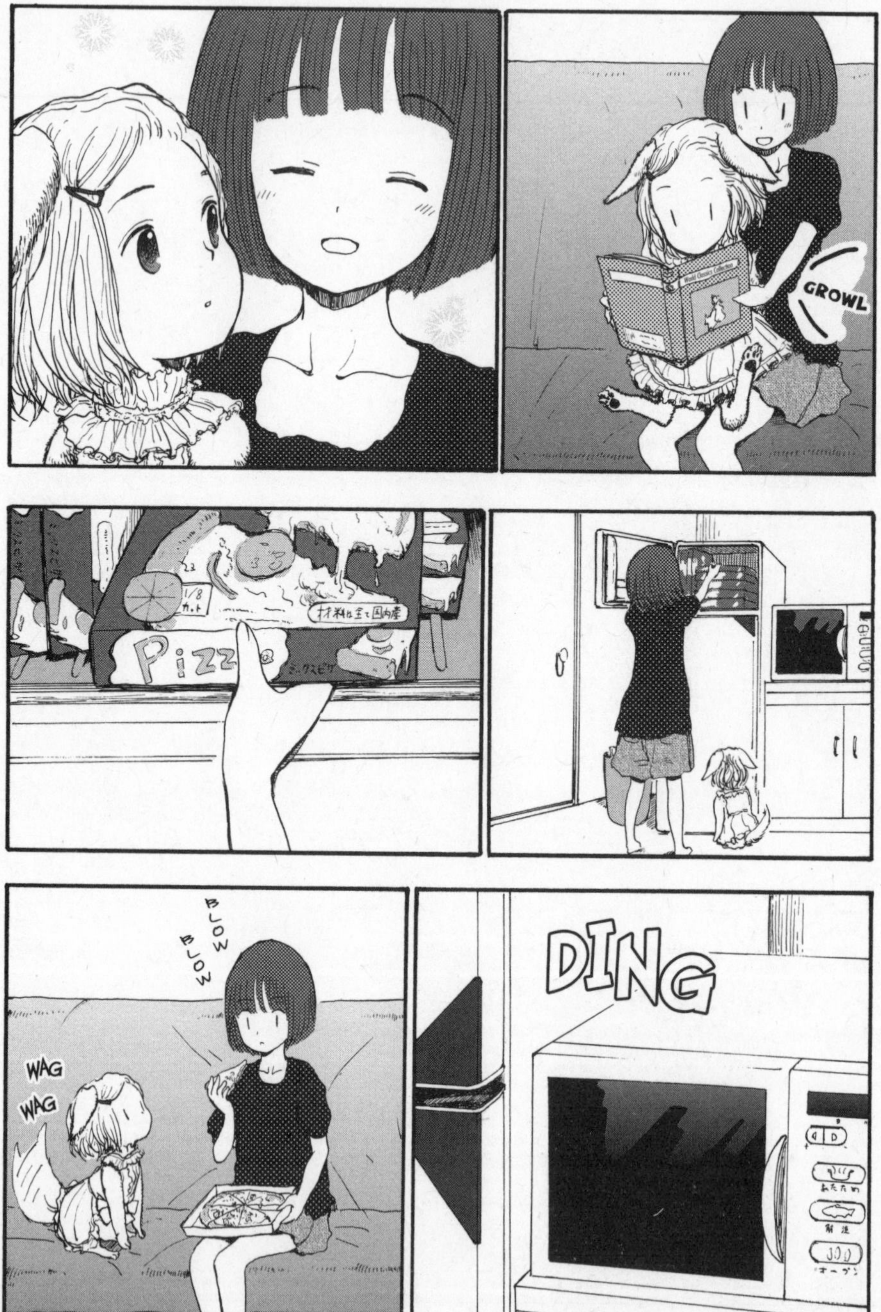
GROWL
1/8 カット
材料は全て国内産
DING
あたため
解凍
オーブン
BLOW BLOW
WAG WAG

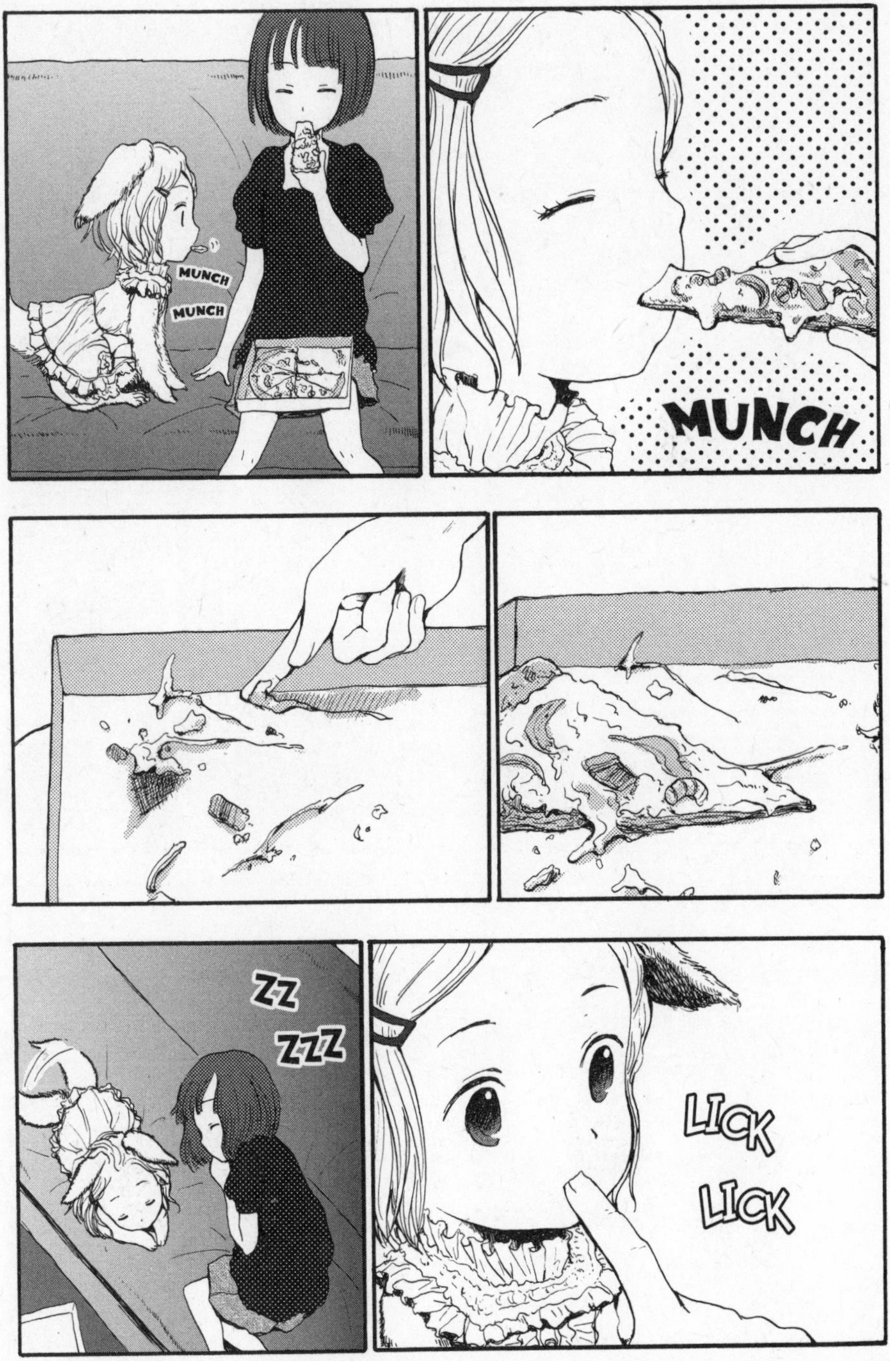
MUNCH
MUNCH
MUNCH
LICK
LICK
ZZ
ZZZ

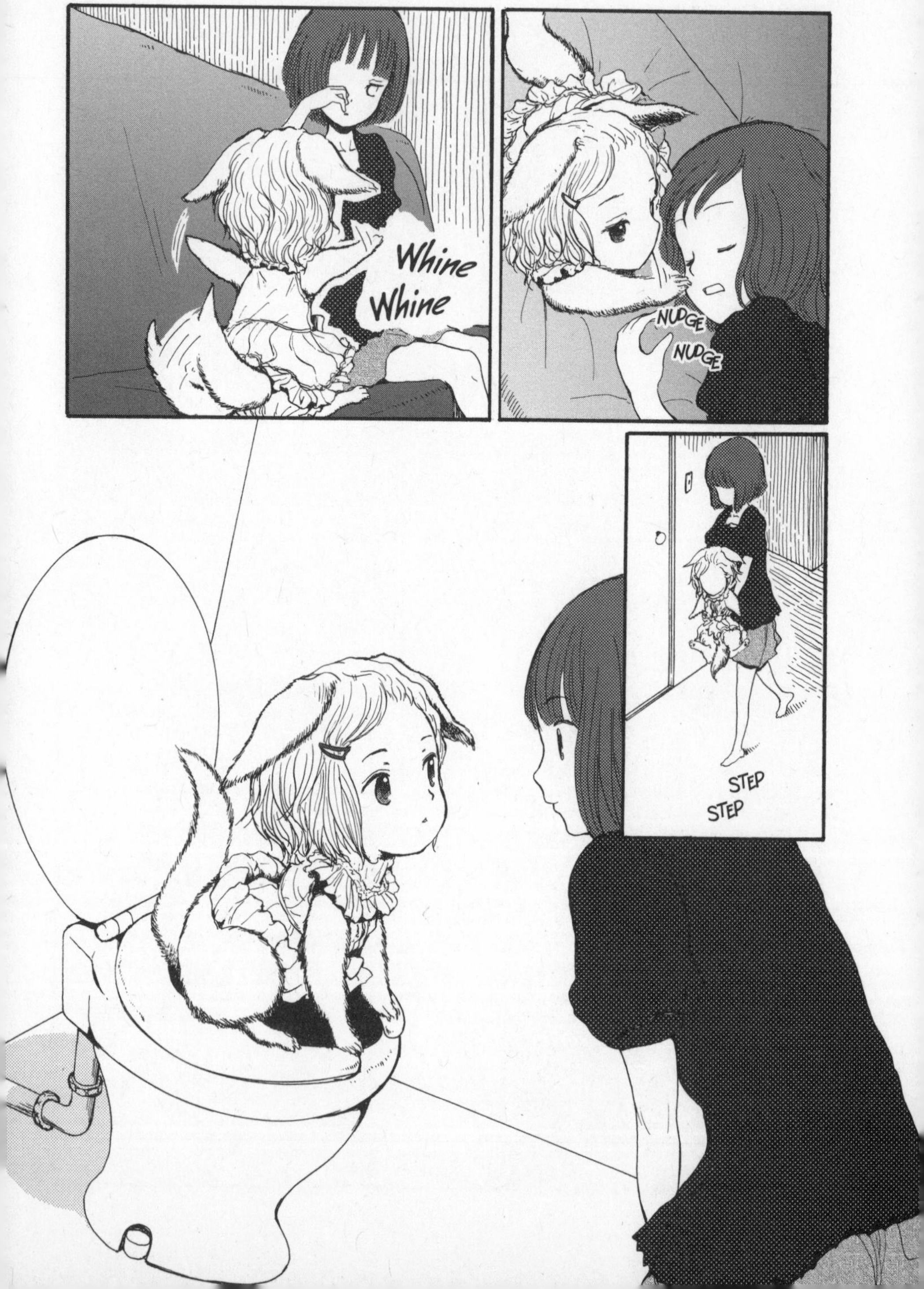
NUDGE
NUDGE
Whine
Whine
STEP
STEP

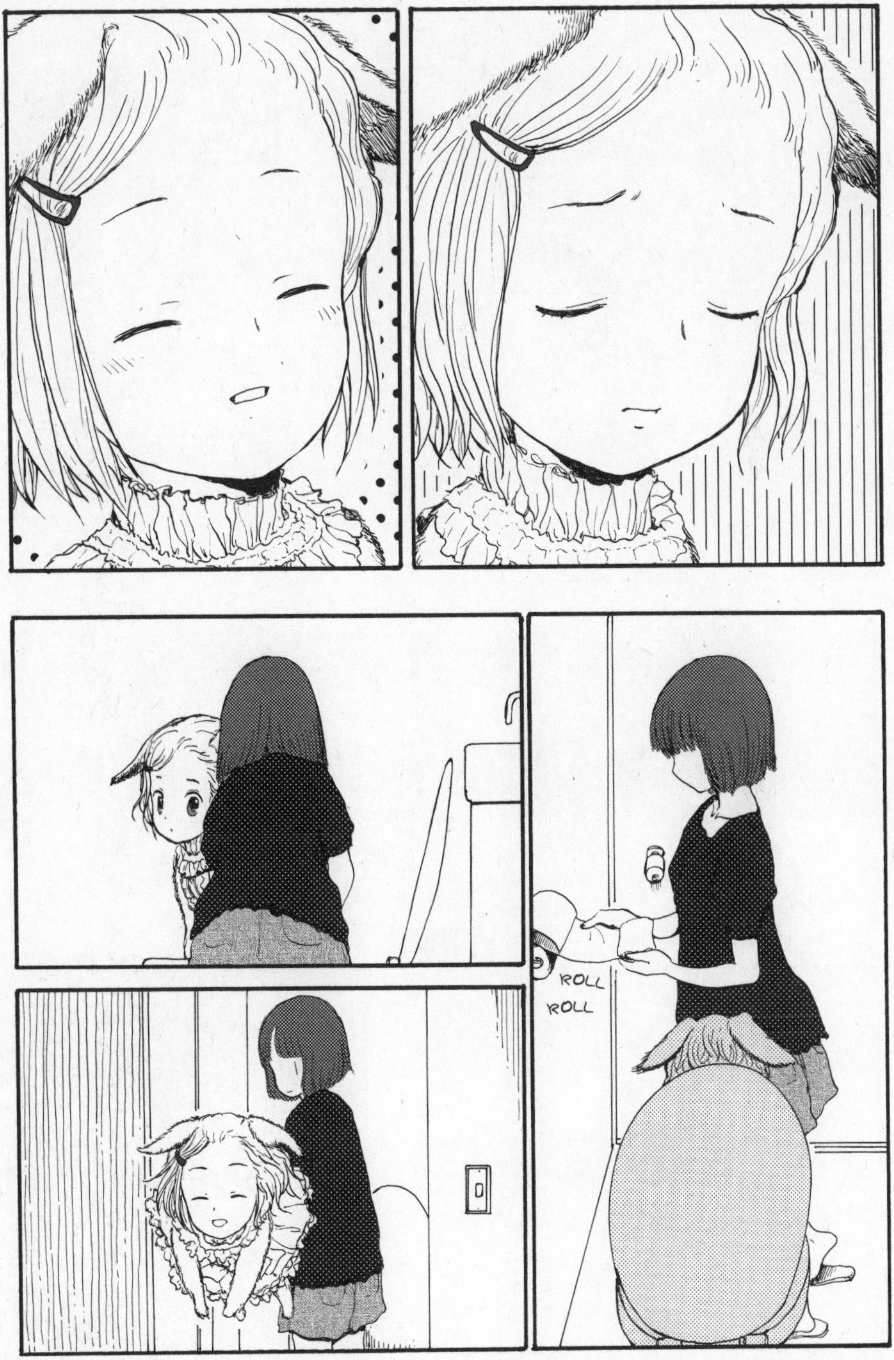
ROLL
ROLL

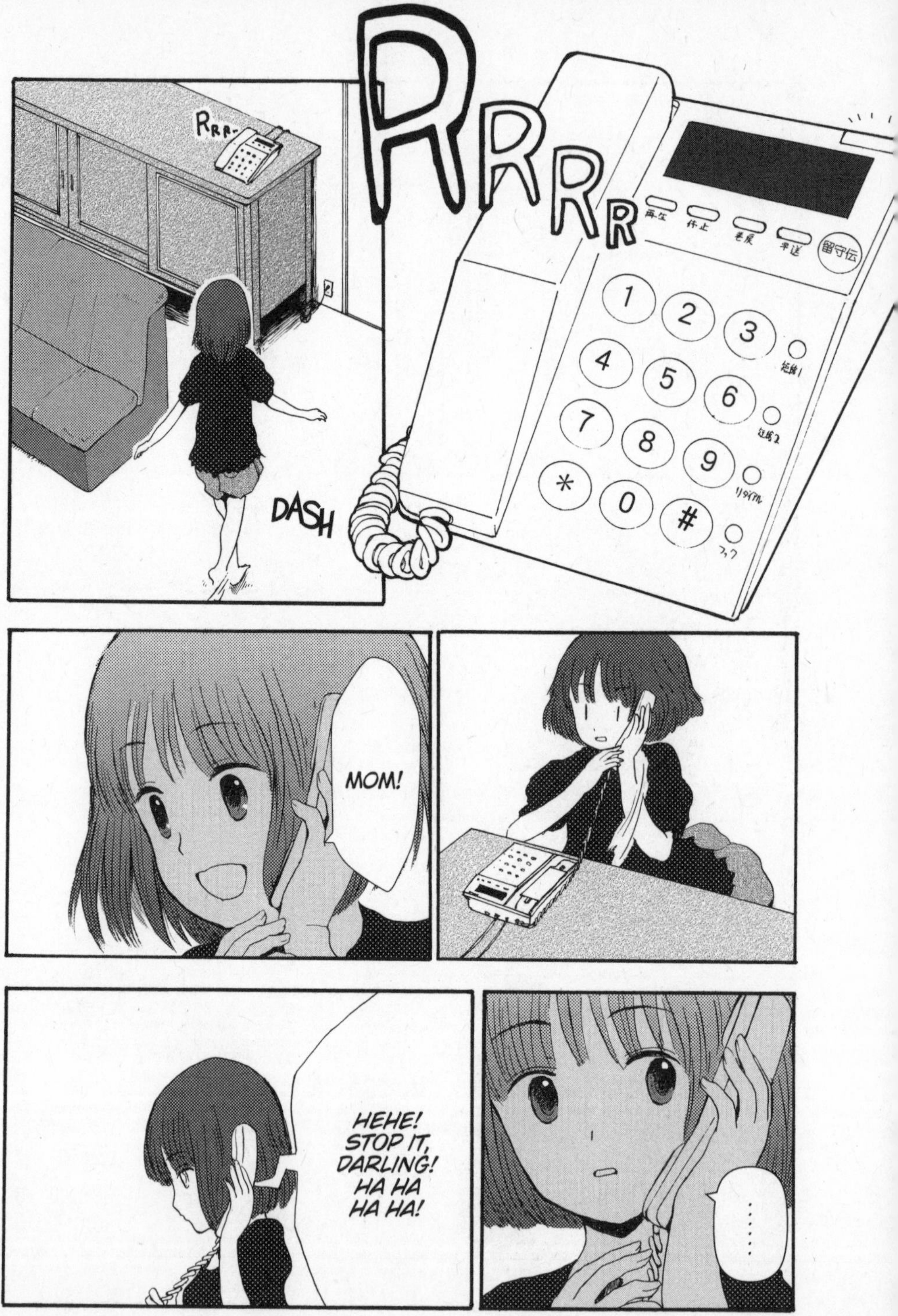
RRRR
Rrr-
DASH
MOM!
......
HEHE! STOP IT, DARLING! HA HA HA HA!

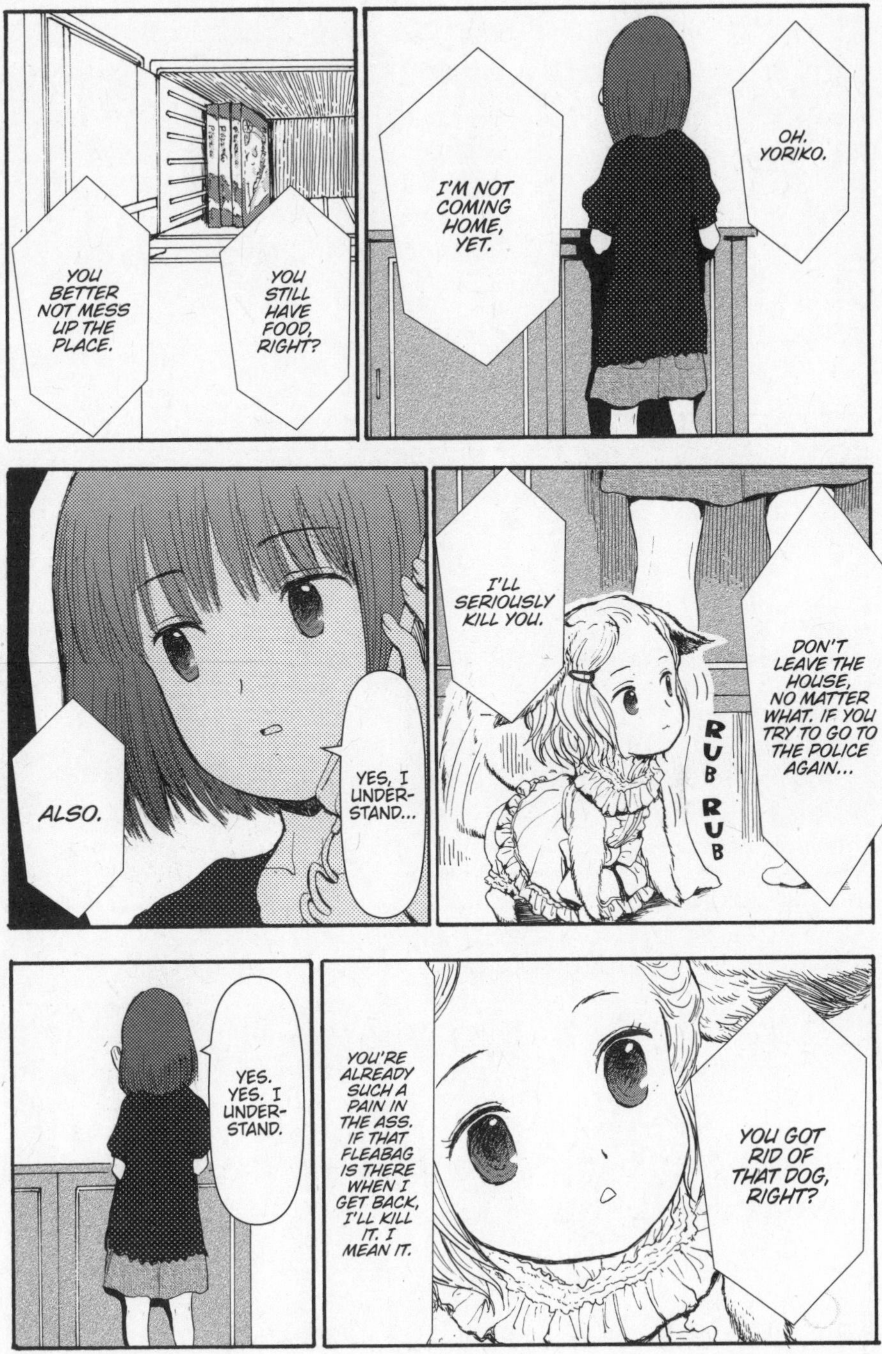
OH. YORIKO.
I'M NOT COMING HOME, YET.
YOU STILL HAVE FOOD, RIGHT?
YOU BETTER NOT MESS UP THE PLACE.
DON'T LEAVE THE HOUSE, NO MATTER WHAT. IF YOU TRY TO GO TO THE POLICE AGAIN...
RUB RUB
I'LL SERIOUSLY KILL YOU.
YES, I UNDER-STAND...
ALSO.
YOU GOT RID OF THAT DOG, RIGHT?
YOU'RE ALREADY SUCH A PAIN IN THE ASS. IF THAT FLEABAG IS THERE WHEN I GET BACK, I'LL KILL IT. I MEAN IT.
YES. YES. I UNDER-STAND.

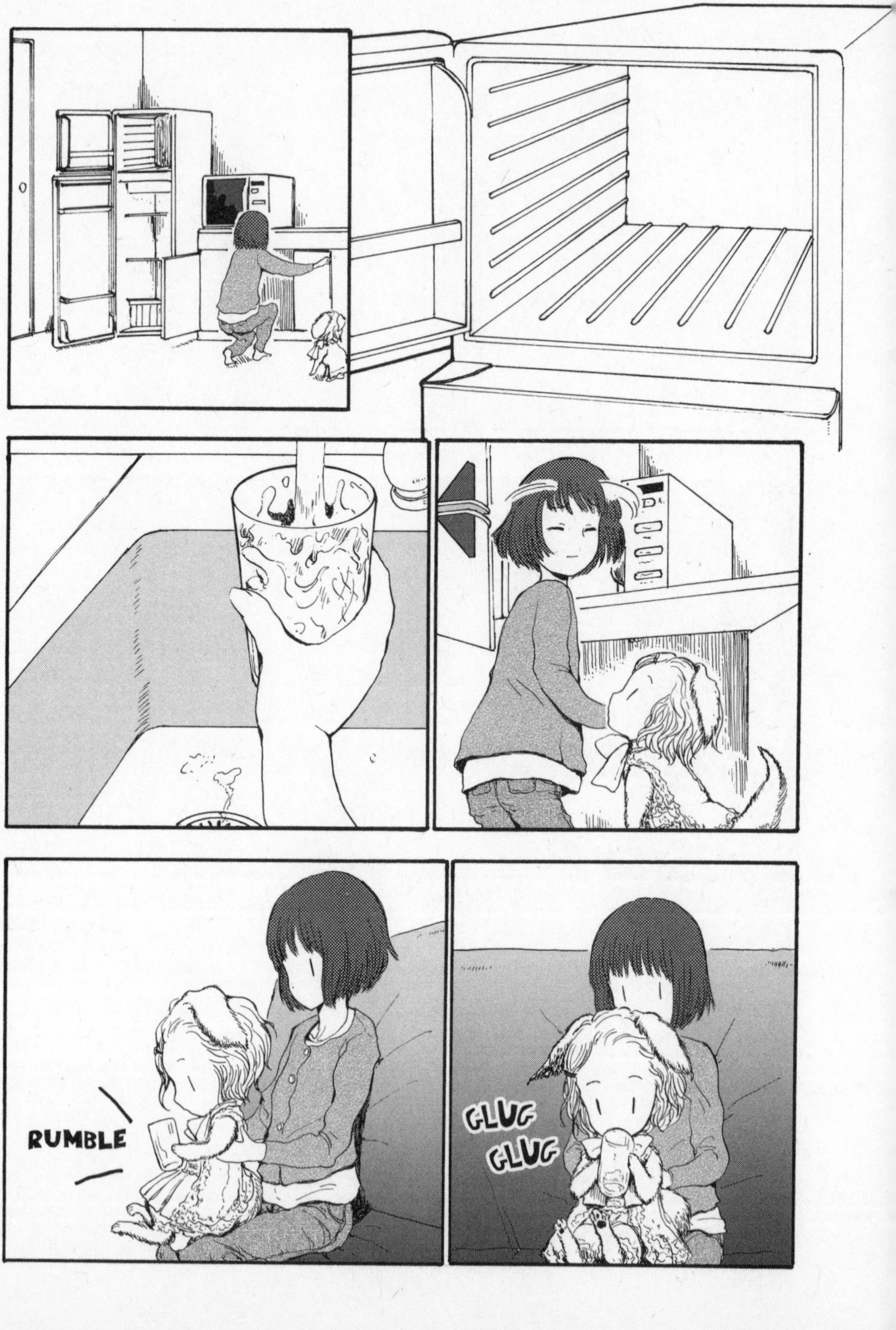
GLUG
GLUG
RUMBLE

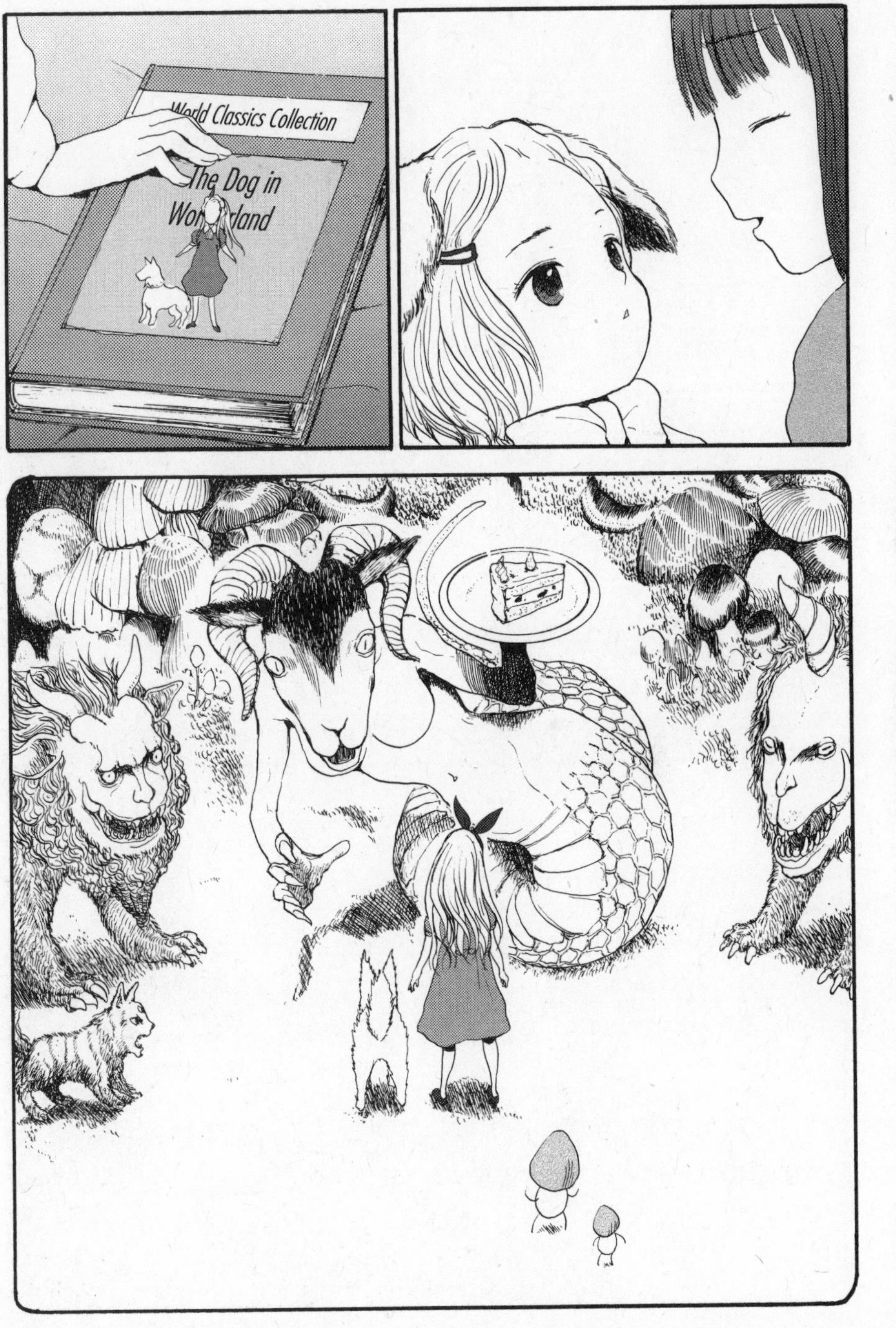
World Classics Collection
The Dog in

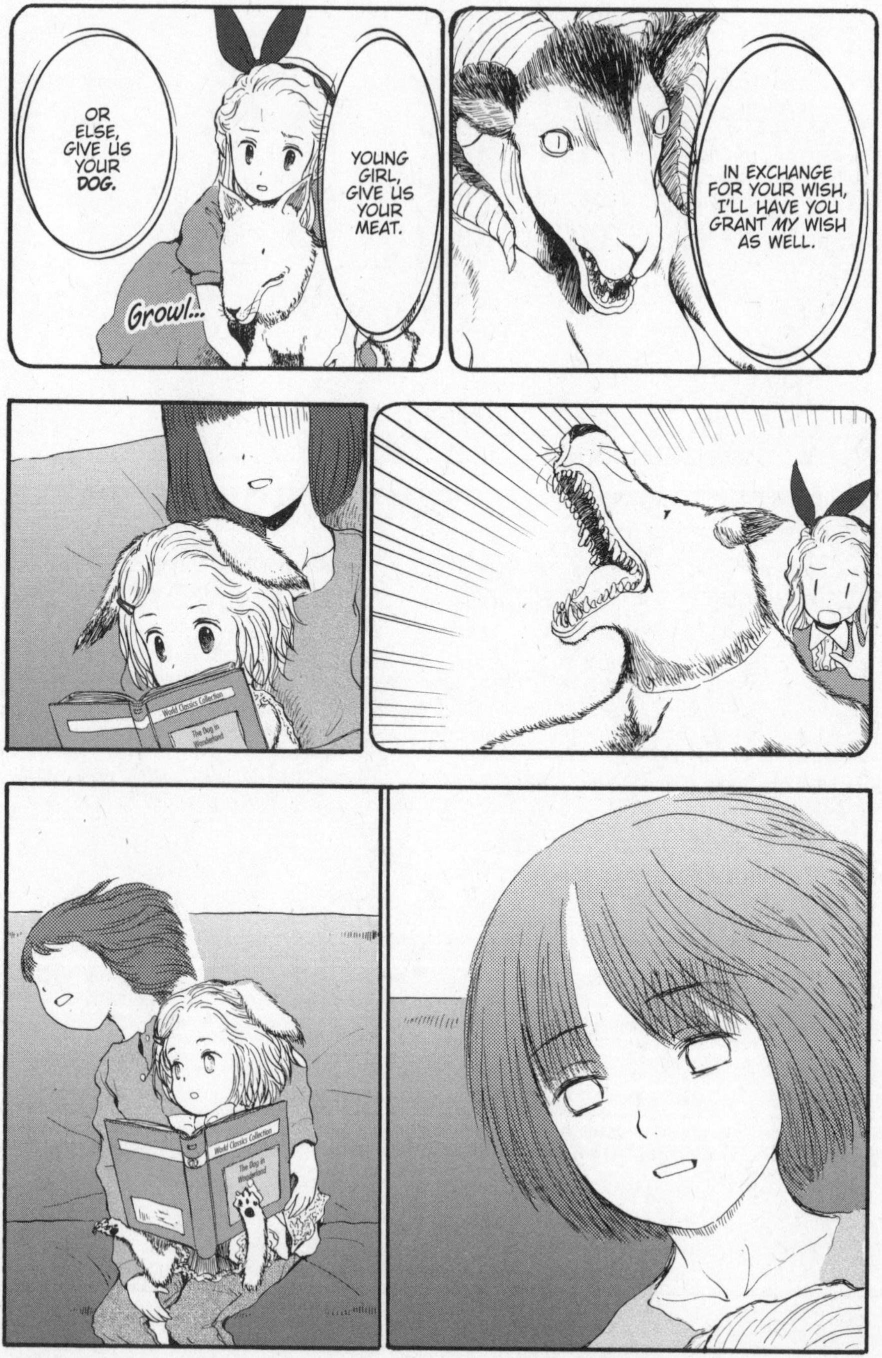
IN EXCHANGE FOR YOUR WISH, I'LL HAVE YOU GRANT *MY* WISH AS WELL.
YOUNG GIRL, GIVE US YOUR MEAT.
OR ELSE, GIVE US YOUR **DOG**.
Growl...
World Classics Collection
The Dog in Wonderland
World Classics Collection
The Dog in Wonderland

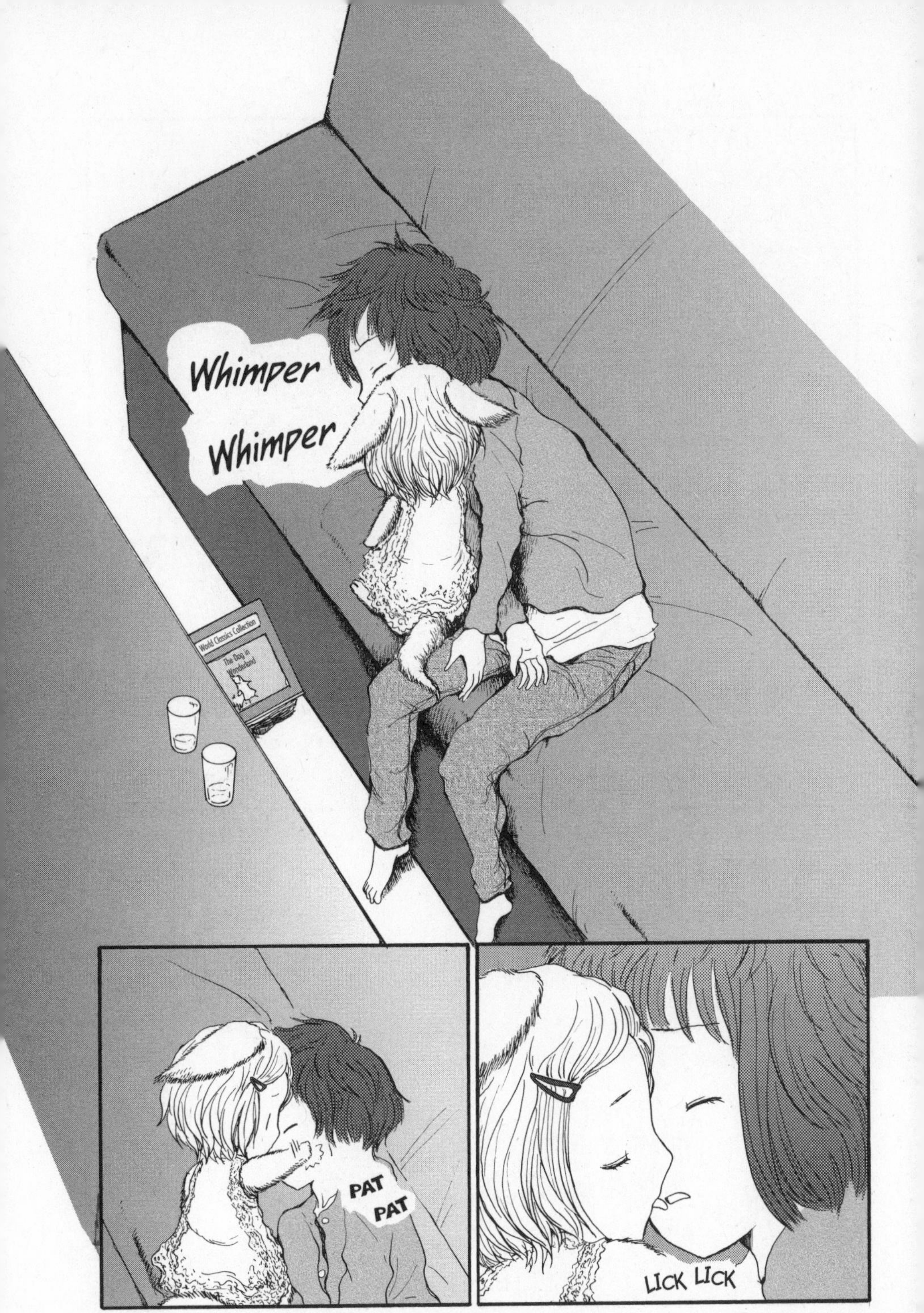
Whimper
Whimper
World Classics Collection
The Dog in Wonderland
LICK LICK
PAT
PAT

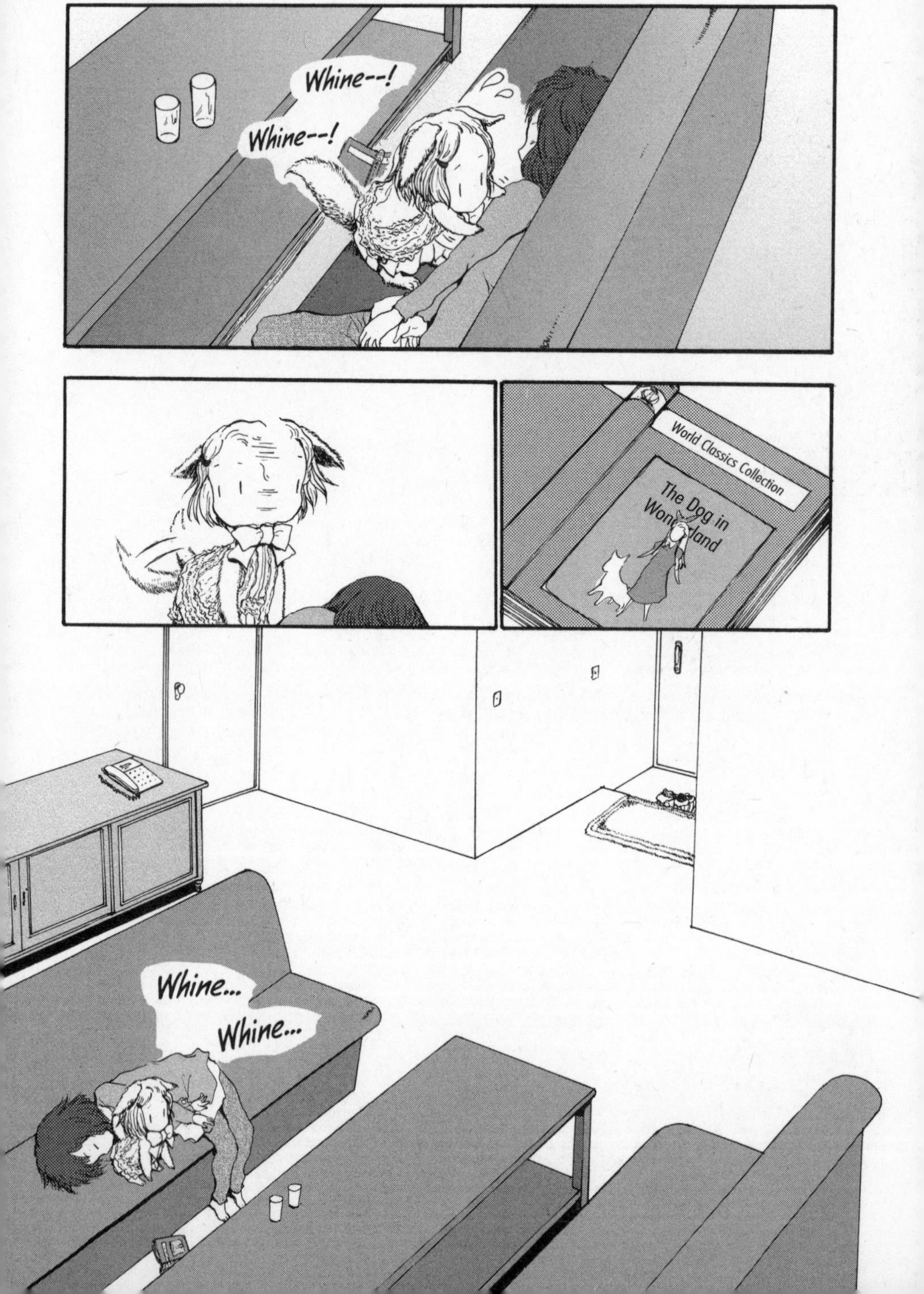
Whine--!
Whine--!
World Classics Collection
The Dog in
Whine...
Whine...

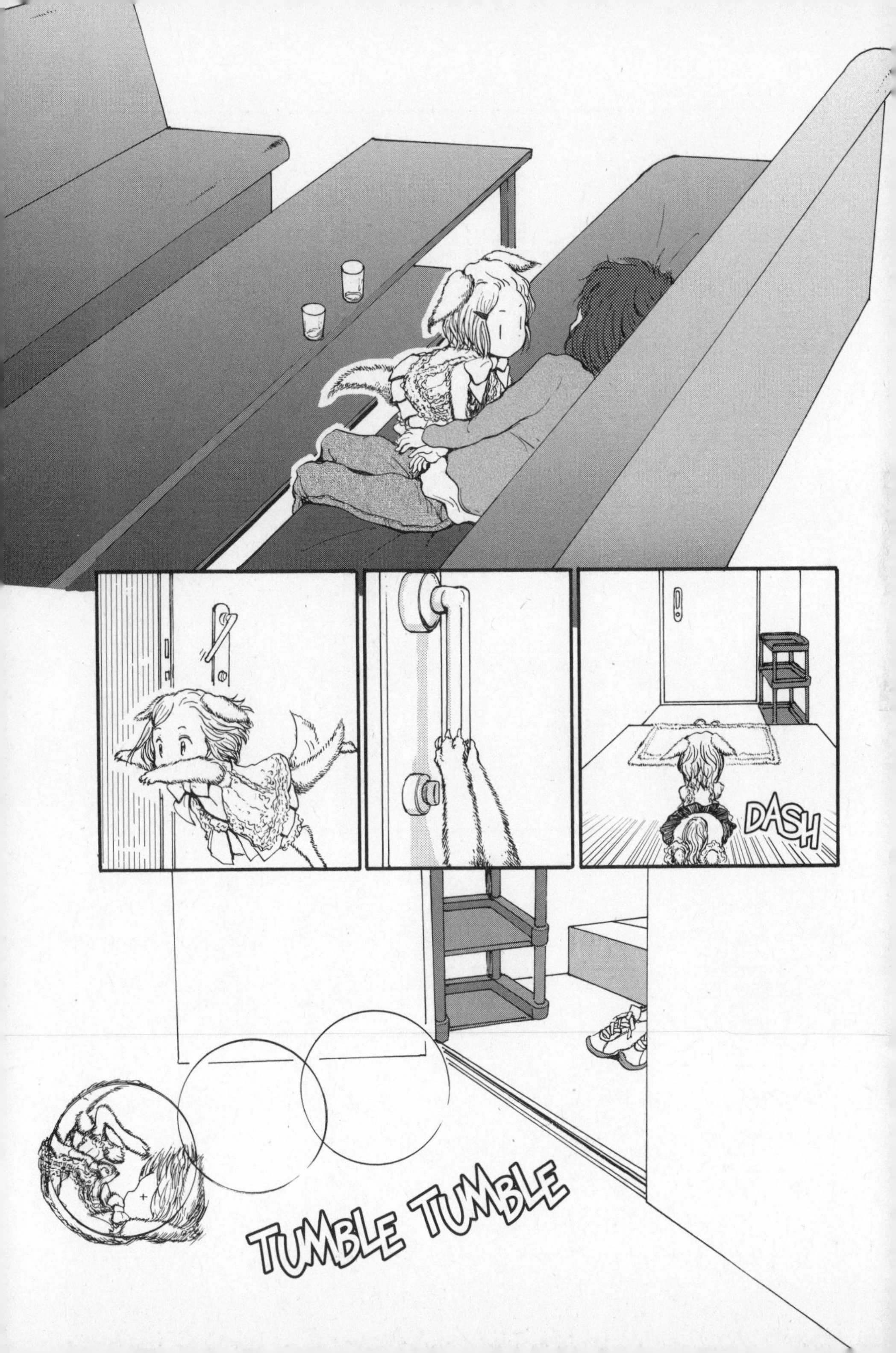
DASH
TUMBLE TUMBLE

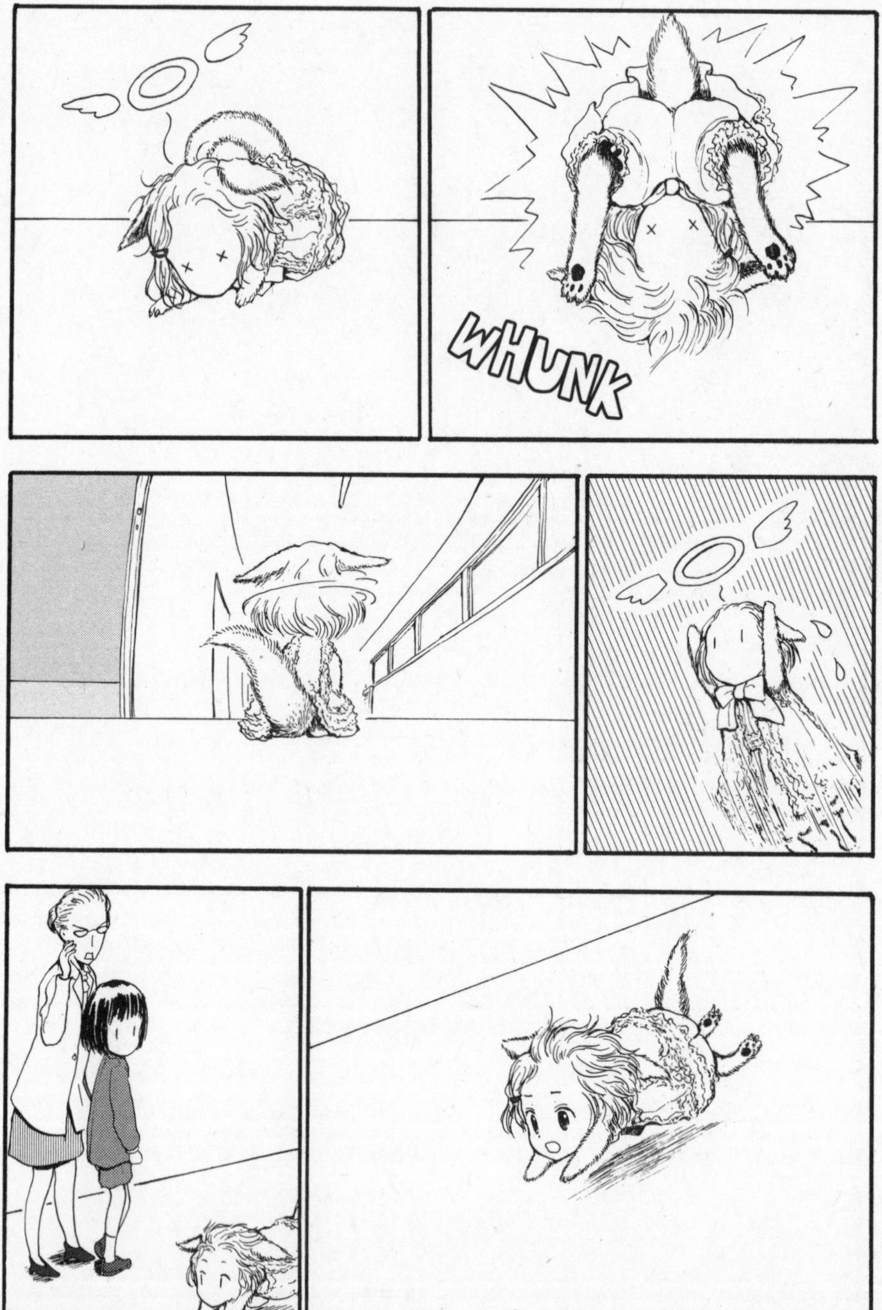
WHUNK

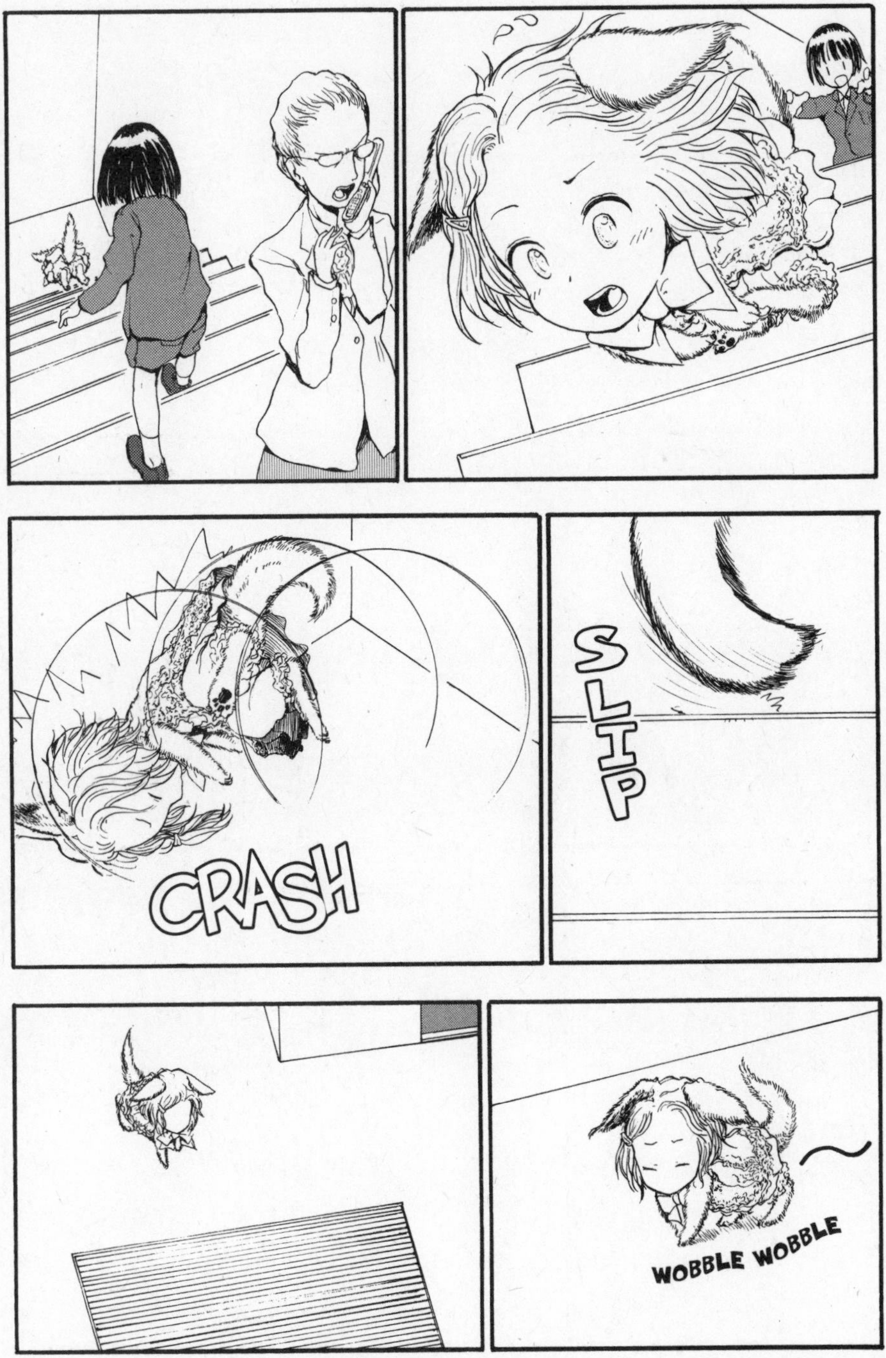
SLIP
CRASH
WOBBLE WOBBLE

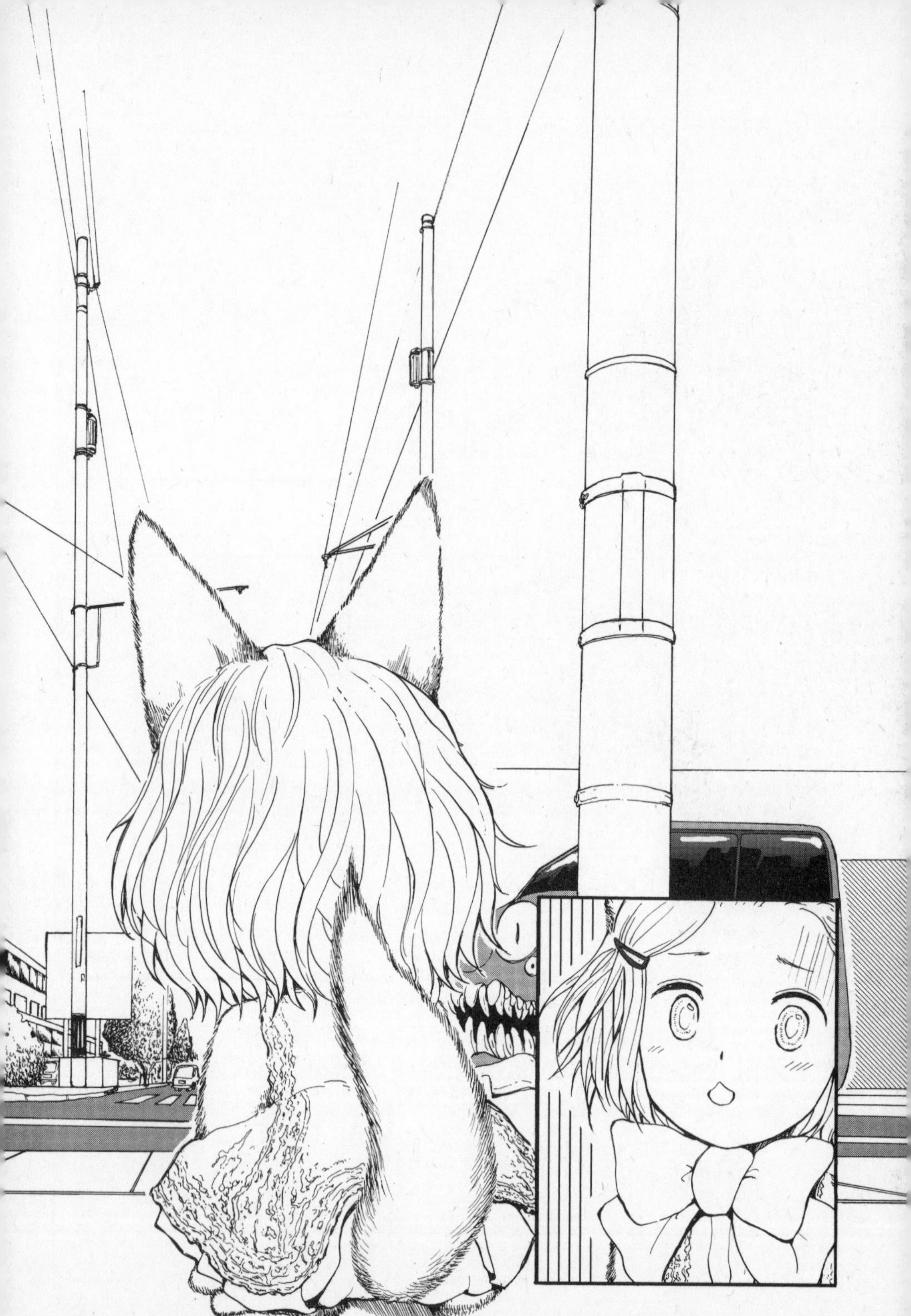

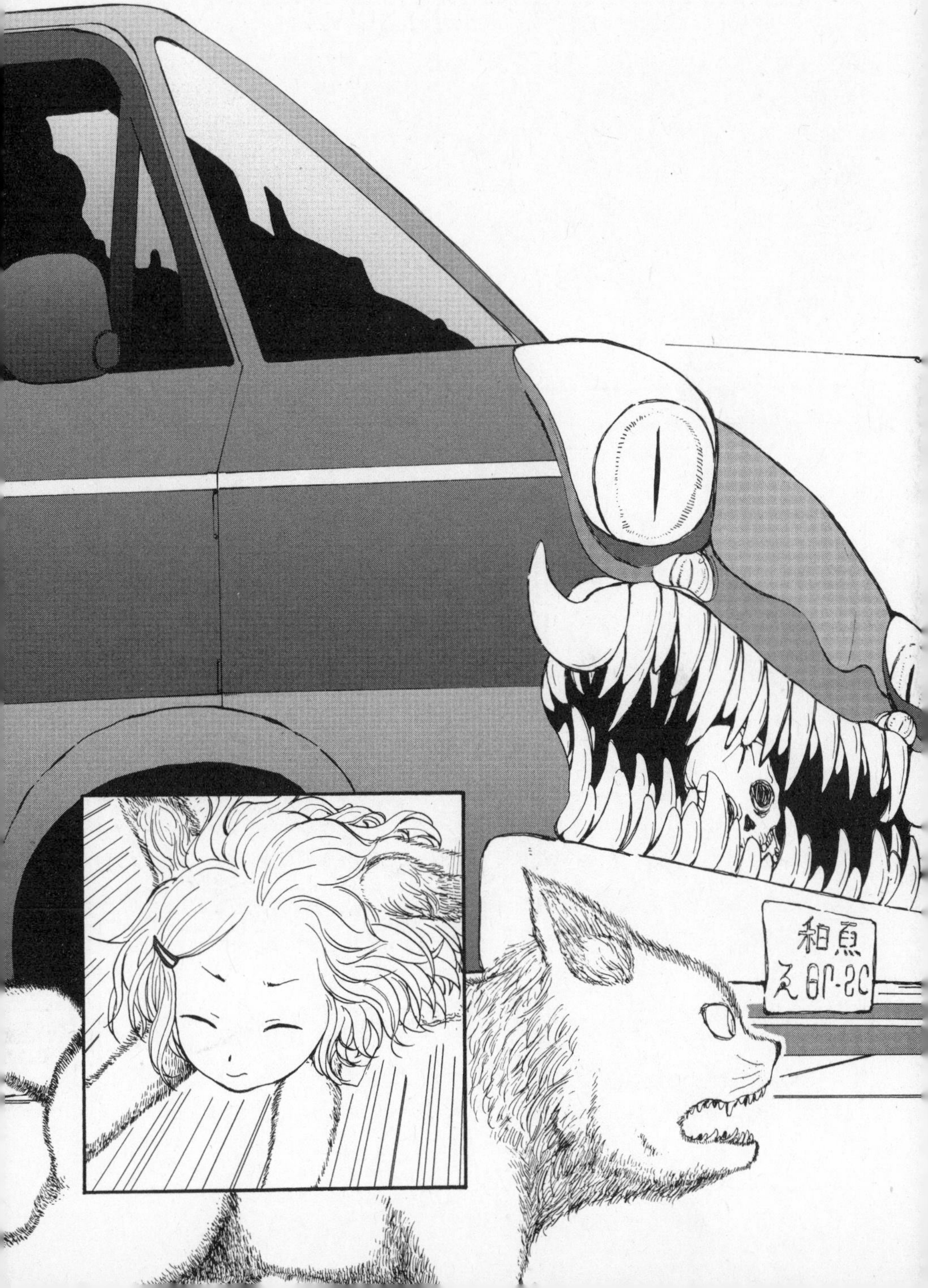

Whine

Whine

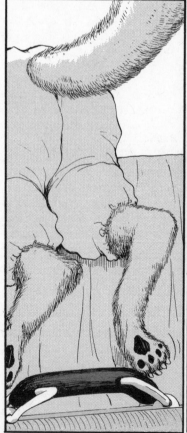

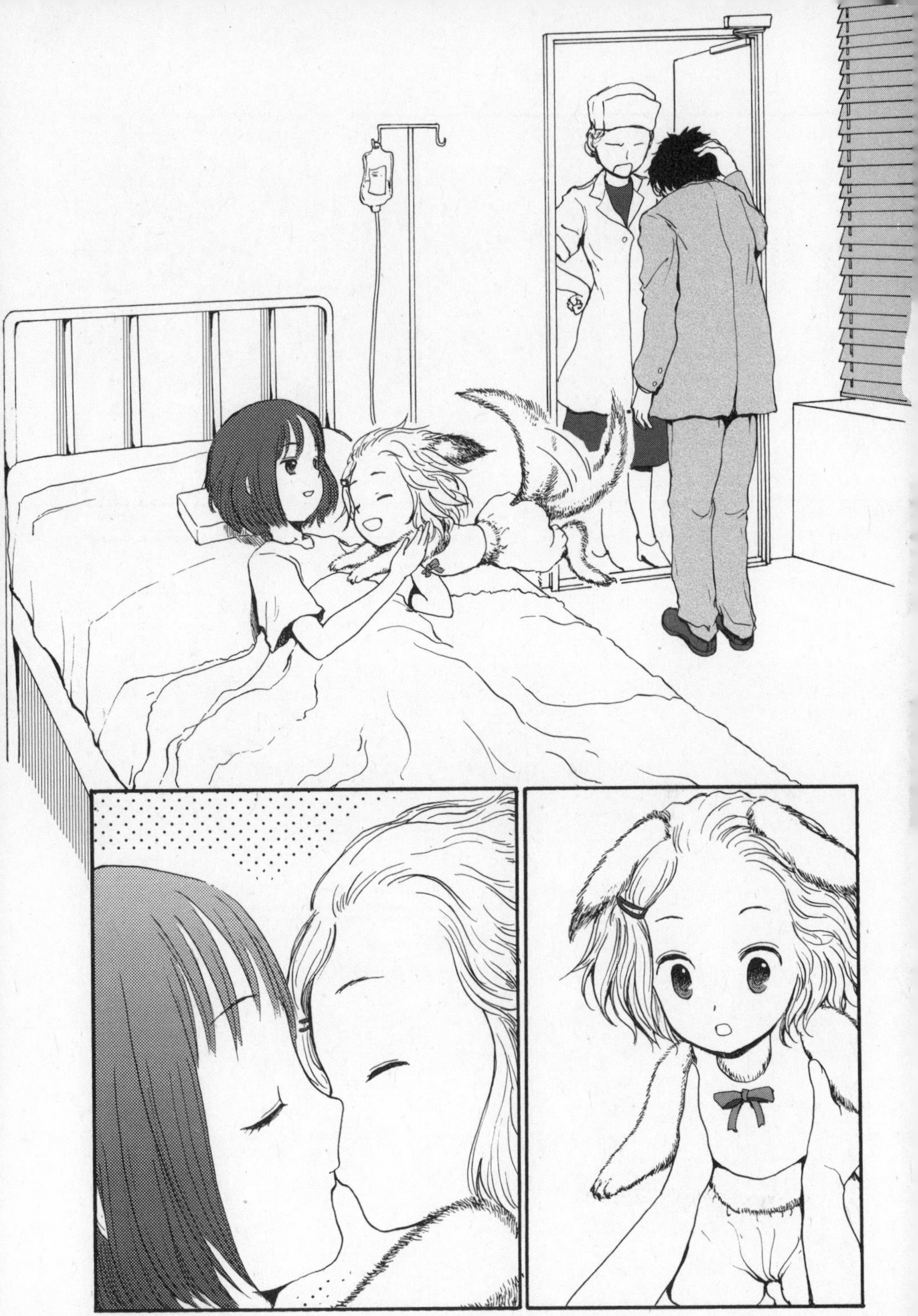

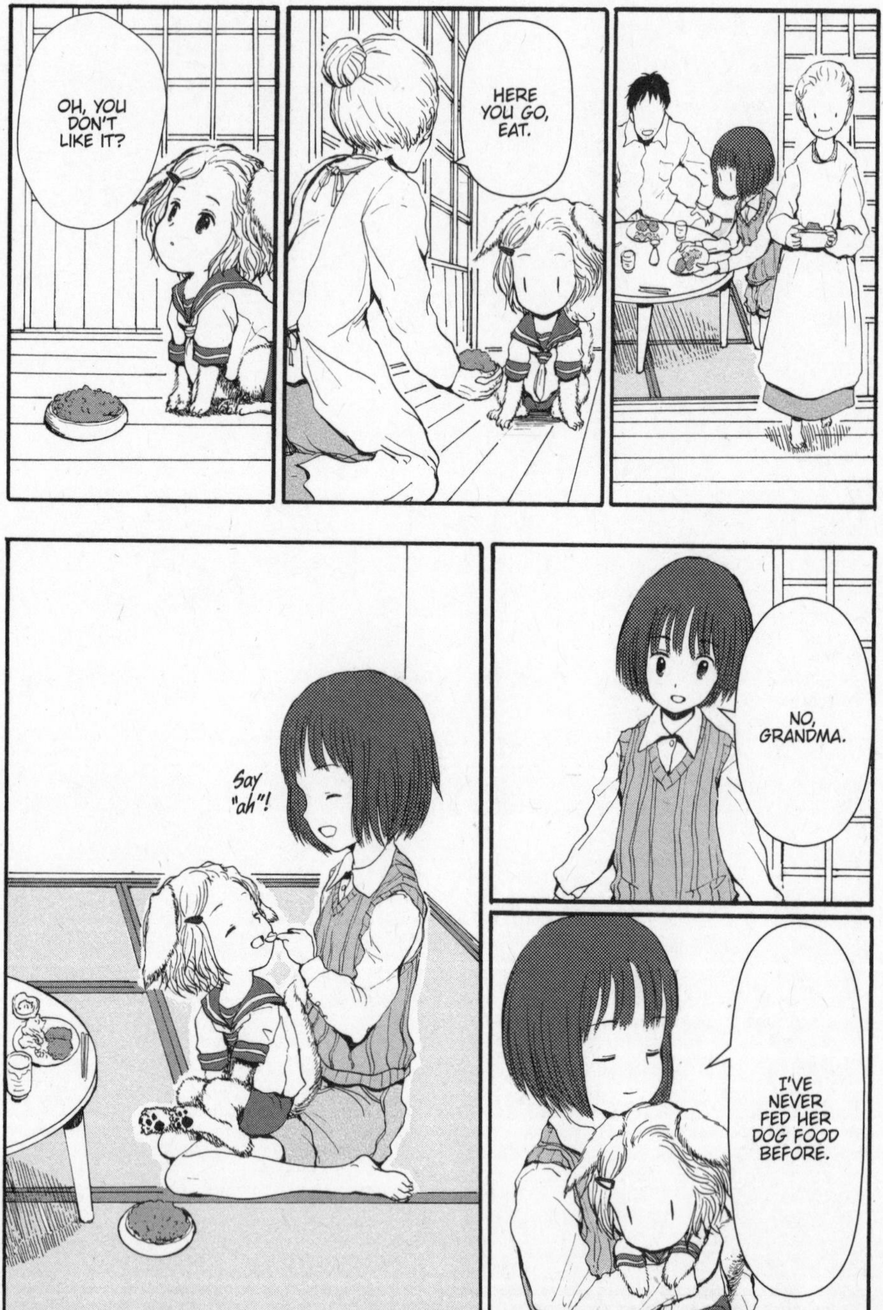
HERE YOU GO, EAT.
OH, YOU DON'T LIKE IT?
NO, GRANDMA.
I'VE NEVER FED HER DOG FOOD BEFORE.
Say "ah"!

A Centaur's Life

AFTERWORD...

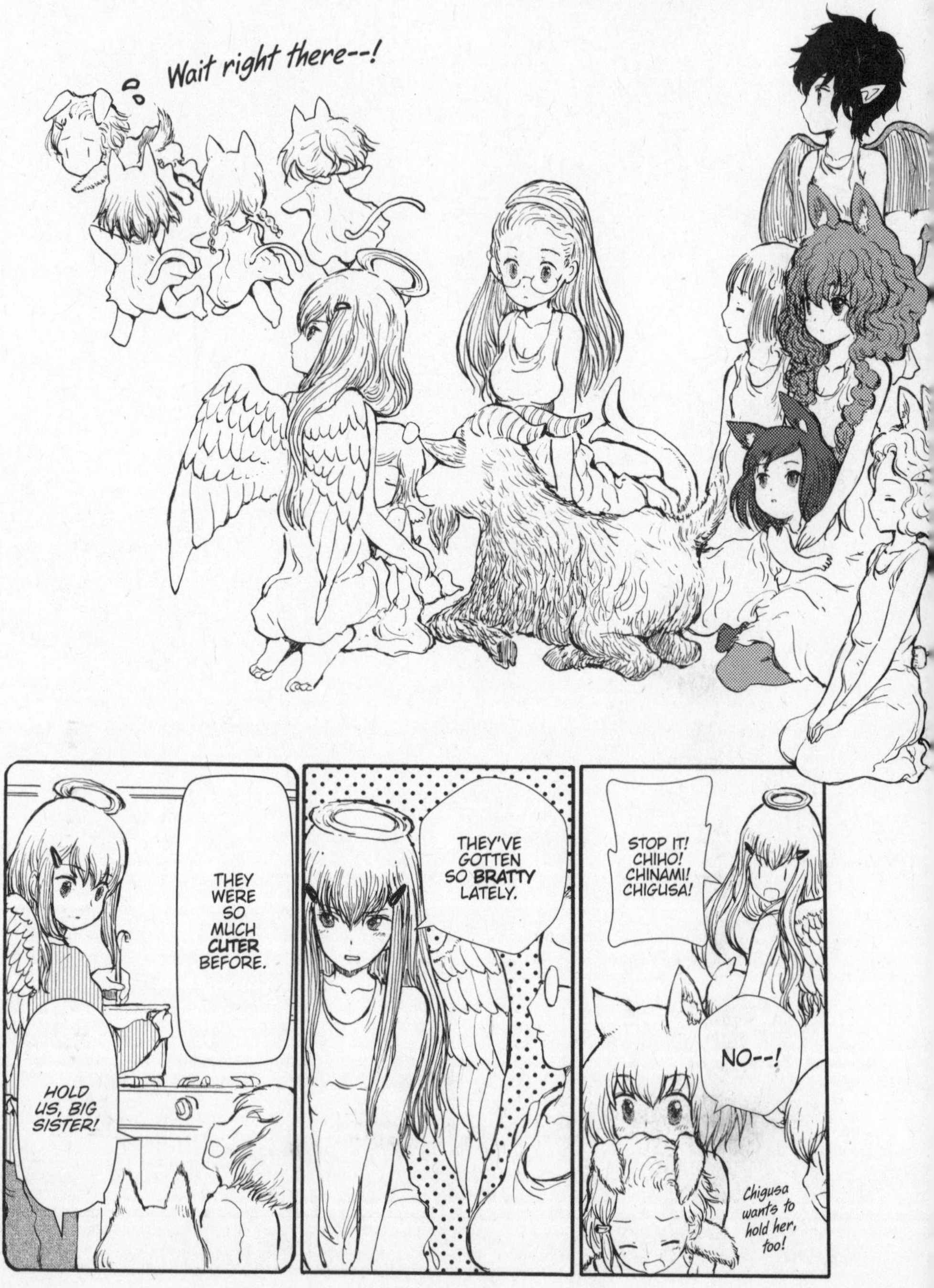

Wait right there--!
STOP IT! CHIHO! CHINAMI! CHIGUSA!
NO--!
Chigusa wants to hold her, too!
THEY'VE GOTTEN SO BRATTY LATELY.
THEY WERE SO MUCH CUTER BEFORE.
HOLD US, BIG SISTER!

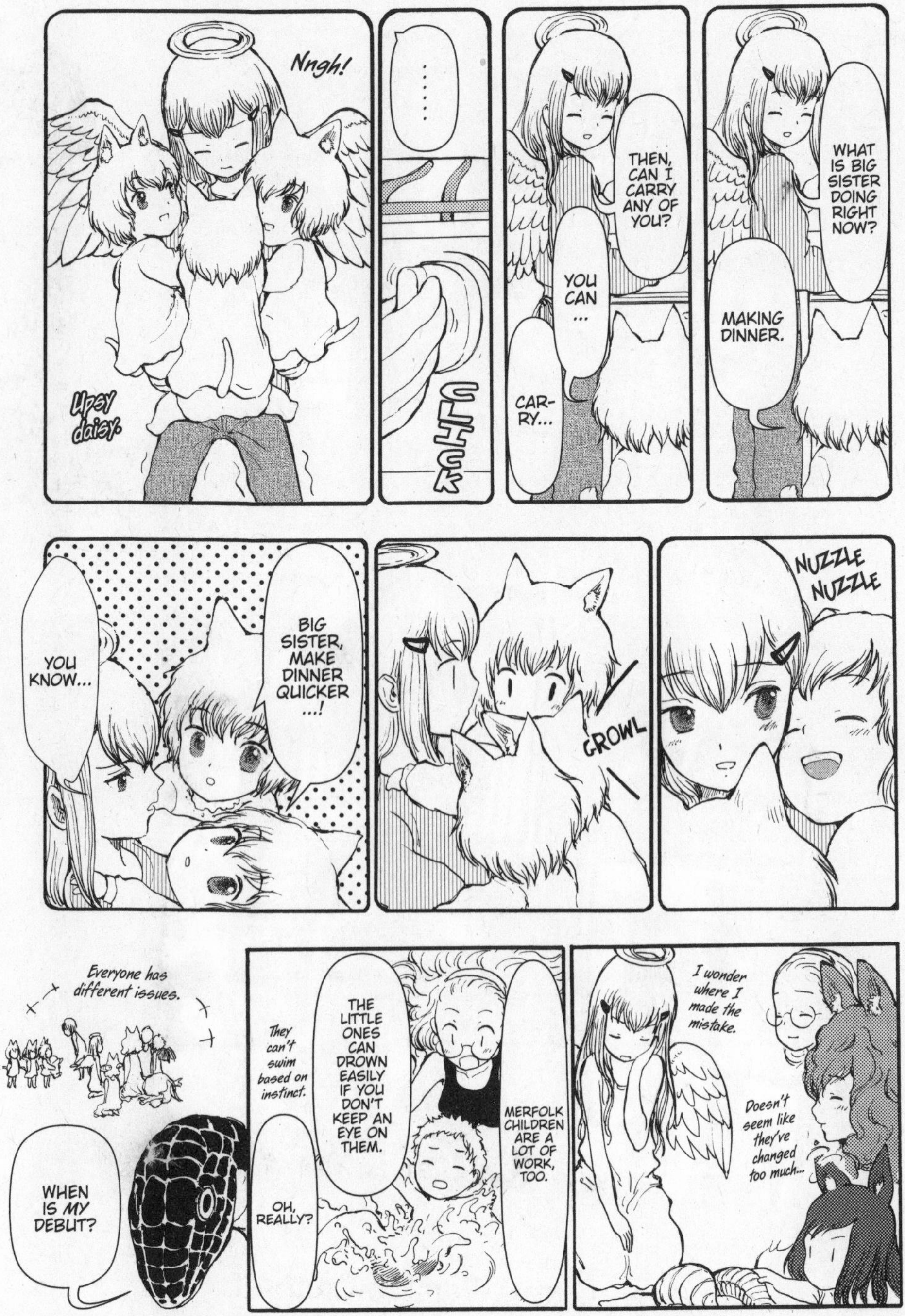
WHAT IS BIG SISTER DOING RIGHT NOW?
MAKING DINNER.
THEN, CAN I CARRY ANY OF YOU?
YOU CAN ...
CAR- RY...
......
CLICK
Nngh!
Upsy daisy.
NUZZLE NUZZLE
GROWL
BIG SISTER, MAKE DINNER QUICKER ...!
YOU KNOW...
I wonder where I made the mistake.
Doesn't seem like they've changed too much...
MERFOLK CHILDREN ARE A LOT OF WORK, TOO.
THE LITTLE ONES CAN DROWN EASILY IF YOU DON'T KEEP AN EYE ON THEM.
They can't swim based on instinct.
OH, REALLY?
Everyone has different issues.
WHEN IS MY DEBUT?

Experience all that SEVEN SEAS has to offer!

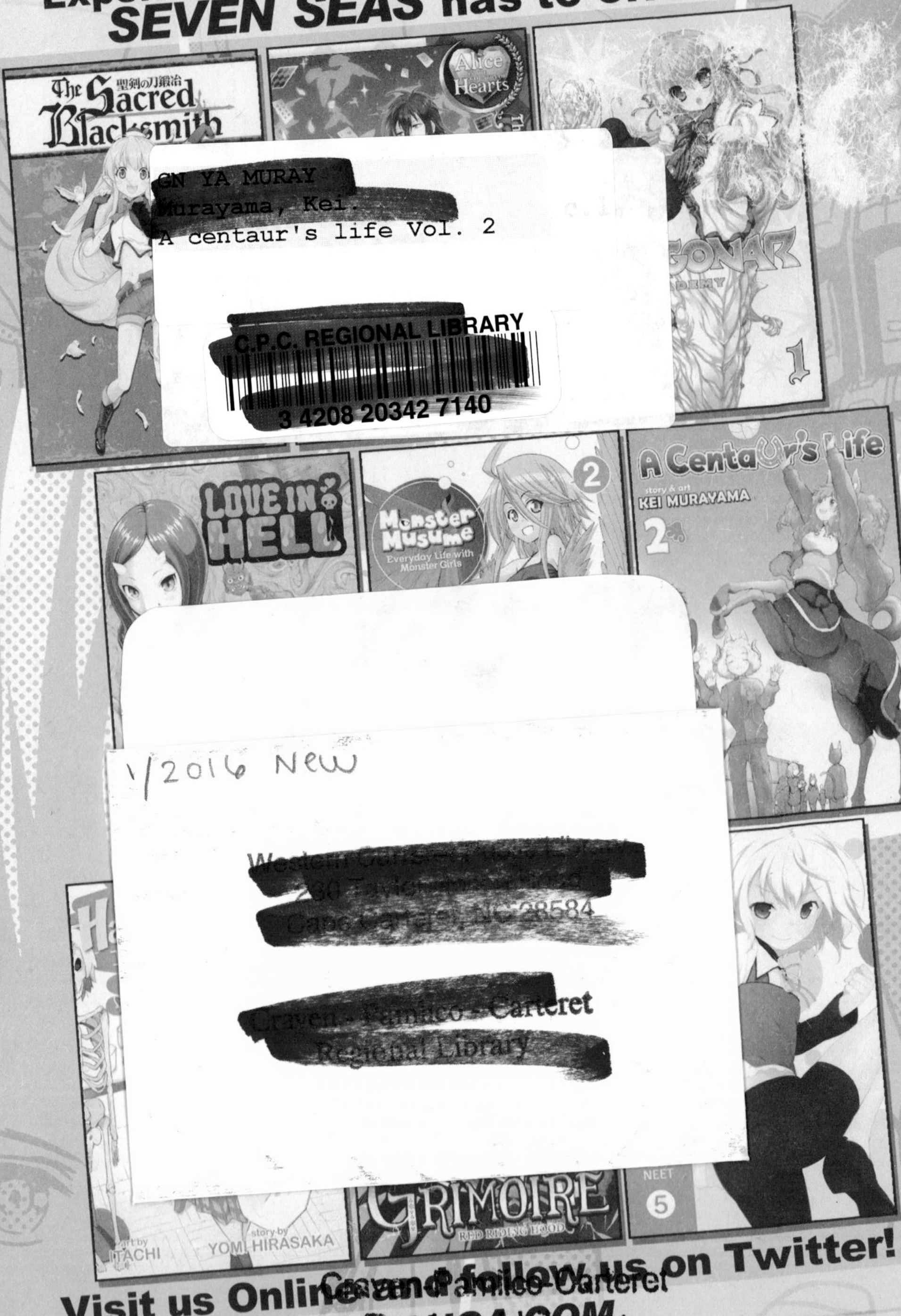

The Sacred Blacksmith
聖剣の刀鍛冶
Alice in the Country of Hearts
GONAR
1
LOVE IN HELL
Monster Musume
Everyday Life with Monster Girls
2
A Centaur's Life
story & art
KEI MURAYAMA
2
GRIMOIRE
RED RIDING HOOD
NEET
5
art by
ITACHI
story by
YOMI HIRASAKA

Visit us Online and follow us on Twitter!

WWW.GOMANGA.COM

WWW.TWITTER.COM/GOMANGA